T0176522

Fundamentals of Big Data Network Analysis for Research and Industry

Fundamentals of Big Data Network Analysis for Research and Industry

Hyunjoung Lee
Institute of Green Technology, Yonsei University, Republic of Korea

Il Sohn
Material Science and Engineering, Yonsei University, Republic of Korea

This edition first published 2016

Registered Office
John Wiley & Sons, Ltd, The Atrium, Southern Gate, Chichester, West Sussex, PO19 8SQ, United Kingdom

For details of our global editorial offices, for customer services and for information about how to apply for permission to reuse the copyright material in this book please see our website at www.wiley.com.

Library of Congress Cataloging-in-Publication data applied for

A catalogue record for this book is available from the British Library.

ISBN: 9781119015581

Set in 10/12pt Times by SPi Global, Pondicherry, India
Printed and bound in Singapore by Markono Print Media Pte Ltd

1 2016

Contents

Preface

The concept of the book was first initiated and sponsored by the Future Steel Technology Forum, where future generations of steel researchers gathered to aggregate their knowledge to address the strategic implications of steel technology and product placement across the global trade community. Under the auspices of the Korea Iron and Steel Association, the authors initiated analysis on the steel commodity trade data and the social network relationships among the countries and products of steel currently being traded across the global frontier. From that initiation, the authors were inspired to provide the general public, industry analysts, and students of data analysis on the methodology of big data analysis using examples of steel product trade relations.

This book is separated into six chapters. Chapter 1 defines big data and how it can be applied to business management for higher productivity and efficiency. Chapter 2 describes the various programs related to big data analysis identifying the pros and cons of the commercially available analysis programs. Chapter 3 deals with network analysis and the basic concepts of the nodes and links related to the structure of social network relations between data. As we reach Chapter 4, details of setting up the research methodology for network analysis, methods of data gathering, and cleansing of unwarranted and unnecessary data is illustrated. In Chapter 5, the centrality analysis, which include degree of centrality, betweenness centrality, closeness centrality, is described in detail and the cohesive subgroup is presented. With the conclusion in Chapter 6, the property of the network and equivalence between node pairs or data pairs is outlined with emphasis on the connectivity of nodes. The appendix in the back of the book provides detailed examples of the network analysis performed using the NetMiner program on steel research topics from keyword analysis of journals published in Wiley.

We have come a long way to reach the final destination to inclusively understand the preceding analyses of big data. The various analyses methods and procedures related to big data network analysis introduced here are the most frequently used methods. This book is designed to comprehensively understand the fundamentals of big data and the expected analysis methods to be conducted within a relatively short time for the beginner and intermediate users. A large part of this effort to complete the book has only been possible through the support and sacrifice of many close to the present authors.

We would like to extend our gratitude to Professor Dong Joon Min for his helpful comments and insights for understanding the limitations of steel data analysis,

Dr. Jae Wook Ryu for his consistent support of the authors, and Professor Doo-Hee Lee for inspiration and the drive for academic excellence.

This book is dedicated to our families, whose sacrifice and support has never been fully appreciated by the authors.

Hyunjoung Lee and Il Sohn

About the Authors

Hyunjoung Lee (Ph.D., Korea University, 2007)
Hyunjoung Lee has published 20 articles on issues related to marketing and social network analysis. She is working on several proposals to study various industrial marketing strategies, focusing on trading network structures and underpinning factors behind those trading network structures. She works at Yonsei University as a research professor and teaches marketing, methodology, and statistics to both graduate and undergraduate students in South Korea.

Il Sohn (Ph.D., Carnegie Mellon University, 2007)
Il Sohn has been a faculty member of the Materials Science and Engineering Department at Yonsei University, Korea, since 2009. He received his doctorate from Carnegie Mellon University and has worked in the steel-related industry and academia for more than a decade at U.S. Steel Corporation and Yonsei University. His experience ranges from fundamental research in continuous casting and steel production to the economic analysis and optimization for raw materials utilization in steelmaking. He is currently an associate professor and the associate director for the Research Institute for Iron and Steel Technology, serves on the board of review for *Metals and Materials Transactions B*, is an advisory board member for Steel Research International and the Korean Institute of Metals and Materials, is an associate editor for the *Journal of Sustainable Metallurgy*, and is the founding chair of the Future Steel Technology Forum of Korea. Professor Sohn has been acknowledged by both the academic and the industrial community, receiving numerous awards for his contributions to the profession, including the AISI Medal, Charles-Herty Award, the Hunt-Kelly Award, Marcus A. Grossman Award, and the Iron and Steel Commendation Award from the Ministry of Trade, Industry, and Energy of Korea.

List of Figures

List of Tables

1

Why Big Data?

There is an enormous amount of data. The increase in unfiltered data that has accumulated so rapidly includes an increase in needless data, which musdt be removed to allow more efficient and unbiased analyses. This requires an ability to extract correct and useful information from the data. Thus, by correctly distinguishing the "gems" from the "pebbles," Big Data analysis would assist an enterprise in obtaining a wider view when starting with a comparably narrow view. Because Big Data bases its significance in the expansion of thought, it is not about volume, velocity, or variety of data but rather about an alternative perspective and viewpoint with respect to the data. If you want to see a forest, you should not leave the forest you should climb to the top of a mountain. Likewise, to obtain meaningful insight from Big Data, we should attempt to broaden our perspective from a bird's eye view. The higher the altitude, the wider is the vision that can be obtained. To see the outside that was never observed from the inside, a different perspective is required to see the forest, and that is where Big Data steps in.

1.1 Big Data

There has been a significant influx of interest in Big Data. Gartner, one of the top marketing analysis institutions in the world, has selected Big Data as one of the top 10 strategic technologies [1] in both 2012 and 2013; in 2014, it selected Big Data and

Fundamentals of Big Data Network Analysis for Research and Industry, First Edition. Hyunjoung Lee and Il Sohn.

Actionable Analytics as the core strategy technology for smart governance [2]. Further, every January at Davos, global political and economic leaders gather at the World Economic Forum to discuss world issues, At the so-called Davos Forum 2012 [3], Big Data was again selected as one of the 10 technologies that have emerged as crucial for future developments. Although we are currently confronted by a financial crisis and partial recovery, along with issues related to climate change, energy, poverty, and security, the selection of Big Data seems to indicate that solutions to global issues require a broad range and amount of data, and the technology to effectively manage and extract useful data is expected to provide much-needed insight into resolving some of these potentially catastrophic global issues.

Of course, when we first encounter Big Data, we focus most of our attention on the word "Big" and become engrossed with the image of a giant being. In reality, however, Big Data is more closely associated with enormity and numberlessness. The term Big Data was defined and widely disseminated by Meta Group (now Gartner) analyst Doug Laney in 2001 to address issues and opportunities in the three dimensions of the rapid data expansion, including data volume, velocity of input/output data, and variety of data type [4]. The concept of Big Data attracting widespread interest in the 2000s can be correlated with the global proliferation of the Internet and the need to analyze the enormous amount data that it generates. The importance of analyzing massive data and converting them into useful information cannot be overstated. Next, a dimension dealing with "value" should be added to the existing three dimensions of data. If Big Data is large, expressed in real time similar to streaming, and includes unstructured data such as text, images, and videos, combining these different types of data and creating value are important. Thus, the amount of reserves is important, whereas the size of the mine is unimportant. The researcher does not need data; he or she needs information. Big Data addresses the size of the data; fundamentally, however, it is more important to analyze and produce meaningful data.

To be considered as Big Data, the data volume must be large in the data set. Although there is no specific size limit that defines Big Data, typically the data set would be a few terabytes for small data sets to as much as a few petabytes for large data sets. Table 1.1 indicates the current data sizes, with the prefixes of peta-, exa-, zetta-, yotta-, bronto-, and geop- used to express the amount of data [5]. If we were to express the amount of data in the books contained in the Library of Congress (in Washington, DC), the total would be about ~15 TB. Through 2012, the human race has accumulated a wealth of data totaling 1.27 ZB. Thus, 1 GpB would suggest an amount of data that is difficult to fathom and would describe an enormous amount of data that are created and distributed.

Another aspect of Big Data is the data velocity and the rate of data accumulation. Twenty years ago, it was expensive not only to install a high-speed data communication network but also to pay its monthly fees. However, now it is relatively easy to use wired and wireless network connections to transfer 1 Gbps (100 Mb/s is possible, at least in Korea) from the home, office, or even the street. Thus, the creation and distribution of data are occurring in the blink of an eye. Recently, natural disasters and various bulletins have first been reported not by the news but by microblogs such

Table 1.1 Data size.

Data	Size		Means				
Bit (b)	1 b	1	Binary digit (1 or 0)				Basic data units
Byte (B)	8 b	2^3	English letter (1 character)				
Kilobyte (kB)	1024 B	2^{10}	1 page				A sheet of paper with 1200 characters
Megabyte (MB)	1024 kB	2^{20}	873	Pages	4	Books	Single digital photo: 3 MB Single MP3 song: 4 MB
Gigabyte (GB)	1024 MB	2^{30}	894,784	Pages	4,473	Books	1–2 hours movie: 1–2 GB
			341	Digital pictures	256	MP3 audio files	
Terabyte (TB)	1024 GB	2^{40}	916,259,689	Pages	4,581,298	Books	Entire volume of books in the library of Congress: 15TB
			349,525	Digital pictures	262,144	MP3 audio files	
			1,613	CDs	233	DVDs	
			40	Blu-ray discs			

(Continued)

Table 1.1 (*Continued*)

Data	Size		Means				
Petabyte (PB)	1024 TB	2^{50}	938,249,922,368	Pages	4,691,249,611	Books	Amount of data Google processes
			357,913,941	Digital pictures	268,435,456	MP3 audio files	Every hour: 1 PB
			1,651,910	CDs	239,400	DVDs	
			41,943	Blu-ray discs			
Exabyte (EB)	1024 PB	2^{60}	960,767,920,505,705	Pages	4,803,839,602,528	Books	Amount of data contained in 100 million copies of a weekly magazine in the US
			366,503,875,925	Digital pictures	274,877,906,944	MP3 audio files	
			1,691,556,350	CDs	245,146,535	DVDs	
			42,949,672	Blu-ray discs			
Zettabyte (ZB)	1024 EB	2^{70}	983,826,350,597,842,752	Pages	4,919,131,752,989,213	Books	The amount of data existing until 2012: 1.27 ZB
			375,299,968,947,541	Digital pictures	281,474,976,710,656	MP3 audio files	
			1,732,153,702,834	CDs	251,030,052,003	DVDs	
			43,980,465,111	Blu-ray discs			

Yottabyte (YB)	1024 ZB	2^{80}	1,007,438,153,012,190,978,921	Pages	5,037,190,915,060,954,894	Books	It would take 11 trillion years to download 1 YB from a high-power broadband
			3843,307,168,202,282,325	Digital pictures	288,230,376,151,711,744	MP3 audio files	
			1,773,725,391,702,841	CDs	257,054,773,251,740	DVDs	
			45,035,996,273,704	Blu-ray discs			
Brontobyte (BB)	1024 YB	2^{90}	1,031,616,699,404,483,562, 415,936	Pages	5,158,083,497,022,417, 812,079	Books	Considering the size of the data that can be collected in real time sensor data of the IoT (internet of things)
			393,530,540,239,137,101,141	Digital pictures	295,147,905,179,352, 825,856	MP3 audio files	
			1,816,294,801,103,709,697	CDs	263,224,087,809,782,414	DVDs	
			46,116,860,184,273,879	Blu-ray discs			
Geopbyte (GpB)	1024 BB	2^{100}	1,056,375,500,190,191,167, 913,919,337	Pages	5,281,877,500,950,955,839, 569,596	Books	Largest data amount that can be fathomed
			402,975,273,204,876,391, 568,725	Digital pictures	302,231,454,903,657,293, 676,544	MP3 audio files	
			1,859,885,876,330,198,730,317	CDs	269,541,465,917,217, 192,562	DVDs	
			47,223,664,828,696,452,136	Blu-ray discs			

as Twitter. Moreover, smart meters in industrial plants, home appliances such as smart TVs and refrigerators, and driverless cars have become increasingly connected via the Internet, allowing the real-time data acquisition of enormous amounts of data, which will continue to accelerate.

Big Data should not be determined just in terms of the size and speed caused by the continuously accumulating variety of data variety. Previously, most of the data we had worked with were well formatted and easy to manage. In other words, the data were well ordered and in a particular form, resulting in structured data. For example, sales, inventory data, or defect ratios during processing are typical data that we observe. However, new types of data cannot be categorized in existing formats and are unstructured. Videos, music, images, location information, text, and so on are data that do not conform to the usual formats; they are unstructured data. These types of data have different sizes and content, which are difficult to organize but have been increasing significantly; thus, they require new processing methods to acquire meaningful data.

Considering Big Data's size, speed, and variety, a typical collection is approximately a few thousand terabytes, produced, distributed, and used at a rate ranging from a few seconds to hours, and this collected Big Data can be in the form of either a structured or an unstructured configuration, which makes it almost impossible to manage and analyze the data by using existing methods. In addition, although Big Data involves an enormous amount and rate with various forms of data, essentially what is most important is to identify meaningful data by analyzing Big Data. Therefore, Big Data includes sets of data that are difficult to manage and analyze using existing methodologies; it also includes human resources, organizations, and related technology to manage and analyze the compounding data that comprise Big Data. Through this process, the resulting creation is the value of Big Data analysis.

In today's connected society, there are infinite amounts of data. However, the existence of larger amounts of data does not necessarily mean that those data should be analyzed. If there are increasing amounts of data, there are also increasing amounts of useless and meaningless data, and special abilities are required to filter the useless raw data into meaningful data sets. Big Data places significance on expanding perspectives and thought and is related not only to the amount, speed, or size of data but also to a sophisticated viewpoint and forecasting. We do not need to leave the forest to see it; instead, we can move up the mountain. Similarly, to gain insight from Big Data, our perspective must be moved above the current perspective. Higher ground allows us to see farther and wider than we can from ground level. To view the outside, which cannot be accomplished from within the group, we must see from a different perspective; to see even more, we must use Big Data. Analysis of Big Data allows our field of vision to be significantly increased from existing ranges.

1.2 What Creates Big Data?

From the past to the present, we have accumulated approximately 1.27 ZB (until 2012), and it is estimated that by 2016, global Internet protocol (IP) traffic will reach approximately 1.3 ZB [6]. The reason for this enormous influx of data cannot be fully comprehended. One reason for this explosive amount of data production is the development of storage devices. With the development of characters, historical records that were once written on plant rinds, animal leather skins, tree fragments (such as bamboo poles), stone plates, clay tablets, and so on, were significantly enhanced with the invention of paper manufacturing and printing. The vast amount of human activities and knowledge that once disappeared without a trace began to be neatly accumulated by characters printed on paper. However, paper-stored information was larger in volume than in amount. With the coming of the twentieth century, analog storage devices such as photographic films, phonographic records, cassette tapes, and videotapes appeared, and information that was once contained on paper was now stored in smaller-volume films or tapes that could hold significant amounts of data. During the 1980s before the digital era arrived, humanity had accumulated approximately 2 620 000 TB of data, 90% or more of which were contained in films and tapes [7]. After 1990, the digital revolution occurred, in which characters, voices, pictures, and images were digitized and there was a dramatic increase in the ability to store data. The floppy disk was the first computer storage devices; later devices included the hard disk and the flash memory. Today we can save and observe tens of GB daily on our smart phone devices to retrieve books, pictures, music, and images on the go at any time. To date, if humanity's accumulated data were recorded on CDs stacked on top of one another, they would span a distance of six times the distance from Earth to the moon. Technological advancements have continued to lower the price of storage. In 1980, it would have cost $213 000 to store 1 GB of data on a hard-disk drive. In 2013, it cost $0.03 to store that same amount of data on a hard-disk drive [8]. This plummeting cost has had a significant impact on the sharp increase in data accumulation (Figure 1.1).

Another reason for the significant growth of data can be attributed to improved connectedness. In the 1960s, computers were rare and valuable, but with the advent of personal computers in the 1980s, their scarcity value dropped. Today, the availability of portable personal computers and devices has rapidly expanded, along with that of smart communication devices such as smart phones and digital pads connected to the Internet, rendering the scarcity value of computers obsolete. Today, many people's smart phones can definitively outperform some of the personal computers produced a few years ago, and the smart phones' improved performance allows users to control various types of equipment through them. In reality, as smart televisions and refrigerators become available in the marketplace, from automobiles to consumer appliances and various equipment, the connectedness of the computer and wireless communication devices is increasingly common and expanding. As a result, the concept of the IoT (Internet of Things), which describes the structural aspect of Internet connectivity technology that gathers data from sensors of objects, has been developed. According to Gartner, in 2009, there were 900 million units of objects that used IoT technology; by 2020, this number is expected to grow to 26 billion units. Cisco speculates that from 2013 to 2022, IoT technology will have an economic value of approximately $14 trillion.

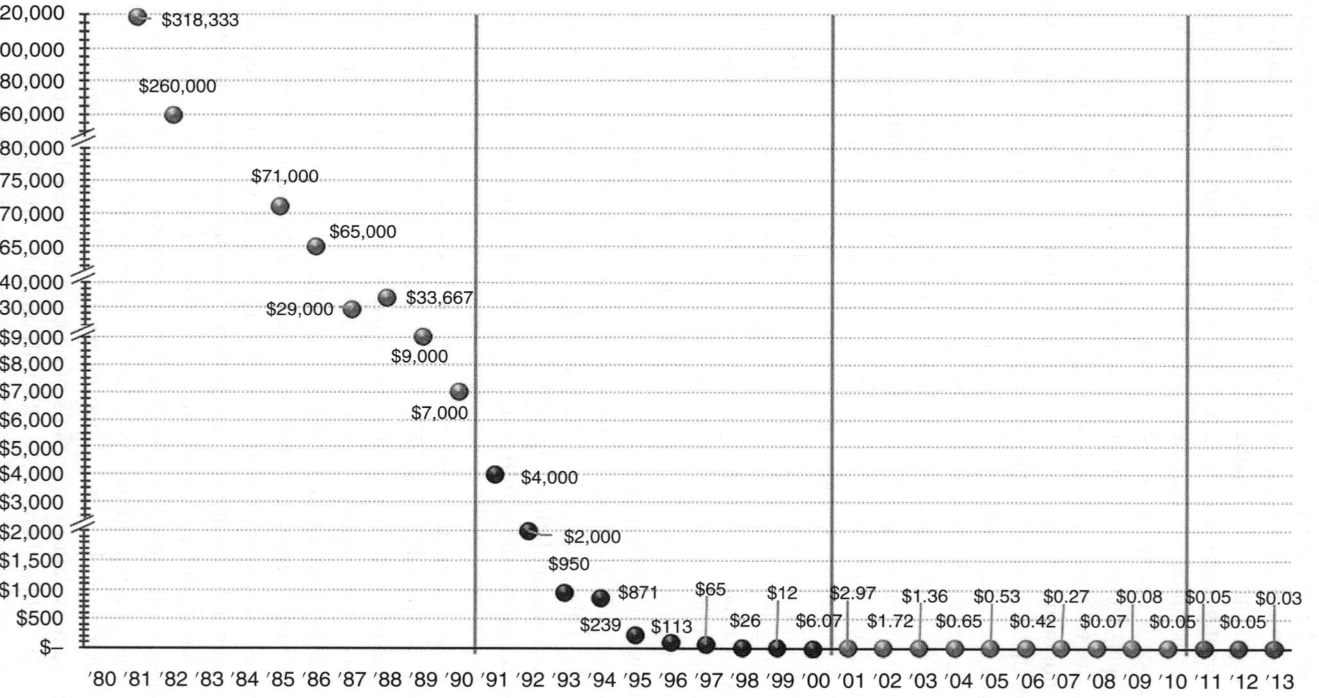

Figure 1.1 Hard-disk drive average cost per gigabytes (unit: US$).

The importance of Big Data cannot be driven solely by the exponential increase in data. Even now, various types of large data are significantly increasing and their speed is becoming faster. What is essential is the extraction of useful information from Big Data. To extract useful information, data management and analysis techniques are needed. Before the 1990s, the size of the digital image database was tens of thousands of images. However, today's online image-sharing sites such as Flicker, Picasa, and Pinterest have digital image databases whose size exceeds our imagination and can include more than tens of billions of images for each database. If image data processing technology did not evolve, even with the development of computer performance, it would not be able to manage the enormously increasing amount of data. Fortunately, the digital image processing technology of analyzing and indexing images has advanced at the pace of the increasing amount of data, and it has become possible to manage and search billions of images per second, allowing the management of vast amounts of data. Similarly, significant advancements in the analysis of various unstructured data and related technology have occurred. These technological developments allowed for recognition of the value of Big Data and are now a topic of interest to many.

Of course, advancements in the technological environment do not always attract the market's attention. Although the technology has long been available, it must match the market environment to become popular with the general public. Numerous types of technology were pioneers of their era and were expected to gain widespread popularity, but they silently disappeared without even entering the market after consumers realized that they were not needed. In that respect, the question of how to apply Big Data to corporate activity became extremely important.

1.3 How Do We Use Big Data?

How can we improve the business environment by using Big Data? Changing our perspective is the first step to improving the business environment. Analyzing Big Data and distinguishing the "gems" from the "pebbles" are not accomplished by evaluating what we know but rather by discovering what we do not know. Evaluation is verifying what we have known from the beginning, but discovery is identifying the right questions to ask through a creative and repetitive exploration process. Discovery is the creation of real value from Big Data. This provides a company with an idea to increase its corporate value [9].

The second step to improving the corporate business environment is to discover the various problems and possible solutions existing within various corporate activities. This involves changes in the corporate thought process and decision-making methods using Big Data. With Big Data, it is possible to find an important, hidden, previously unknown truth. Finding meaningful truth in Big Data that cannot be ascertained through cognitive human abilities is Big Data's problem-solving process. Forecasting is another area that is actively being pursued within Big Data. The future exists in the present. The future is not disconnected to the past or to the present. Things chosen in the past exist in the present, and things selected in the present will move to the future. Because the past, present, and future are not segmented, if the present can be ascertained, future doors can be opened. The analysis of the various past forms of Big Data can make it much easier to glimpse possible outcomes and future circumstances. From enormous amounts of data, people can discover new knowledge and events, and through this discovery, they can connect the present and the future. Thus, forecasting is enabled if data are correctly analyzed. A classic example is that of market basket analysis, which involves analyzing customers' purchasing behavior and merchandise related to cross- and up-sold items, the sale of which are optimized by selective placement. By analyzing customer purchasing behavior, it was found that people who purchase diapers also had a propensity to buy beer, and before a hurricane, both flashlights and sweet snacks are widely bought. These findings facilitate the optimal placement of products for consumers to purchase more effectively. By analyzing purchasing behavior, beer is placed next to diapers and strawberry cake is placed next to flashlights, resulting in increased sales. An important element of Big Data analysis that has increasingly been highlighted is the visualization of results. Visualization is a technique and method that allow analyzed data to be easily understood at a glance. A corporation's employees must clearly understand what has been discovered through the Big Data analysis; this need renders visualization extremely useful.

Data exist in every corporation, and the availability of data provides an opportunity to improve corporate productivity. By implementing different perspectives on existing data, the third step in improving the corporate business environment is to improve the practical use of existing data and information technology to improve work productivity. Improving productivity has often been used and could sound like a cliché. However, productivity enhancement is an important issue in the corporate environment. The methods of using Big Data for improved corporate productivity can be classified into two categories. First, by using sensor technology, data on the movement of materials can be identified and managed, resulting in lower labor, inventory, and logistics costs. Second, through Big Data analysis, unnecessary efforts in the work flow of the value chain can be minimized, allowing restructuring of the work process that optimizes work productivity. So far, the productivity enhancements in industry have been accomplished by substituting for the human work force with machines and computers; however, in the Big Data world, the raw materials, product, machines, and so on, are outfitted with various sensors and tags that enable real-time interactions and the accumulation of data to enhance productivity. Unlike in the past, the data have become more robust, quickly produced, and accumulated to allow a different dimension on increasing productivity. Through real-time data production and acquisition from various sensors, much more detailed and micro forecasting and control are possible, allowing precise management. For example, there is a bullwhip effect in SCM (supply chain management). Incorrectly assessing the supply of raw materials results in a greater error in production output forecasting at the next step of the supply chain, resulting in an increased gap between actual sales amounts. Therefore, through accurate forecasts and controls using real-time data, the gap between supply and demand can be minimized and can lower inventory and logistics costs, which can increase productivity. In reality, the next-generation power management system–labeled Smart Grid–which is the convergence of information technology (IT) with existing power grid systems, is installed with various sensors and meters in the power system that provide information on real-time power-consumption trends, allowing increased productivity and efficient management of power production. Through mutual communication, it is possible to perform detailed control and remote equipment examination of power flow. Automatic restoration during disruptions is also possible, allowing increased energy efficiency and providing optimal distribution of power according to consumption and increasing the ability to react during emergency situations. In the United States, raw materials and manufacturing service companies have moved from their previously used traditional methods of making repairs after equipment failures to a "state-based monitoring" method in which engineers actively monitor the state of equipment before failure. Waiting until failure creates an unexpected problem in productivity, and the production line is halted during a repair. However, by monitoring the temperature, vibration, production amount, and so on, and sending the data to the system for analysis, engineers can preemptively prepare for the problem and provide solutions that will not affect the production line to a great extent. Structured data are useful, but unstructured data can also assist in increasing productivity. The production and distribution of company documents can be analyzed and, by improving document use productivity, can be enhanced. Making the location of documents or images easier can minimize the cost and time to retrieve information, which is another application characteristic of Big Data.

The fourth step in improving the corporate management environment is to provide an objective viewpoint to a corporation's decision makers. In attempting a new endeavor, several decisions must be made, during which many conflicts arise. If objective, observed data exist, the decision maker can overcome prejudice and weak points, thus resulting in rational consensus within the organization. Decision making will always be a manager's essential duty, and the failure of many corporations is a result of a failure in decision making. The intuition of an experienced person is very important, but sometimes intuition can be an obstacle to making rational decisions. If intuition can be supplemented by a Big Data analysis, a more appropriate result can be deduced. For example, in the oil and gas industry, oil and gas fields are searched for and developed by installing large-scale sensor networks in the earth's crust to identify with precision the possible locations and structure of oil fields. This results in lower development costs and improved oil transportation costs. To effectively use Big Data in the corporate decision-making process, an appropriate handling flow for data processing is necessary. Because Big Data itself does not assist in the decision-making process, an optimal decision-making process flow must exist within the corporation to effectively use Big Data. The final step to improve the corporate management environment is to create new value and to ensure that this created value is connected to a new business plan. The smart utilization of data allows the creation of a new business management paradigm. The ultimate goal of using Big Data is to identify what was missed in the past and to identify the hidden value of the dynamic client or create a new value and provide for the client. In the energy industry, networked sensors and an automated feedback mechanism are used to alter energy consumption patterns. By installing smart meters at power facilities in the industry, real-time energy consumption and costs can be verified, allowing the identification of peak times of energy use during work hours and providing optimal control of overloading in the power grid. Through these efforts, energy-intensive processes could be rearranged to a lower energy load time. Example is that of recent advancements in automotive navigation systems. These systems now surpass the mere combination of an electronic map and global positioning system (GPS) with the addition of accumulated information from road sensors that is transmitted to the navigation system, which is then transmitted to the central server and analyzed for traffic conditions, after which the customer is resupplied with the optimal and shortest distance to the destination of choice. Through these technological innovations and a Big Data analysis, the vehicle's fuel efficiency is improved and customers are provided with more efficient use of their time than being stuck in bumper-to-bumper traffic. It seems that in the near future, a navigation system could be developed to identify a driver's schedule and moods and to provide the optimal directions before the driver requests them. In the background of these evolutions, we cannot stress enough the importance of detailed data collection and analysis.

However, to maximize the effect of Big Data application, technology to effectively process Big Data is required. Simply, what problem should pass through a particular process, and who will manage that process to achieve the highest productivity. We typically concentrate not on the problem itself but on how quickly we can solve it. That said, the most important aspect is to identify the actual problem. To discern information about a problem, analysis of Big Data may be helpful. Generally, there are three steps for Big Data analysis. The first step is observation. Analyzing Big Data does not require collection of huge amounts of data. The data become meaningful only when they are analyzed. Therefore, through observation, we must initially decide what data to accumulate. Next, a quantifying process is needed. This is necessary to allow a systems-based observation that goes beyond simple data accumulation. In Big Data analysis, a broader and variable method of quantification is required. Finally, a process for deductive reasoning is needed. For example, the amount of data has significantly increased with the proliferation of smart phones. However, we also must use deductive reasoning about why people use smart phones.

Additionally, an increase in human resources for Big Data analysis is needed. According to McKinsey, in 2018 in the United States alone, there will be a deficiency of 14000 to 19000 data scientists who have the ability to deeply analyze Big Data and a deficiency of 1.5 million managers with the know-how to use Big Data to make informed decisions for greater productivity [10].

Today, there are infinite amounts of data. In the Big Data warehouse, there are clues for solving immediate problems. However, solutions do not involve Big Data sets exclusively. As previously mentioned, a greater amount of data will require an increasing amount of filtering. Therefore, by finding a gem within the enormous data size, we can effectively analyze Big Data to broaden corporate insight of the corporation at the next level.

1.4 Essential Issues Related to Big Data

Big Data's future is not necessarily uniformly bright. Big Data seems to show potential for use that excites many of its followers; however, there is much skepticism regarding the use of Big Data in such a wide range. Understanding these issues correctly and how we respond to them will determine whether Big Data will be a useful company asset or an enormous hassle.

The most widely disputed issues related to Big Data are personal privacy and protection issues. Because "Big Brother"[1] is often associated with Big Data and the use of Big Data has increased rapidly, we begin to wonder what boundaries of personal information and range of rights must be fulfilled before its use; these issues have found their way into the courtroom, with heated debate on both sides.

Another issue from a different perspective on Big Data is data abuse. With larger amounts of data, information can be fabricated to manipulate a person's true identity. The 2002 movie "Minority Report" depicted a cutting-edge crime prevention system, "Pre-crime," which enabled crime to be prevented using forecasting. The problem was that the probable event was considered to be an actual event, which a government agency then used as evidence to "suppress" so-called future perpetrators. This story demonstrates that total trust in Big Data can actually lower a company's productivity. We must realize and acknowledge that Big Data analysis provides a probability and likelihood that we can use to direct our actions.

Data acquisition and sharing are additional issues that have been contested. These issues involve intellectual property rights in open data, which seem to be addressed differently by the laws of different countries. Generally, open data used "as is" without processing is considered illegal, but once the data have been processed, creating new value, there seems to be a tendency to consider it legal. However, there remain gray areas in which different countries have different notions of how much processing is required to create new value and how to define the concept of new.

Because the United States considers freedom of speech and information distribution as more important than personal rights, there are many legal precedents that enable the distribution and use of personal data if they provide a public service, even if they infringe on personal rights. Therefore, if Big Data–related companies follow correct procedures for consent and provide anonymity, then data can be used without significant issues. Conversely, the European Union (EU) has a more conservative approach to human-rights protections and has actively promoted a law enforcing the "right to be forgotten [11]." In January 2012, the EU decreed that individuals had the right to remove personal information possessed by Internet companies without legal consent and finalized its data protection amendments, and in May 2014, the EU's highest court, the Court of Justice, approved the right to be forgotten. Many are well aware of the "Google Spain" trial, in which the Court of Justice ordered Google to delete a search result that consisted of a newspaper article on a 16-year-old incident

[1] Big Brother is a character of George Orwell's novel *1984*. Big Brother is taken a role that is monitoring the citizen through telescreens and deliver to the absolute. In the real world, Big Brother has become meaning of social control.

in which the plaintiff experienced foreclosure due to delinquent federal tax payments. The contents of the foreclosure auction were legal and open to the public. In the foreclosure auction process, all information must be provided pursuant to constitutional rules and regulations. If this procedure and information availability are not respected, the court official or government office may be considered to have unjustly executed the foreclosure, unjustly violated the rights of the debtor, or possibly acted to illegally accumulate wealth. Nevertheless, the Court of Justice judged that the search for information on past foreclosure information is unlawful and does not reasonably justify the acquisition of that data; it then ordered Google to remove the content. However, there exist many still-unresolved legal regulations addressing the complex and various types of Big Data being produced and created.

References

1 Gartner (2013) Gartner Identifies the Top 10 Strategic Technology Trend for 2013, http://gartner.com/newsroom/id/2209615 (accessed 22 May 2005).

2 Gartner (2014) Gartner Identifies the Top 10 Strategic Technology Trends for Smart Government, http://www.gartner.com/newsroom/id/2707617 (accessed 22 May 2005).

3 World Economic Forum (2012) Big Data, Big Impact: New Possibilities for International Development, http://www3.weforum.org/docs/WEF_TC_MFS_BigDataBigImpact_Briefing_2012.pdf (accessed 22 May 2005).

4 Laney, D. (2001) 3D Data Management: Controlling Data Volume, Velocity, and Variety, Meta Group(Gartner), http://blogs.gartner.com/doug-laney/files/2012/01/ad949-3D-Data-Management-Controlling-Data-Volume-Velocity-and-Variety.pdf (accessed 22 May 2005).

5 The Economist (2010) All Too Much: Monstrous Amounts of Data, The Economist (Feb. 25 2010), http://www.economist.com/node/15557421 (accessed 22 May 2005).

6 Cisco (2014) The Zettabyte Era: Trends and Analysis, 2014 June 10, http://www.cisco.com/c/en/us/solutions/collateral/service-provider/visual-networking-index-vni/VNI_Hyperconnectivity_WP.pdf (accessed 22 May 2005).

7 Hilbert, M. and López, P. (2011) The world's technological capacity to store, communicate, and compute information, *Science*, **332**(6025), 60–65.

8 Komorowski, M. (2014) A History of Storage Cost, http://www.mkomo.com/cost-per-gigabyte-update, reproduced (accessed 22 May 2015).

9 Hahm, Y.K. and Chae, S.B. (2014) *Big Data, Changing the Business*, Seoul: SERI.

10 McKinesy Global Institute (2011) Big Data: The Next Frontier for Innovation, Competition, and Productivity, http://www.mckinsey.com/insights/business_technology/big_data_the_next_frontier_for_innovation (accessed 22 May 2015).

11 Right to be forgotten is a concept that an individual has the right to request that his or her personal data to be removed from accessibility via a search engine European Commission (2014) Factsheet on the "Right to be Forgotten" Ruling, 2014 May 2013, http://ec.europa.eu/justice/data-protection (accessed 22 May 2015).

2

Basic Programs for Analyzing Networks

Up to now, our viewpoint on data was focused on the actor's attribute. However, since an actor's behavior is not always independent, it is necessary to observe the actors from a network relation perspective. There is a traditional saying in Korean classics: *Myungshimbogam*, of "if you want to know a person, first look at his friends." This word transforms our perspective from a single actor's attributes to a network. To analyze Big Data from a network perspective, a program is available for network analysis. Some widely used network analysis programs are introduced such as UCINET (University of California Irvine NETwork), NetMiner, R, Gephi, and NodeXL. UNICET and NetMiner are comprehensive programs that can use various techniques for network analysis. NodeXL focuses more on software for the statistics calculation, while R focuses on statistics calculation and Grephi focuses on visualization. Through NodeXL, network data can be retrieved by using Excel Template for basic analysis and visualization.

2.1 UCINET

UCINET [1] is a software program developed by Linton Freeman for different types of network analysis. The UCI initials in the acronym acknowledge Freeman's position as a professor at the University of California Irvine. The software was later enhanced in collaboration with Steve Borgatti and Martin Everett and is currently the most widely used network analysis software on the market. UCINET allows the

Fundamentals of Big Data Network Analysis for Research and Industry, First Edition. Hyunjoung Lee and Il Sohn.

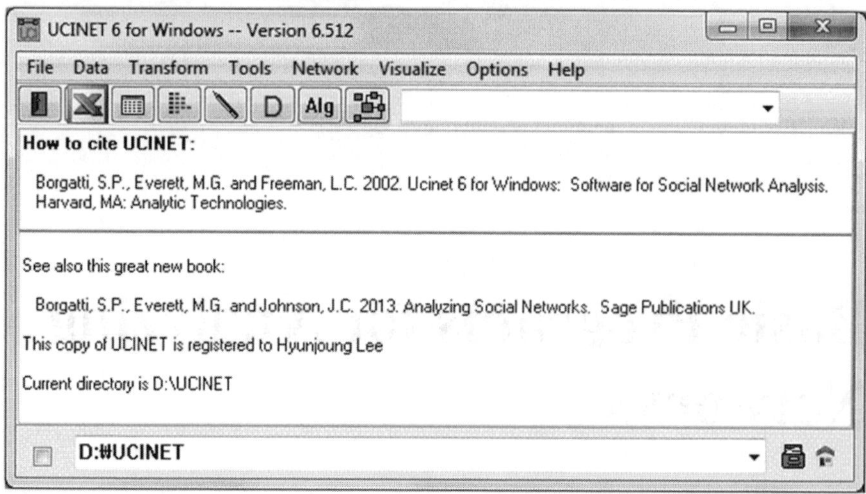

Figure 2.1 UCINET 6 interface.

researcher to use various analytical techniques such as topography measurement including density and clustering and structural equivalence including the structural, automorphic, and regular characteristics of the entire network. In addition, data transformation is readily accomplished through characteristic functions, and statistical analysis related to network analysis can be performed within the program. UCINET is available for download from the www.analytictech.com web site.

The recently updated UCINET6 has an interface similar to the format illustrated in Figure 2.1 above. Once the program has been installed, a small drop-down window is used to open data within the document folders and shows the current default folder. The menus at the top of the window include the *File, Data, Transform, Tools, Network, Visualize, Option,* and *Help* tabs of the program. The [File] menu includes operations to change the default folder or edit data files. Choosing the *File > Change Default Folder* command allows the researcher to change the preexisting default folder, while choosing the *File > Text Editor* command allows the Microsoft Notepad application to execute. Within the Notepad program, data files are easily edited by the user.

The [Data] tab contains commands within the program to open and save data files. UCINET is able not only to import and analyze network data from Excel and text programs but also to import other network analysis software data such as from DL(Data Language), Krackplot, Mage, Pajek, and Metis. Furthermore, analyses can also be performed using data in edge and node list formats, which enables the program to handle large network data sets. DL data form, which is compatible with UCINET, describes the language of the data set form. DL files can be composed within Notepad and can be called on within the software. The format of the DL file is presented in Table 2.1A, B[1]; dl indicates that the file is a dl file and describes a matrix size in which nr is the number of rows and nc is the number of columns. For a square matrix, nr=4 or nc=4 can be expressed as n=4 format=fullmatrix. Variable names are shown in the

[1]To explain the data, trading data of the steel product have been used. See Table 5.1.

Table 2.1 DL data format.

A. DL_Matrix format

```
dl nr=9, nc=9
labels
S. Korea Japan Brazil Canada China Mexico Singapore Thailand USA
data:
0      22823  0  0      14831  0      0      0      28725
63107  0      0  0      28114  0      0      19641  27989
0      0      0  0      0      0      0      0      10851
0      0      0  0      0      0      0      0      30789
36613  15227  0  0      0      0      12257  0      37296
0      0      0  0      0      0      0      0      18369
0      0      0  0      0      0      0      0      0
0      0      0  0      0      0      0      0      0
0      0      0  45999  0      29782  0      0      0
```

B. DL_Edgelist format

```
dl nr=7 nc=8 format=edgelist2
labels embedded
data
China     Singapore  12257
Brazil    USA        10851
China     USA        37296
Mexico    USA        18369
Canada    USA        30789
Japan     China      28114
Japan     Thailand   19641
Japan     S.Korea    63107
S. Korea  China      14831
Japan     USA        27989
S. Korea  USA        28725
S. Korea  Japan      22823
USA       Mexico     29782
USA       Canada     45999
China     Japan      15227
China     S.Korea    36614
```

labels, and the data can be entered in the adjacent column. When entering the variable names and data, users should take care not to leave any spaces between them.

For data that are not in the DL format, the internal function of *Data > Data editors > Excel Matrix Editor* or *Data > Data editors > UCINET Spreadsheet* can be used to directly insert and edit the data. The node name can be inserted in the first row and column in the illustrated UCINET Spreadsheet. The command *Data > Export* selects and saves data in the desired software data format. The *Data > Display* command allows the researcher to view network data within UCINET; when the command is executed, ucinetlog files are opened and general information on the results of the analysis and the data information can be retrieved. The saved UCINET data is stored in dual file system in which the actual data file has the ##h extension, and the file with the data information has the ##d extension. The file with the ##h extension is used for data analysis.

Commands for transforming the data or setting up a relationship matrix, such as dichotomize, symmetrize, recode, and reverse, are available under the [Transform] tab. The dichotomize command allows the data to be reconfigured as 1s and 0s, with a value of 1 is given indicating that the data satisfies a particular condition and a value of 0 indicating that the condition is not satisfied. The symmetrize command transforms the original data to consider only connections and ignores direction. Dichotomizing and symmetrizing the data in UCINET is performed with the commands *Transform > Dichotomize, Symmetrize,* and the transformation conditions can be selected after the option has been chosen.

The [Tools] tab includes the commands for network data analysis and statistical analysis. Analyses available through the lower portion of the Tools pull-down menu include multidimensional scaling, cluster analysis, correspondence analysis, singular value decomposition, factor analysis, measures of similarity and dissimilarity, and univariate analysis. There are also commands for scatterplot and dendrogram.

For example, the *Network > Density > Density* overall command can be used to determine the density and degree of centrality of the dichotomized data presented in Table 2.1. No. of Ties represents the number of relationships in the network and Avg Degree represents the degree of the average connection (Figure 2.2a). Centrality can be obtained by using the command *Network > Centrality* and *Power > Degree,* which is summarized in Figure 2.2b. The results of the analysis indicate that Japan and China export steel products to four countries in an out-degree analysis, whereas the United States imports from six countries in an in-degree analysis with a centralization index of 0.5938, which suggests a high centralization index among importing nations from the perspective of an in-degree analysis.

One limitation of the program is that the [Visualize] command is unable to visually present the network analysis results directly within the program but must be used with external visualization software such as NetDraw, Mage, and Pajek. When the *Visualize > NetDraw, Mage, Pajek* drop-down menu is selected, a separate window is opened, and the researcher selects the data to visualize. NetDraw is a visualization software program developed by Steve Borgatti, one of the UCINET developers; it includes various algorithms for visualizing the network in 2D space and can be considered to be a data visualization expansion of the UCINET software. Figure 2.3 illustrates the steel product export network for the data presented Table 2.1, which was obtained using NetDraw.

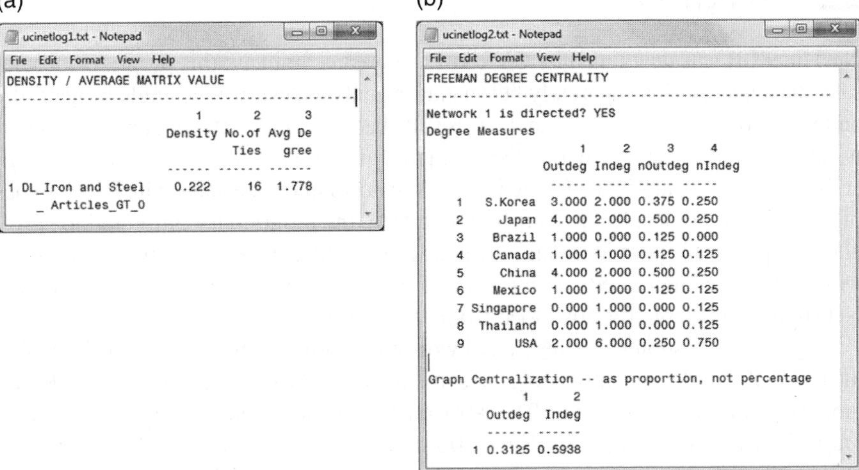

(a)

ucinetlog1.txt - Notepad

DENSITY / AVERAGE MATRIX VALUE

	1 Density	2 No.of Ties	3 Avg Degree
1 DL_Iron and Steel_Articles_GT_0	0.222	16	1.778

(b)

ucinetlog2.txt - Notepad

FREEMAN DEGREE CENTRALITY

Network 1 is directed? YES

Degree Measures

		1 Outdeg	2 Indeg	3 nOutdeg	4 nIndeg
1	S.Korea	3.000	2.000	0.375	0.250
2	Japan	4.000	2.000	0.500	0.250
3	Brazil	1.000	0.000	0.125	0.000
4	Canada	1.000	1.000	0.125	0.125
5	China	4.000	2.000	0.500	0.250
6	Mexico	1.000	1.000	0.125	0.125
7	Singapore	0.000	1.000	0.000	0.125
8	Thailand	0.000	1.000	0.000	0.125
9	USA	2.000	6.000	0.250	0.750

Graph Centralization -- as proportion, not percentage

	1 Outdeg	2 Indeg
1	0.3125	0.5938

Figure 2.2 Results of density and degree centrality using UCINET. (a) Density and (b) degree centrality.

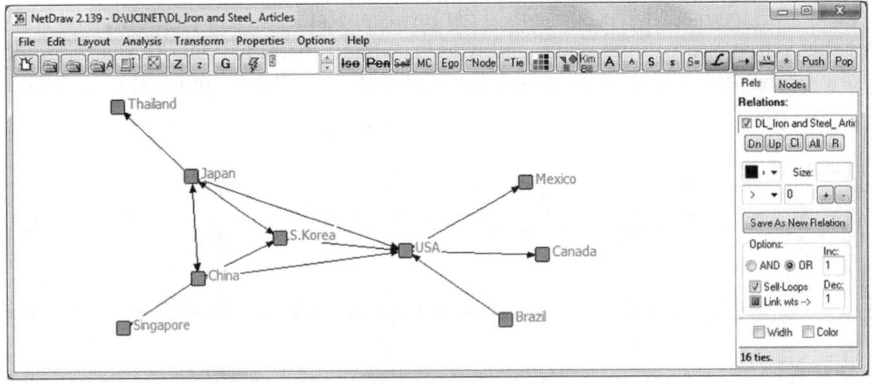

Figure 2.3 Visualization using NetDraw.

In addition to the visualization programs identified above, Mage, which was developed for use in molecular modeling [2], is able to visually present a 3D image. The program must be installed on the computer before use. Pajek, which means "spiders" in Slovak, describes a complex encrypted network structure that mimics the Web arrays that spiders weave and traverse freely; this program allows a researcher to perform a simple analysis that decrypts the complex network structure. The visual interpretation created by Pajek is optimized to be compatible with programs such as Photoshop, which has the advantage of enabling the researcher to create high resolution graphics through simple conversions.

The [Options] tab provides commands to create and edit default folders for software connected to UCINET.

2.2 NetMiner

NetMiner [3] was developed by CYRAM, a Korean company; this program does not save the analysis files separately but manages analysis results in a single project file, and visual presentation of the analysis results based on the network analysis indexes is relatively easy, which makes the program fairly robust for network analysis. In addition, the program is well suited to the Windows interface and includes a number of analytical modules. In the NetMiner4 version, the program is configured to easily allow repetitive operations and provides a Python programming-based script workbench for increased researcher friendliness during analytical operations. NetMiner is available for download from http://netminer.com.

Figure 2.4 illustrates the NetMiner4 work environment. The ❶ **Title Bar** identifies the name of the file currently being executed within NetMiner. NetMiner files take the nmf (NetMiner File) extension. The ❷ **Main Menu** bar includes the *File, Edit, Data, Map, Transform, Analyze, Statistics, Mining, Visualize, Chart, Window,* and *Help* commands for data input and output, data management, data analysis, and data visualization. The ❸ **Tool Bar** provides shortcuts for the commands.

The [File] tab in the Main Menu includes commands related to data import and export. In addition to text and Excel data files, several other compatible network analysis software files can be imported or exported into NetMiner, and imported data can be in Edge list, Matrix, or Linked list formats. The Edge list data format consists of the source node, target node, and weight, while Linked list data format is in the form of the source node, target node1, target node2, … Furthermore, the researcher

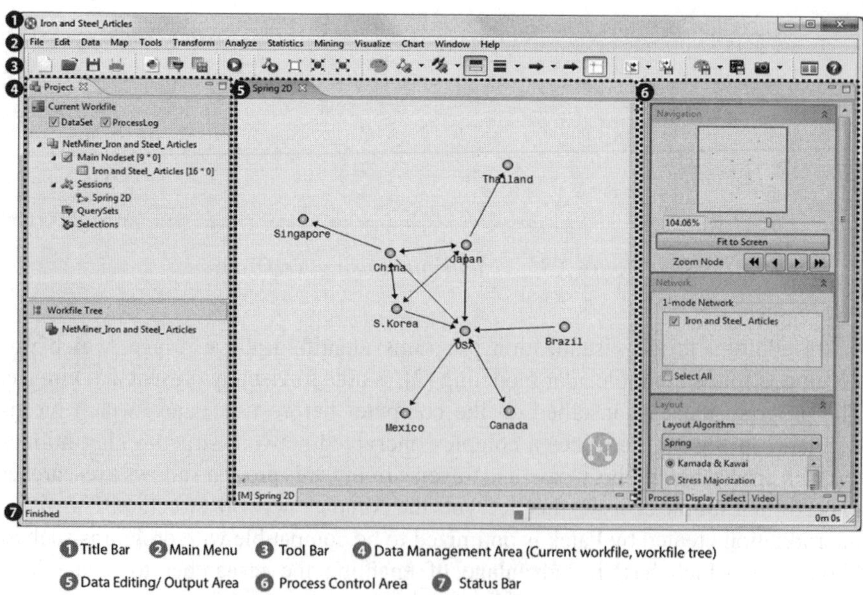

Figure 2.4 NetMiner4 work environment.

is able to input new data directly by selecting the *File > New > Project > Blank Project, Singleton Project* or *File > New > Workfile commands*. The Blank Project command is used to organize independent data sets, and the Singleton Project command is used to directly insert data into untitled nodesets and networks generated by the program.

The [Edit] command allows the researcher to edit data, and the Data command is used to create new data or import and export data. The [Map] command is used to expand or contract visual network maps or change the direction within the network. The [Tools] menu includes commands such as script workbench functions allowing repetitive operations, matrix calculators, and query composer. The [Transform] menu includes commands to change the network direction and values, extract node and link data, separate and merge networks, and transform the network category (e.g., change a two-mode network to a one-mode network).

The [Analysis] menu provides a number of analytical modules for network analysis. The density and degree of centrality analyses performed by UCINET are also performed by NetMiner. Density analysis is performed by executing the command *Analyze > Properties > Network;* the results of the analysis are presented in Figure 2.5. The degree of centrality analysis is performed by executing *Analyze > Centrality > Degree,*

(a)

- **Output Summary**

NETWORK PROPERTIES

	# of Links : O(m)	Density : O(m)	Average Degree : O(m)
Trade relationships	16	0.222	1.778

(b)

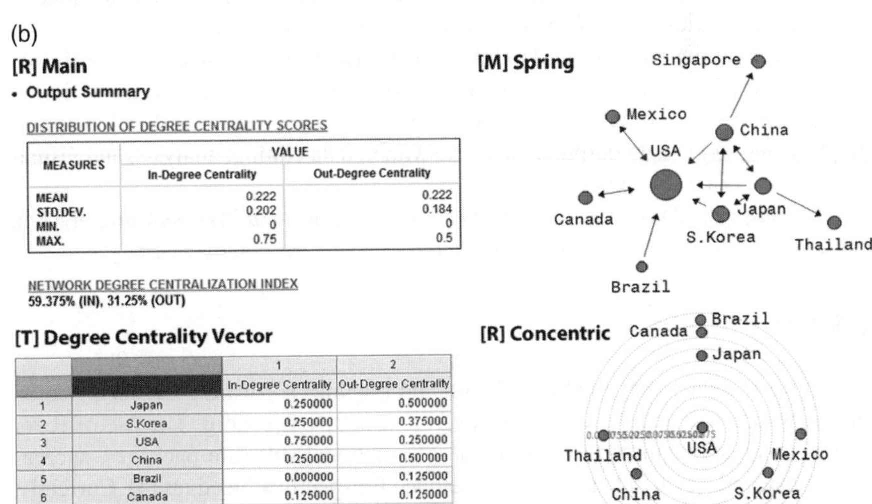

[R] Main

- **Output Summary**

DISTRIBUTION OF DEGREE CENTRALITY SCORES

MEASURES	VALUE	
	In-Degree Centrality	Out-Degree Centrality
MEAN	0.222	0.222
STD.DEV.	0.202	0.184
MIN.	0	0
MAX.	0.75	0.5

NETWORK DEGREE CENTRALIZATION INDEX
59.375% (IN), 31.25% (OUT)

[T] Degree Centrality Vector

		1	2
		In-Degree Centrality	Out-Degree Centrality
1	Japan	0.250000	0.500000
2	S.Korea	0.250000	0.375000
3	USA	0.750000	0.250000
4	China	0.250000	0.500000
5	Brazil	0.000000	0.125000
6	Canada	0.125000	0.125000
7	Mexico	0.125000	0.125000
8	Singapore	0.125000	0.000000
9	Thailand	0.125000	0.000000

Figure 2.5 Results of density and degree centrality analyses in NetMiner. (a) Density and (b) degree centrality.

which results in the subordinate tabs of [R]Main, [T]Degree Centrality Vector, [M] Spring, and [M]Concentric, where [R] represents Report, [T] represents Table, and [M] represents Map. The Map incorporates the Spring Layout Algorithm developed by Kamada and Kawai [4], in which node positions are approximately proportional to the minimum path distance and which assumes an ideal distance even for nonadjacent node pairs.

The [Statistics] menu provides commands for different types of statistical analyses of networks. Table 2.2 presents the commands (i.e., algorithms) used in the NetMiner4. The [Mining] command identifies the patterns exhibited by the network data, and the [Visualize] and [Chart] menu commands provide different visualization and chart algorithms to visually illustrate the network. The [Windows] menu enables the researcher to hide or display subordinate windows, and the [Help] command opens the help menu for general NetMiner questions and updates.

The ❹ **Data Management Area** is composed of the [Current Workfile] and [Workfile Tree]. The [Current Workfile] consists of the basic units of analysis and visualization in NetMiner, which include the data set and process log. The data are based on the data set, which consists of the main-nodeset, sub-nodeset, 1-mode network data, and 2-node network data, which are used to analyze and visualize the network. The collective node in the 1-mode network is the main nodeset, and the collective node in the 2-mode network is the sub nodeset. Analysis results are recorded in the process log. Changes in the Current Workfile can be saved as a new Workfile, and several work files can be managed at once as a list of Workfiles in the [Workfile Tree]. Including several work files in a single project makes researcher data management easier. Figure 2.6 presents the data structure and data set for the sample *Iron and Steel_Articles*[2] data. The two-mode network data diagrams indicate that all of the nine countries export *Iron and Steel* and *Articles of Iron and Steel.*

The data editing area of the ❺ **Data Editing/Output Area** window is activated when of one of the data sets in the [Current Workfile] is selected, and the activated data can be directly edited or added in NetMiner. Analysis and visualization results are presented in the data output area. In NetMiner, data editing, analysis, and visualization occurs in a single domain.

The analysis and visualization options are selected. In the ❻ **Process Control Area,** and different options are activated depending on the analysis commands.

2.3 R

R is an open source statistical calculation and graphics software program based on scripts, which is available for download from www.r-project.org. The use of R for network analysis requires the installation of additional software packages, such as sna, igraph, and egrm, that have been developed for specific objectives [5]. Currently, 5738 packages can be installed on R, which makes it one of the most comprehensive analysis and visualization programs available. Figure 2.7 illustrates the initial screen displayed when R is executed.

---

[2] To explain the data, trading data of the steel product have been used. See Table 5.1.

Table 2.2 Algorithms implemented in NetMiner4.

Transform	Analyze	Clique	Role	Statistic	Visualize
Direction	Neighbor	n-Clique	SimRank	MDS	Layout
Symmetrize	Degree	n-Clan	Position	Correspondence	Drawing
Transpose	Ego-network	k-Plex	Blockmodel	Decomposition	Spring
Value	Structural hole	k-Core	Brokerage	Covariance matrix	MDS
Dichotomize	Homophily	Lambda set	Bow-tie model	Principal component	Clustered
Reverse	Assortativity	Community	Expand/collapse	Factor analysis	Layered
Normalize	Equicentrality	Cohesive block	Properties	Frequency	Circular
Recode	Subgraph	s-Clique	Network	Gini coefficient	Simple
Missing	Dyad census	Centrality	Group	Power law	Two mode
Diagonal	Triad census	Degree	Models	Descriptive	Spring
NodeSet	Triad combination	Coreness	Dyadic interaction(p1)	Crosstabs	Chart
EgoNetwork	Connection	Closeness	ERGM (Exponential Random Graph Model)(p*)	ANOVA	Pie chart
Reorder	Shortest path	Decay	Blockmodel	Correlation	Matrix diagram
LinkSet	All path finding	Betweenness	Two mode	Autocorrelation	Area bar
Incidence	All cycle finding	Flow betweenness	Degree	Regression	Box plot
Line Graph	Dependency	R.W. betweenness	Degree centrality	Logistic regression	Scatter plot

(Continued)

Table 2.2 (*Continued*)

Link reduction	Connectivity	Load	Betweenness centrality	Mining	Contour plot
Link reduction simulation	Minimum cutset	Information	Closeness centrality	Frequent subgraph	Surface plot
Matrix	Maximum flow	Eigenvector	Eigenvector centrality	Classification	Network contour plot
Vectorize	PFNet	Status	Maximum matching	Regression	Network surface plot
Layer	Topological sort	Power		Collaborative filtering	
Split	Influence	Effects		Reduction	
Merge	Accessibility	PageRank		Clustering	
Multiplex	Diffusion	Generalized PageRank		Anomaly detection	
Mode	Influence network	HITS		Text	
2-mode network	Linear threshold	Community			
Onemode network	Cohesion	Equivalence			
Main node attribute	Component	Structural			
Tree construction	Bi-component	Regular			

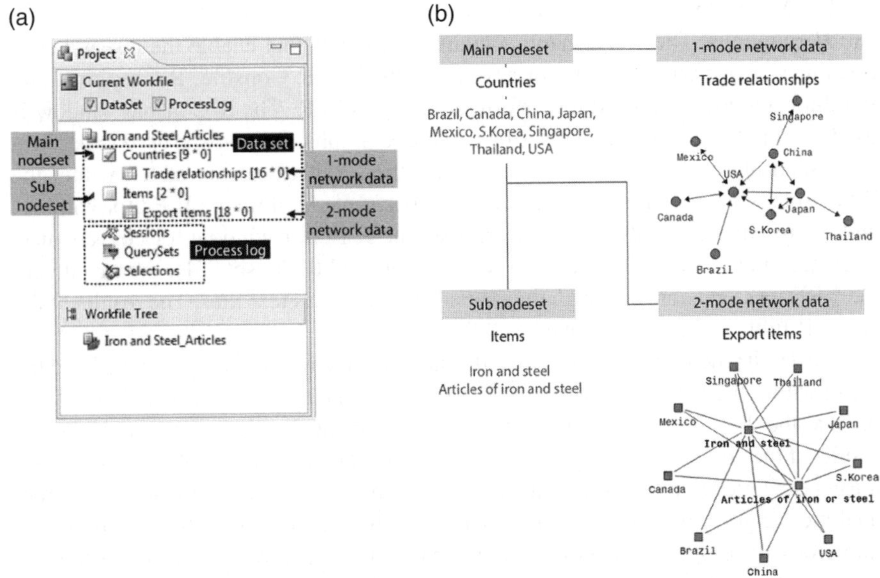

Figure 2.6 NetMiner data structure and data set. (a) Data structure and (b) data set.

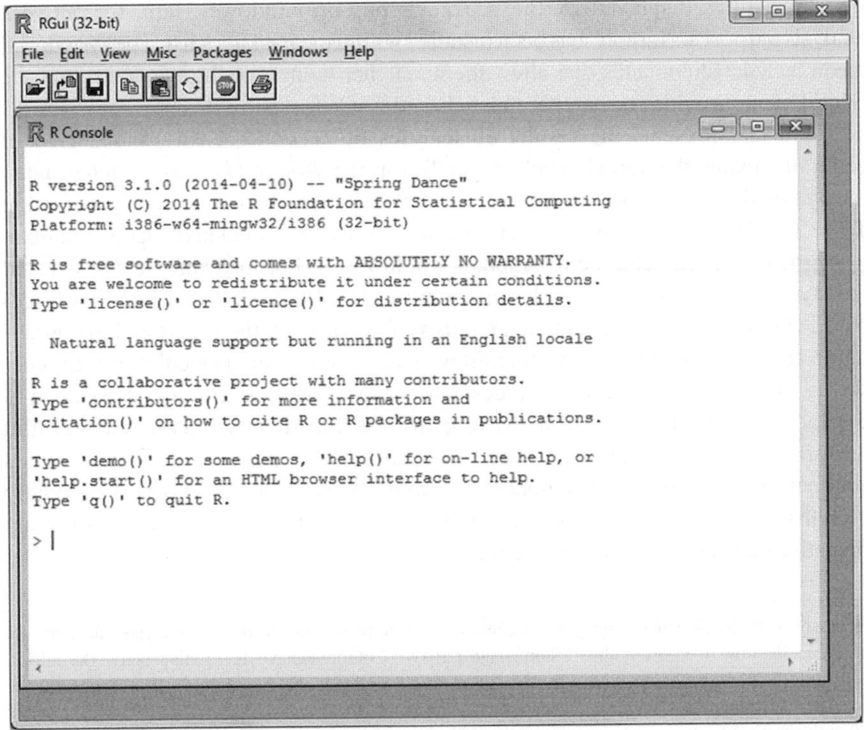

Figure 2.7 The R interface.

The Main Menu of R consists of *the File, Edit, View, Misc, Packages, Windows,* and *Help* menus. The [File] menu contains commands that enable the researcher to open new script windows and or saved scripts. The R Console, R Graphics, and R Editor windows are used to perform an analysis in R. The R Console window is used to input the actual analysis script, and the R Graphics window is used to perform the visualization analysis. However, because the script cannot be edited within the R Console window, editing and executing is performed within the R Editor window, and the researcher is advised to incorporate the R Editor window for convenience. Each activated window is saved as a separate file, and R Console files are saved with the *.RData extension, although they can also be saved as text files. The results of the active R Editor window are saved as *.R files.

The [Edit] menu includes commands that allow the researcher to edit data and the script within the R Console window. The [View] menu allows the researcher to view or hide the Tool bar and Status bar. The [Misc] menu includes commands for the results of the console window, suspending current calculations, and buffering options during execution. The Packages menu includes commands for downloading different analytical algorithms and executing them in R. In addition to the basic R program, numerous developer packages exist, which requires the researcher to install the appropriate software package for the purpose of the analysis. To install packages, the researcher must select the command *Packages > Install Packages,* which activates the [CRAN[3] mirror], select the appropriate country, and follow the package installation procedures displayed by the package's pop-up windows. Here, for network analysis purposes, "igraph" has been installed within the Packages list. The [Windows] menu includes commands that allow the researcher to arrange the windows, and the [Help] menu provides researcher manuals and FAQs for using R.

Table 2.3 presents the results of analyses of network density and degree of centrality using the igraph package in R for the *Iron and Steel_Articles* data.[4] Analyzing data in R requires that the researcher write a script, which is presented in Table 2.3. For clarity, the network visualization is also provided in the table, although it is provided in the separate R Graphics window in R. For the example, we selected the layout algorithm developed by Fruchterman and Reingold [6], which is a force-based algorithm that assumes that a repulsive force acts on the vertex and that gravitation acts on the edge; the resulting graph is based on iterated calculations. In other words, an existing link between nodes at a distance below a criterion is assumed to exhibit a repulsive force while an existing link above a criterion is assumed to exhibit an attractive force, similar to a spring. If no link exists, repulsive forces are assumed to repel the node from other nodes. The initial position of the node is randomly established; as the graph becomes stable, the algorithm iterates the positioning operations until equilibrium is achieved.

---

[3] R is software developed by many researchers and developers, and the related analysis packages are available for download from the R homepage CRAN (Comprehensive R Archive Network) mirror. Selecting the country/region within the CRAN mirror downloads the R program and packages in the appropriate language.

[4] To explain the data, trading data of the steel product have been used. See Table 5.1.

Table 2.3 R Script (in italics) and results.

```
> library(igraph)
> #Create a directed graph using adjacency matrix
> Iron_and_Steel_Articles<-
graph(c(5,3,6,3,4,2,4,8,4,1,4,3,2,3,7,3,1,4,1,2,2,1,2,4,1,9,3,6,1,3,3,7),directed=T)
> V(Iron_and_Steel_Articles)$name<-c("Japan", "S.Korea", "USA", "China",
"Brazil", "Canada", "Mexico", "Singapore", "Thailand")
> data
IGRAPH DN– 9 16 --
+ attr: name (v/c)
> plot(Iron_and_Steel_Aricles, layout=layout.fruchterman.reingold)
```

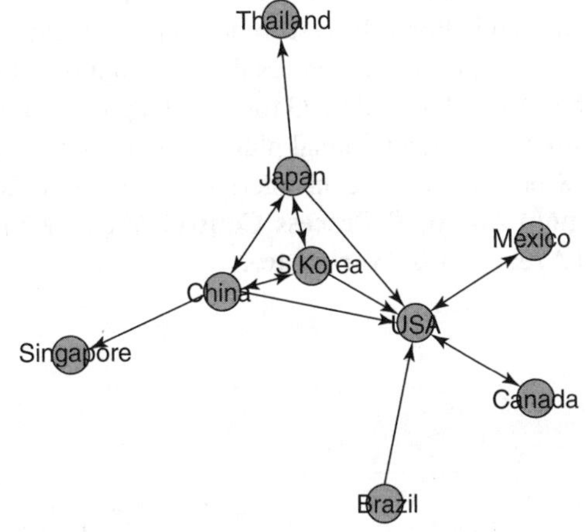


```
> graph.density(Iron_and_Steel_Articles)
[1] 0.2222222
> degree(Iron_and_Steel_Articles)
Japan S.Korea USA China Brazil Canada Mexico Singapore Thailand
6 5 8 6 1 2 2 1 1
> degree(Iron_and_Steel_Articles, mode=c("in"),loops=FALSE,
normalized=TRUE)
Japan S. Korea USA China Brazil Canada Mexico Singapore Thailand
0.250 0.250 0.750 0.250 0.000 0.125 0.125 0.125 0.125
> degree(Iron_and_Steel_Articles, mode=c("out"),loops=FALSE,
normalized=TRUE)
Japan S.Korea USA China Brazil Canada Mexico Singapore Thailand
0.500 0.375 0.250 0.500 0.125 0.125 0.125 0.000 0.000
```

2.4 Gephi

Gephi [7] is open source software developed by students at the University of Technology of Compiègne, France, in 2008, that allows dynamic network visualization, search, and analysis. Although several software programs for the visualization and analysis of network data are available, the Gephi software focuses on node attributes and uses the different colors and sizes for different nodes to provide a more intuitive visual analysis.

Gephi is not limited to network analysis and visualization, but addresses various types of networks such as biological networks, communications networks, Internet topology, P2P (peer-to-peer) file-sharing networks, on-line social networks, financial networks, semantic networks, and organizational networks. In addition, Gephi supports spreadsheets, CSV, DL(UCINET), VNA(NetDraw), NET(Pajek), GML, GEXF, TIP, GDF, and ZIP files and allows the researcher to import and export several types of data. The esthetically expressed visual results also support different file formats and output files in the SVG, PDF, and PNG formats. Gephi is available for download from http://gephi.github.io[5], and additional plug-ins make it easy to apply additional functions. Figure 2.8 presents the Gephi interface, which consists of the **❶ Main Menu, ❷ Management Menu, ❸ Process Control Area, ❹ Visualization Area, ❺ Analysis Output Area, and ❻ Workspace.**

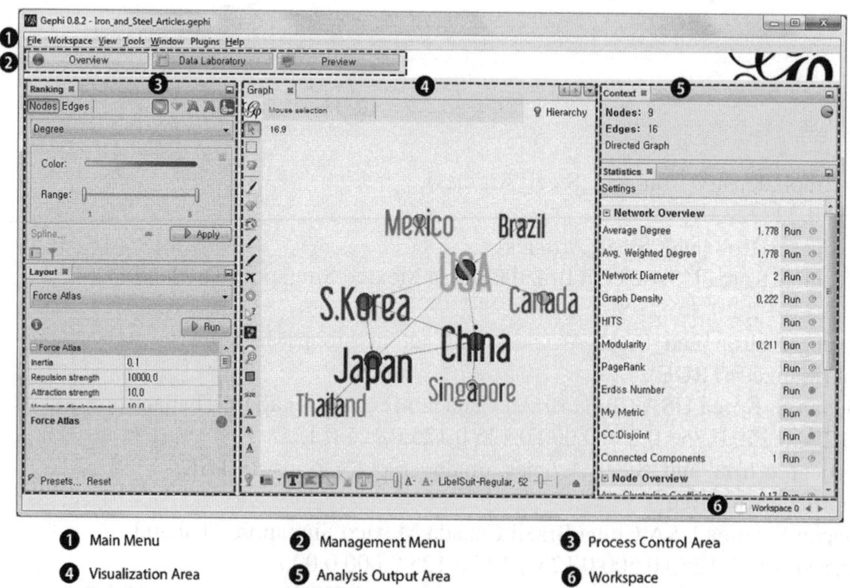

Figure 2.8 The Gephi interface.

[5]The information provided in the text is based on Gephi 0.8.2, which is the most current version.

In the ❶ **Main Menu** (*File, Workspace, View, Tools, Windows, Plug-in, Help*), the [File] menu includes commands for opening existing or saved Gephi files and for creating new Gephi files, importing external data, and saving current Gephi files. Files created with Gephi are saved with the *.gephi extension. The [Workspace] functions similar to the Workfile Tree in NetMiner. If the researcher wishes to manage new data in the Gephi file, a new Workspace can be opened, and data can be imported into the Workspace. Movement of data between Workspaces can be performed with ◀▶ in the ❻ **Workspace.** The [View] menu enables the researcher to observe the currently active window in full page mode and the [Tools] menu includes commands for adding functions from plug-ins and software set-up options and languages. Gephi currently supports English, French, Russian, Spanish, Portuguese, Chinese, and Japanese. The [Windows] menu includes analysis and visualization commands such as Clustering, Context, Data Table, Console, Filter, Graph, Hierarchy, Layout, Partition, Preview, Preview Setting, Ranking, Welcome, Statistics, Timeline, Configure Windows, and Close Windows. When commands are selected, new tabs for ❸ **Process Control Area,** ❹ **Visualization Area,** ❺ **Analysis Output Area** appear, and additional commands can be executed. The [Plugins] menu provides additional commands available through the installation of various plug-ins. [Help], updating commands for the software is given.

The Gephi ❷ **Management Menu** provides Overview, Data laboratory, and Preview buttons. The Overview screen is where most of the operations are performed and where visual results can be moved, corrected, and edited. The visual results from the [Overview] window can be previewed in the Preview window for verification, and detailed information regarding the analytical results is provided in the Data Laboratory screen. The [Data Laboratory] window is the data management area for visual interpretation of the data selecting the Run command. In addition, Gephi allows the researcher to import data in CSV format and export data tables. Prior to outputting visual results, items for final specification can be modified in the [Preview] screen. Figure 2.9 presents the Data Laboratory and Preview screens.

In the ❸ **Process Control Area,** the execution Tab that appears when the Windows command is selected displays the command options. The Process Control Area, Visualization Area, and Analysis Output Area all appear in the Overview screen of the ❷ **Management Menu;** the Analysis Output Area appears in the Data Laboratory screen, and the lower portion of the Data Table Tab provides commands that allow the researcher to insert, modify, and edit data.

The ❹ **Visualization Area** presents the results of the data visualization and provides options for customizing visualizations. The *Windows > Ranking* command creates a new Tab within the Process Control Area that allows the researcher to control the color and size of nodes, edges, and labels. Gephi allows 2D and 3D visualization, and the researcher is able to choose various layout algorithms such as Fruchterman-Reingold, ForceAtlas, Yifan Hu Multilevel, Circular, Radial Axis, Geolayout. In addition, the Layout Adjust command included in the layout algorithm can be selected to selectively perform layout algorithms; if this command is selected, the labels for the visual results do not overlap. Some visualization algorithms require installation of additional plug-ins.

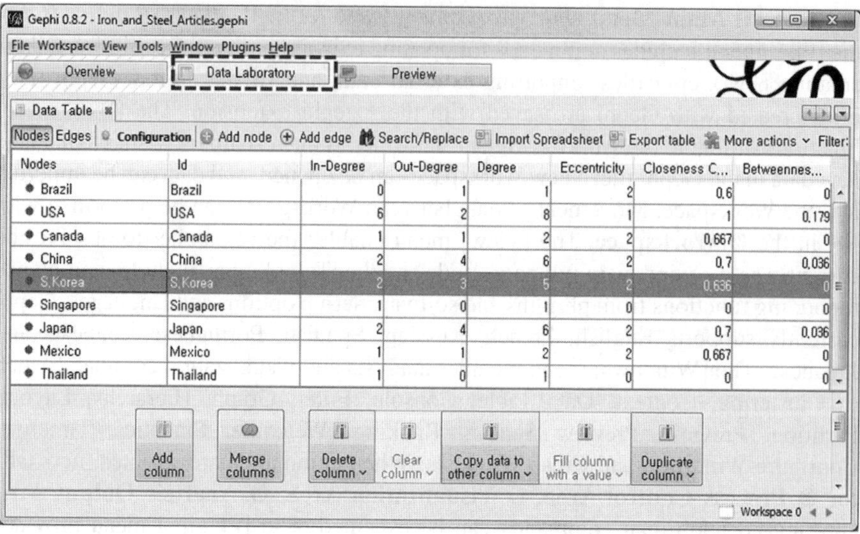

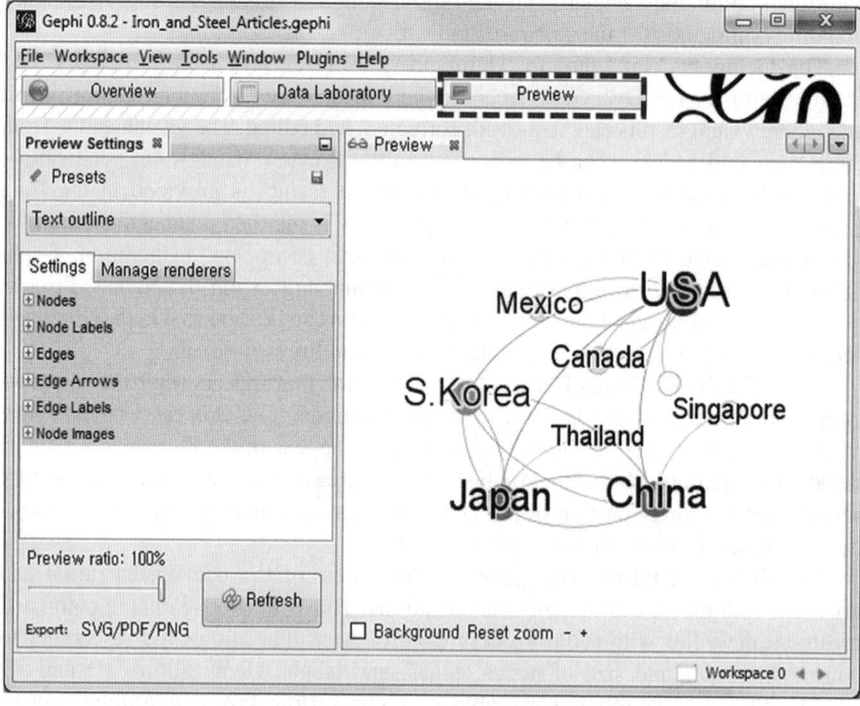

Figure 2.9 Gephi data laboratory and preview screens.

The number of nodes and edges and graph characteristics (directed or undirected) are indicated through the Context Tab in the ❺ **Analysis Output Area.** The Statistics Tab provides some of the analyses performed by Gephi. Analysis results can be verified by selecting the Run command. In Gephi, density analysis results are verified by the *Statistics > Network Overview > Graph Density* commands, and the degree analysis of individual nodes is verified by the *Data Laboratory > Data Table* commands. To analyze and visually interpret the *Iron and Steel_Articles* data, the researcher would first import the data in CSV format and select the *Data Laboratory > Data Table Tab > Import Spreadsheet* commands, which open a window to select the file to be imported. Data options regarding separators, Edges or Node tables, and Charset must be chosen. After the data have been imported, the visual results are presented in the Overview and Preview screens. The visual results of the *Overview > Graph Tab* commands are presented in Figure 2.8, and the visual results of the *Preview > Preview Tab* commands are presented in Figure 2.9. The *Overview > Statistics Tab* commands that confirm the results of the analysis results are presented in Figure 2.8; the *Data Laboratory > Data Table Tab* commands that confirm the results of the analysis results are presented in Figure 2.9.

In addition, the Timeline command (*Windows > Timeline*) in Gephi makes it possible to exhibit dynamic networks because the command allows the researcher to add and remove nodes and edges as a function of time. Furthermore, in Gephi, the current researcher environment is saved and when the Gephi is reexecuted later, the past researcher environment is applied and a researcher specific analysis and visualization environment can be created.

2.5 NodeXL

NodeXL [8] is a free, open-source template that utilizes the Microsoft Office Excel Template to collect, analyze, and visualize network data. NodeXL was developed by the Social Media Research Foundation and has been continuously updated through researcher donations. NodeXL imports and exports files from UCINET, GML, Pajek, matrix formats and collects network data from Twitter, YouTube, Flicker or email. In addition, plug-ins enable data to be retrieved from Facebook personal pages, Facebook Fan pages, Facebook group networks, the MediaWiki Network, the Exchange Server Network, the ONA Survey Network, and the VOSON Hyperlink Network. NodeXL is available for download from http://nodexl.codeplex.com/. As Figure 2.10 indicates, Excel is executed when the NodeXL template is selected, and the NodeXL menu is added to the Ribbon menu. In NodeXL, data are exhibited in one area, and a separate Document Actions area exhibits the graph.

The NodeXL Main Menu consists of the *Data, Graph, Visual Properties, Analysis, Options,* and *Show/Hide* menus. The [Data] menu provides commands for data creation and data input and output, and the [Graph] menu provides commands for selecting the Layout Algorithm used to generate the graph in the Document Actions area. The [Visual Properties] menu includes commands to define the style of graph edges and vertices, and the Autofill Columns command allows the researcher to

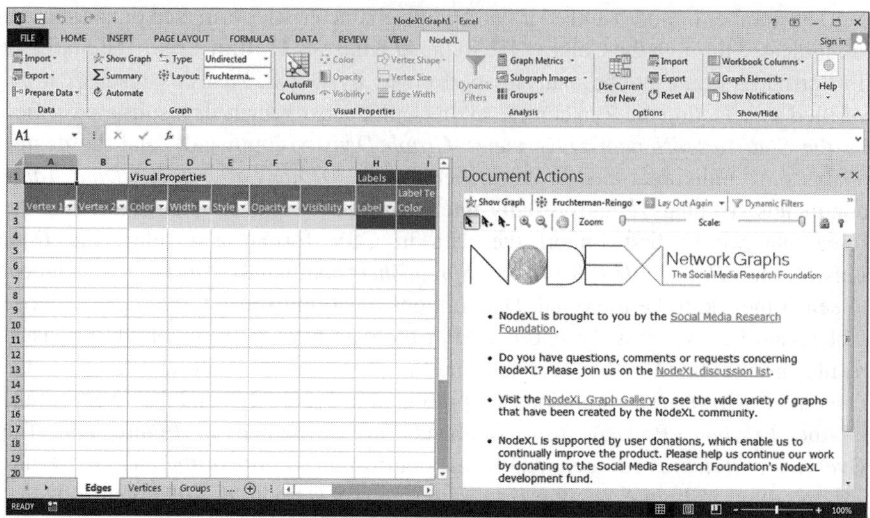

Figure 2.10 NodeXL interface.

simultaneously define the resulting analytical values and the size, color, shape of edges and vertices based on edge attributes. When the Graph Matrix command is selected from the [Analysis] menu, different network analyses can be performed, including the overall graph metrics, degree, betweenness and closeness centrality, and clustering. The [Options] menu provides commands for importing and exporting data based on researcher specifications. The [Show/Hide] menu provides commands that enable the researcher to show and hide data tables and graphs.

When NodeXL is used to analyze and visualize the *Iron and Steel_Articles* data, the Vertices tab appears in the lower portion of the screen, and the results of the analysis for the individual nodes are provided. The Overall Metrics Tab presents the overall characteristics of the network generated by the analysis. To verify the resulting graph, the researcher may select the Document *Actions > Refresh Graph* or *Layout (Algorithm) > Layout Again* commands.

References

1 Borgatti, S.P., Everett, M.G., and Freeman, L.C. (2002) *Ucinet6 for Windows: Software for Social Network Analysis*, Harvard, MA: Analytic Technologies.

2 Richardson, D.C. and Richardson, J.S. (1992) The kinemage: a tool for scientific communication, *Protein Science*, **1**(1), 3–9.

3 Cyram (2014) *NetMiner4*, Seoul: Cyram Inc.

4 Kamada, T. and Kawai, S. (1989) An algorithm for drawing general undirected graphs. *Information Processing Letters*, **31**(1), 7–15.

5 Butts, C.T. (2008) Network: a package for managing relational data in R, *Journal of Statistical Software*, **24**(2), 1–36.

6 Fruchterman, J.T. and Reingold, E. (1991) Graph drawing by force-directed placement, *Software Practice and Experience*, **21**, 1129–1164.

7 Bastian, M., Heymann, S., and Jacomy, M. (2009) Gephi: an open source software for exploring and manipulating networks. International AAAI Conference on Weblogs and Social Media.

8 Smith, M., Milic-Frayling, N., Shneiderman, B. *et al.* (2010) NodeXL: A Free and Open Network Overview, Discovery and Exploration Add-In for Excel 2007/2010, http://nodexl.codeplex.com/ from the Social Media Research Foundation, http://www.smrfoundation.org (accessed 22 May 2015).

3

Understanding Network Analysis

While existing research is based on an actors' independence, network analysis assumes that the actors are interdependent. Based on that assumption, network analysis aims to quantitatively measure regular patterns. Network analysis assumes that the actions of actors are not independent or autonomous, but interdependent, where the relationship among the actors works as a conduit for flow or transfer of (material or immaterial) resources. Also, the difference from previous research methods is that a position of an actor in a group can place limitations on his or her actions or provide an environment for coincident to occur. In other words, actors are interdependent, resource is circulated through relationships and a social network is formed, but actions can vary according to the position of the actor in a group. Therefore, even if an analysis is basically initiated from an individual actor, it actually covers not only the actor but also the groups and connection relation between a group and an actor.

3.1 Defining Social Network Analysis

Society includes actors such as nations, corporations, groups, and individuals, who interact with one another within an organization or society. These interactions produce social relationships that are referred to as social networks. A relationship might begin with mere acquaintance and might be expressed in many ways,

Fundamentals of Big Data Network Analysis for Research and Industry, First Edition. Hyunjoung Lee and Il Sohn.

depending on the relevant subject and context. For example, role relationships are exhibited by exporting and importing countries, manufacturing companies and companies supplying raw materials, and by students and teachers. There are also cognitive or emotional relationships that are established on the basis of factors such as acknowledgement, friendship, respect, and exclusivity. A relationship can also be established and classified in terms of actions such as selling, buying, conversing, supporting, and moving.

The actors within a social relationship affect one another, which can maintain or extend the relationship. When individuals select a particular product or develop a new technology, they often obtain advice from others and collaborate toward a common goal rather than deciding or acting individually. Therefore, it is necessary to understand social participants' effects on one another. To date, however, our perspective has been limited to actors' individual characteristics rather than the value and importance of the actor's relationships. Consequently, an actor is assumed to be reserved or introverted and unaffected by relationships with other actors in the network, and changes in the relationship or the situation are not taken into account. This assumption has been more predominant for social networks with greater numbers of actors and more complicating and varying relationships among actors. This assumption has also been due to a lack of interest, the extent of the data available, and the complexity of the relationships.

What sorts of relationships can be identified? In 2000, different social network services such as Twitter and Facebook generated interest in social networks and relationships. With advances in computer technology and the proliferation of personal communication and infra systems on the Internet, it became possible to obtain big data. Simultaneously, **Social Network Analysis** (**SNA**) techniques for analyzing relationships were developed and usyed, making the fundamental tools needed to understand social networks available. SNA, which is context specific, provides an intuitive and clear analysis of dynamic interactions in relationships and their effect on network structure.

SNA is a method for modeling relationships between actors through nodes and links to identify network typologies and evolution. Its roots can be found in the sociometric research conducted by Dr. Moreno, an Austrian-born psychiatrist, in the 1930s [1]. Moreno used sociometry to measure like and dislike behavior between individuals and to identify the dynamics of inclusion and exclusion for an actor within a group. These measurement techniques provided a sociomatrix that identified the status of a particular actor within a group; the matrix could be used to calculate a group cohesiveness index. More recently, research has analyzed the dynamic evolution of network structure and has expanded to research areas beyond the social sciences such as engineering and the natural sciences.

Although earlier empirical research in the social sciences has been based on individual characteristics and independent actors, SNA assumes that actors are mutually dependent and establish relationships that exhibit systematic patterns that can be quantified and measured. SNA holds that the behavioral patterns exhibited by a network of actors are not independent or autonomous but are mutually dependent and that relationships between actors serve as a conduit or resources that are materials or nonmaterial. Furthermore, the claim that the social position of the actor in the group can limit or provide opportunities for group behavior patterns distinguishes SNA from other existing empirical research methodologies. In other words, SNA assumes that actors within a group are mutually dependent, that resources are distributed through relationships, and that the behavior patterns of group actors are limited or encourages by the actor's social position within the group. Thus, although SNA begins with individual actors, it also includes the group and the relationships of individual actors within the group.

Recently, the application of SNA has expanded to areas such as knowledge management, human resources and organization management, criminal investigation, marketing and customer relationship management, Internet services, and structural biology.

3.2 Basic SNA Concepts

3.2.1 Basic Terminology

1. *Actor or node*: The actor is the person, company, social organization, country, product, animal, or entity that is expressed as a node in SNA. Although we use the word "actor," the actor does not necessarily have to physically perform or intend to perform a duty or an action within the network.

2. *Relationship or link*: The actor is socially connected, and this relationship is expressed as a link in SNA. Social relationships can be categorized as functional relationships, cognitive or emotional relationships, and behavioral relationships [2].

3. *Dyad relation*: Because a relationship involves two distinct actors, a network is an ensemble of several pair or dyad relations. Therefore, the basic unit of analysis in SNA is the dyad relationship. The dyad relationship is a connection between the paired actors and their potential connections. Analysis of a dyad relation focuses on the interactivity and the uniqueness of the relationship.

4. *Triad relation*: A triad relation involves the analysis of the connections between three actors and potential subgroup categories. Analysis of a triad relation focuses on transitivity and balance in the relationships of the actors. The transitivity of a triad relation involves the potential transfer of an existing dyad relation to another dyad relation in a triad relationship [3]. For example, in a triad relationship between "i," "j," and "k," if actor "i" likes actor "j" and actor "j" likes actor "k," then it can be inferred that actor "i" likes actor "k." The balance within a triad relationship is the psychological balance within the actors of the triad relationship and the status of the actors in maintaining this balance. Thus, if actors "i" and "j" exhibit mutual affection for one another, the evaluation of third-party actor "k" would tend to be similar, but if "i" and "j" exhibited mutual dislike of each other, the evaluation of third-party actor "k" would be different.

5. *Subgroup*: A group is the set of all actors connected within the network. Subgroups are a subset of connections of actors and their subsequent connections. Thus, a subgroup might consist of actors connected through dense, direct, and reciprocated choice relations that enable actors in the subgroup to share information, create solidarity, and act collectively. Numerous direct contracts among subgroup actors, combined with few or no ties to outsiders, dispose a group toward homogeneity of thought, identity, and behavior. Examples of subgroups include military platoons, sports teams, work teams, terrorist cells, and criminal gangs.

6. *Network*: A network is composed of a set of actors (nodes) and their relationships (links), which can be specifically defined with respect to the actor, group, and relationship. A network can be analyzed as a whole-network that includes all nodes or as an ego-network that describes the network from the perspective of a central individual node. In a whole-network analysis, the internal structure of the entire network and the distribution course are identified. In an ego-network analysis, the characteristic local network connections for a focus node or ego with other nodes are identified.

3.2.2 Representation of a Network

1. *Graph and matrix*: A graph intuitively illustrates a network by visually displaying nodes and links. In addition, a graph can represent a matrix that allows the mathematical and statistical analysis of a complex network. A node on a matrix or a graph can be related to itself, which is termed a self-loop or a reflexive tie. In a graph, a self-loop is represented as a directed or undirected link to itself (Figure 3.1a). In a matrix, self-loops are represented by the values along the diagonal (Figure 3.1b).

2. *Path and distance*: The connections between nodes of a network involve paths and distance. A path, which identifies the connection between two nodes, is an important parameter for data measurement. In a path, a node and

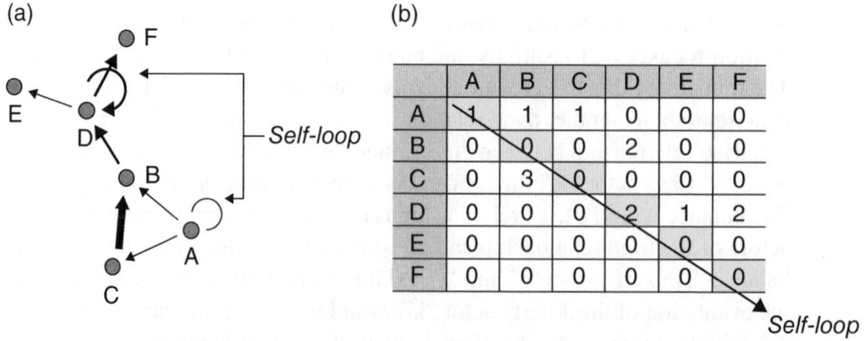

	A	B	C	D	E	F
A	1	1	1	0	0	0
B	0	0	0	2	0	0
C	0	3	0	0	0	0
D	0	0	0	2	1	2
E	0	0	0	0	0	0
F	0	0	0	0	0	0

Figure 3.1 A network graph and matrix. (a) Graph (b) matrix.

link cannot be passed more than once. Therefore, several paths that connect two nodes might exist in a single graphical representation, and the shortest path between the two nodes is identified as the path with the fewest links. In network analysis, distance does not refer to the physical distance between nodes but rather to the number of links between the nodes for a particular path. Thus, two nodes connected by a single link are considered to be "directly connected," and two nodes connected through several links are considered to be "indirectly connected." In Figure 3.2a, node A is directly connected to nodes B, C, F, and is indirectly connected to node G. There seem to be two indirect paths between nodes A and G: Path 1 (A → F → G) and Path 2 (A → B → E → G), where Path 1 is the shortest path.

3. *Degree*: Two nodes connected through a link are referred to as mutually adjacent, and the number of mutually adjacent nodes is termed degree centrality. Thus, the degree of a node in a network reflects the node's activity or influence on other nodes within a network. A node that is not connected to other nodes is termed an isolated node. Degree takes a minimum value of 0 and a maximum value of g – 1 in a network with g nodes. In the graph presented in Figure 3.2b, node E is an isolated node without any connections and node C, with a degree of 3, exhibits the highest degree centrality. The maximum degree that can occur in this five-node network is a degree of 4. Node B receives arrows from nodes C and A and sends an arrow to node D, exhibiting two in-degree connections and one out-degree connection. In contrast, node D receives an arrow from node B and sends an arrow to nodes E and F, exhibiting one in-degree connection and two out-degree connections.

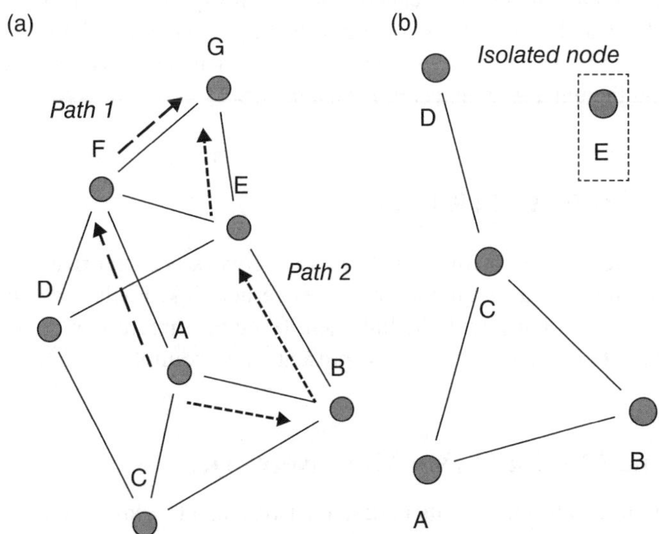

Figure 3.2 (a) Path and (b) degree.

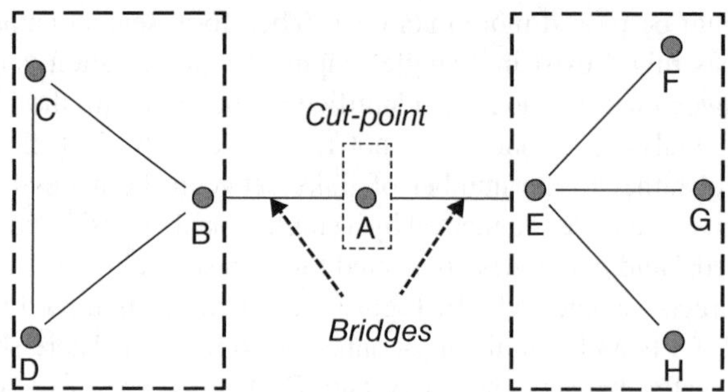

Figure 3.3 Cut-point and bridges of a network component.

The concept of degree centrality reflects the number of links between individual nodes, where the maximum number of links is determined by the number of nodes, and the proportion of links within a network is identified as the density. Based on the density, we can determine the number of connections between all the nodes of a network. Density is defined as the ratio between the actual number of links and the greatest possible number of links (which results in a maximum density of unity). When calculating density, typically self-loops are not considered, and the maximum possible number of links equals the number of nodes × (the number of nodes − 1).

4. *Component*: A network that has no disconnected nodes within a group is identified as a component. A node that separates a component from two or more components is termed the cut-point, and the specific link between the cut-point and a component is called a bridge. In Figure 3.3, A is a cut-point and the B–A and A–E links are bridges. If the cut-point and the bridges are not connected, there will be two separate components: one with nodes B, C, and D and the other with nodes E, F, G, and H.

3.3 Social Network Data

To organize the data for network analysis, the network is categorized based on the nature of the node as a one-mode or two-mode network. Each node and link can exhibit specific attributes, with the link identifying the direction of the relationship and its weighted value. Figure 3.4 presents an example of a network data structure.

3.3.1 One-Mode and Two-Mode Networks

Depending on the attributes of its nodes, a network can be classified as a one-mode network in which all the nodes in the network share the same attribute or a two-mode network with two different node attributes within a network [4]. For example, in a

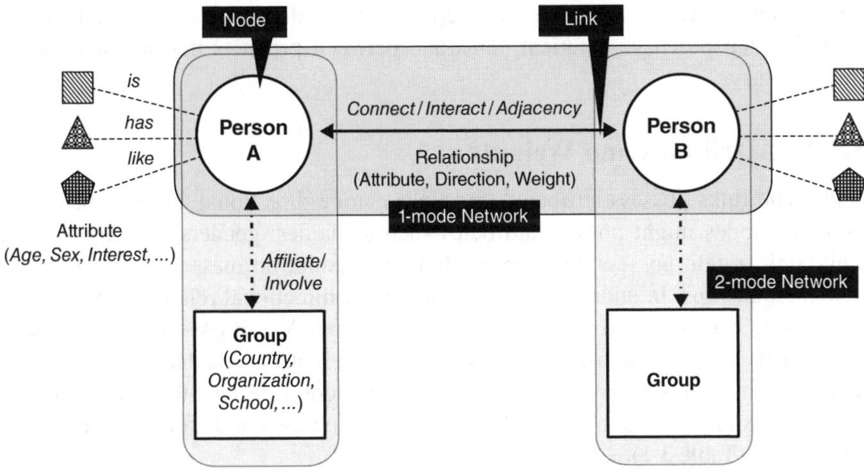

Figure 3.4 Structure of the network data.

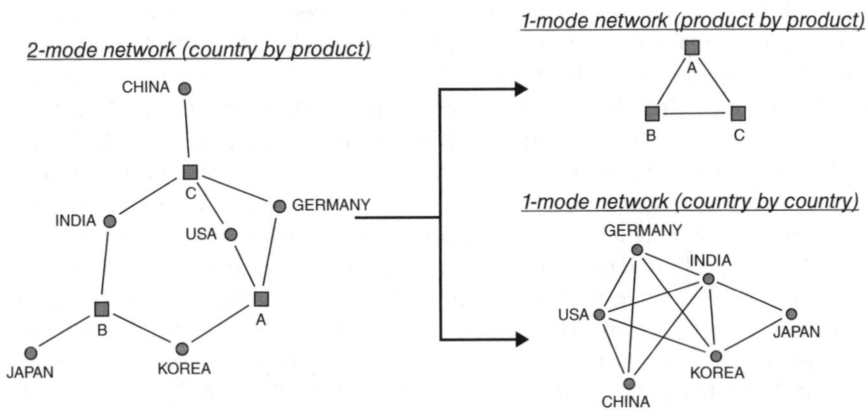

Figure 3.5 Transformation of a two-mode network into a one-mode network.

one-mode network, the node–attribute relationship might be "person by person, country by country," and in a two-mode network, the node–attribute relationship might be "person by country." Currently, most network analysis is based on one-mode networks, so to fully analyze a two-mode network, the two-mode network must be transformed into a one-mode network. Consequently, direct relationships between nodes with different attributes in a two-mode network are transformed into indirect relationships in one-mode networks with identical node attributes, to increase the efficiency of the network analysis. Figure 3.5 presents the direct relationship of products A, B, and C for the different countries in the two-mode network of "product by country," which is transformed and distinguished as the indirect relationships of two one-mode networks of "country by country" and "product by product"; direct relationships between countries are replaced by indirect relationships between countries that purchase identical items and between products that are sold to the same country.

3.3.2 Attributes and Weights

Nodes and links possess attributes, and links can be directional and weighted. For example, nodes might possess attributes such as names, genders, and affiliations, while links might possess attributes such as friendship, business relationships, and trust relationships. In addition, links can represent directional relationships such as "A likes B," which would be expressed as a link from A to B ($A \rightarrow B$). To represent the intensity of the relationship, the link is given a weight. A node that links to another node is termed the source node, and the receiving node is termed the target node. In the above example, A is the source node and B is the target node for the relationship "A likes B" (Table 3.1).

3.3.3 Network Data Form

Network data take the form of a matrix. However, depending on the format, network data might also take the form of a linked list or an edged list, which provides the same information as a matrix. A linked list format for data simplifies the node relationship in the matrix into "source node by target node 1, target node 2, … target node n," which has the advantage of efficiently representing data in which many nodes exist. However, the weights of the links between source and target nodes cannot be fully expressed in the linked list format. In an edged list format, the data are represented as mutually connected pairs of nodes in which the weight of the relation can be expressed. For data in the form of a matrix, an existing relationship in the $m \times n$ cell takes the value of "1 or the weighted value" or a value of "0" if no relationship exists. Typically, network data take the form of a matrix, but this data format is less appropriate when the number of nodes is extremely large. The first line of the left side of the matrix represents the source node, and the first column represents the target node. The diagonal values are the values of a self-loop between each node and itself (Table 3.2).

Table 3.1 Link direction and weight.

	Unweighted	Weighted
Directed	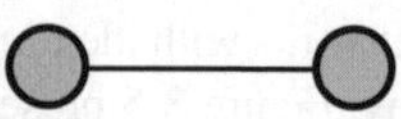 O——O	O━━▶O
Undirected	 O——O	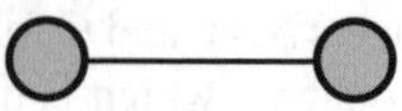 O——O

Table 3.2 Network data formats.

	One-Mode Network	Two-Mode Network
Graph		

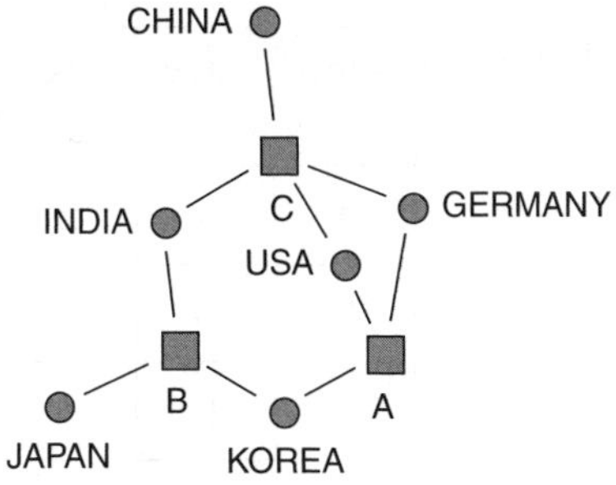

Matrix

One-Mode Network:

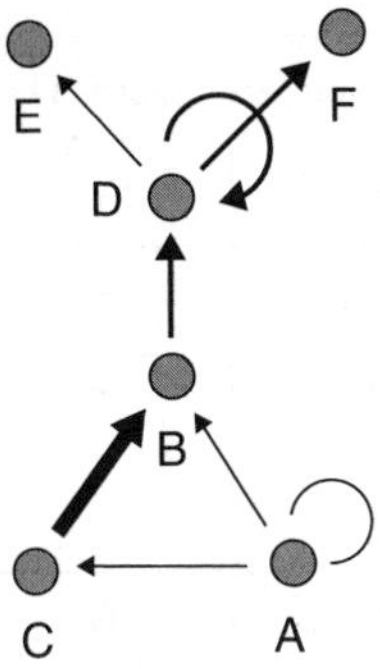

	A	B	C	D	E	F
A	1	1	1	0	0	0
B	0	0	0	2	0	0
C	0	3	0	0	0	0
D	0	0	0	2	1	2
E	0	0	0	0	0	0
F	0	0	0	0	0	0

Two-Mode Network:

	A	B	C
KOREA	1	1	0
JAPAN	0	1	0
USA	1	0	1
CHINA	0	0	1
INDIA	0	1	1
GERMANY	1	0	1

Edged list

One-Mode Network:

Source	Target	Weight
A	B	1
D	F	2
C	B	3
A	C	1
B	D	2
D	E	1
A	A	1
D	D	2

Two-Mode Network:

Source	Target	Weight
KOREA	A	1
USA	A	1
GERMANY	A	1
INDIA	B	1
JAPAN	B	1
KOREA	B	1
INDIA	C	1
GERMANY	C	1
USA	C	1
CHINA	C	1

(*Continued*)

Table 3.2 (*Continued*)

<table>
<tr><th></th><th>One-Mode Network</th><th>Two-Mode Network</th></tr>
<tr><td>Linked list</td><td>

Source	Target 1	Target 2	Target 3
A	A	B	C
B	D		
C	B		
D	D	E	F

</td><td>

Source	Target1	Target2
KOREA	A	B
JAPAN	B	
USA	A	C
CHINA	C	
INDIA	B	C
GERMANY	A	C

</td></tr>
</table>

References

1 Barabási, A.-L. (2002) *Linked: The New Science of Networks*, Cambridge, MA: Perseus Publishing.

2 Knoke, D. and Kuklinski, J.H. (1982) *Network Analysis: Quantitative Applications in the Social Sciences*, Sage Publications: Beverly Hills, CA.

3 Wasserman, S. and Faust, K. (1997) *Social Network Analysis: Methods and Application*, New York: Cambridge University Press.

4 Borgatti, S.P. and Everett, M.G. (1997) Network analysis of 2-mode data, *Social Networks*, **19**(3), 243–269.

4

Research Methods Using SNA

Research related to network analysis starts from recognizing research problems through empirical studies and developing hypotheses to prove empirical evidence. To set up a hypothesis, attribute variables as well as related variables among actors can be considered. In performing a network analysis, not only are related variables considered, but it is also possible to set up a hypothesis considering a variety of aspects including relational features among actors, which can affect the actors' attribute variable and have an effect on the actors' relations. A research plan is constructed by considering the network modeling of defining nodes and links within the network as well as determining a means of collecting data. Depending on the form of network data that would be collected by a researcher, a variety of methods to collect data, including a survey, interview, observation, web-log, bibliographic data, and so on, can be used. Collected data are basically expressed within the matrix, and data cleansing is necessary to make it available for network analysis. The process of data cleansing is essential, as unstructured data have recently been gathered and used to a greater extent. In addition, there is a process to confirm whether a hypothetical relationship is supported, which is formed by using various indexes and techniques of network analysis. Finally, social network analysis can be completed after interpretation of the research results to draw a

Fundamentals of Big Data Network Analysis for Research and Industry, First Edition. Hyunjoung Lee and Il Sohn.

conclusion for the problem at hand. However, because a network is continuously changing and not fixed, there needs to be research, which consistently reflects the dynamic features of the network.

4.1 SNA Research Procedures

Research on social networks generally seeks to identify patterns of relationships between nodes and links and to determine the effects produced by these relationships. Thus, research on social network building empirically examines relationship data by identifying a problem and developing hypotheses that are tested with empirical data. In developing hypotheses, both actor relationship variables and actor attribute variables must be considered. It cannot be assumed that only relationship variables are relevant for network analysis; other factors, such as the variables related to actor attributes and the effects of actor attributes on the relationships, also must be addressed when developing hypotheses.

Testing research hypotheses requires identifying an appropriate research design that defines the nodes and links of the network for network modeling and selects the method to be used to collect the data. Methods used to collect network data include questionnaires and surveys, interviews, observations, web-logs, and literature surveys. Because the raw data are typically in matrix form, data cleaning is necessary to transform the raw data into a format appropriate for network analysis. Moreover, it is necessary to transform the network data into unstructured data.

The next research stage involves the use of different network analysis methods to test the hypotheses regarding network relationships. Subsequently, the research results are interpreted, and the conclusions are applied to the problem under investigation. However, because networks are not static but dynamic entities, follow-up research is necessary to determine the extent to which network characteristics continue to evolve (Figure 4.1).

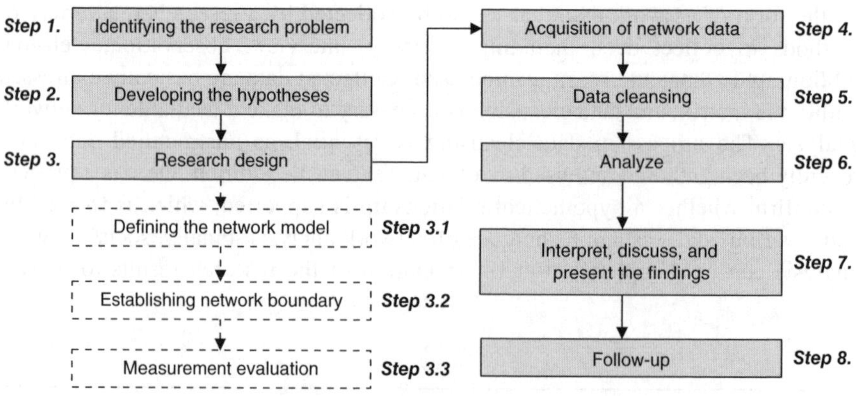

Figure 4.1 Research procedure.

4.2 Identifying the Research Problem and Developing Hypotheses

4.2.1 Identifying the Research Problem

To date, most research involving network analysis has focused on associations between actor attributes and patterns of behavior. However, rather than assuming that similar actors engage in similar actions, we identify existing relationships among actors and examine the characteristic behaviors related to these relationships to empirically establish relationships. As a result, network research investigates actor attributes and relationships between actors; this focus is different from most earlier social science research, which has focused solely on actor attributes. Relationships between actors can be used to identify relationships between attributes. When people act, they often interact with other people to form relationships; within these relationships, an individual might serve both as the target of an action and also as an actor. By repeating the process of identifying individual relationships, it is possible to discover a common feature shared by a group of people who exhibit similar behavioral patterns. Relationships do not only exist between individuals; trade relationships exist between countries in the form of foreign trade, and an individual country might be the source or target in a trade relationship. In addition, countries with similar national incomes seem to be similar with respect to the products traded in the economy. Based on the type of products traded, the nation's influence, and the direction of that influence, it is possible to determine a nation's developmental status. Network research requires that we not lose focus on the objective of the research but precisely understand and answer the question being investigated. The research question must seek to determine the extent to which relationships exists between two or more variables, and in network research, the research problem should include relationship variables. Furthermore, the research question must be formed in such a way that the answer can be clearly and directly provided on the basis of empirical evidence.

4.2.2 Developing Hypotheses

Once the researcher has identified a research question, research hypotheses must be developed. A hypothesis is a proposed explanation of the relationship between variables. If the research problem seeks to determine cause-and-effect relationships between variables, the hypothesis proposes an answer to this question. However, a hypothesis is not formed simply by proposing that a relationship between variables exists. Creating a meaningful hypothesis requires the researcher to determine how to measure the hypothesis variables and obtain data that will test the hypothesis. In addition, a hypothesis should be stated in simple and general terms that allow it to be empirically confirmed if it is to be useful for describing the present situation and predicting the future.

Network research investigates actor attributes and their associations with relationships, and the attributes might be nodes, mutual relationships, overall networks, or groups. Relationship might be categorized as involving similarities, social relationships, interactions, and flow. Similarity relationships might involve locations (e.g., identical space time continuums), affiliations (e.g., the same company or club), or attributes (e.g., shared gender or age). Social relationships might involve kinship (e.g., parents or siblings), roles (e.g., friends, superiors, competitors, or students), emotions (e.g., fondness or dislike), or cognitive activities (e.g., mutual knowledge or knowledge with respect to a particular topic). Interactions include activities such as conversing, advising, helping, and harming in which data, resources, faith, and/or human resources are exchanged. By investigating subject attributes and types of relationships, network research is able to explain the structural patterns exhibited by relationships, the effect of attributes on relationships, and effects due to the existence of a relationship. In particular, network research is able to identify the attributes and relationships of nodes or groups, such as characteristic changes in node relationships that are related to attributes (e.g., centrality increases with age or advertising exerts a greater effect purchasing for clients with higher betweenness compared to clients with higher degree centrality), change in node attributes that are associated with relationship properties (e.g., turnover decreases with increased centrality in organizations), and connections between relationship characteristics (e.g., organizations with greater centralization exhibit lower organizational density) (Table 4.1).

Table 4.1 Types of hypotheses in network research [1].

	Independent Variables	Dependent Variables	Example
Node level	Network property	Network property	*Degree centrality → betweenness centrality*
	Network property	Actor attribute	*Closeness centrality → performance*
	Actor attribute	Network property	*Physical attractiveness → degree centrality*
Dyad level	Network tie	Network tie	*Working together → friendship*
	Network tie	Attribute similarity	*Friends → attitude toward organizational justice*
	Attribute similarity	Network tie	*Smoking → friendship*
Group level	Network property	Network property	*Group density → group average path length*
	Network property	Group attribute	*Group density → group performance*
	Group attribute	Network property	*Group proportion of women → group density*

4.3 Research Design

4.3.1 Defining the Network Model

After identifying the relationships between variables and generating hypotheses based on these relationships, relevant nodes, and relationships must be clearly defined. Network modeling transforms a complex reality into a set of simple network connections of nodes and links.

1. *Defining the node*: To define the node, identify the focus of the analysis (e.g., people, objects, or countries), and identify attribute types and levels. For example, when analyzing companies, the nodes might be organization members, departments, or companies, with organization members as the smallest unit and companies the largest unit of analysis. Note attributes might include names, gender, departments, positions, organizational structure of a department, or company sales revenue.

   Generally, the smallest unit of analysis is preferred for data collection (e.g., the organization member). When data are obtained for the smallest unit of analysis, it is relatively easy to expand the range of the analysis to units of greater size. After the node level has been selected, the next step is to generate a one-mode or two-mode network, depending on the characteristics of the nodes that comprise the network. Various network forms are consistent with a particular of dataset. Because different evaluation indices are associated with different types of networks, preliminary consideration of the network form should be done to verify the hypothesis. Finally, the researcher should identify the node attributes to be used in the analysis. Beginning with the characteristics of the population statistics, the behavioral variable of the individual node might be included in the attributes and the resulting value of the network analysis can be transformed into the node attributes and used.

2. *Defining the link*: The researcher must be able to measure links and apply links to each node within the network. To define the link, the researcher must identify the different types of relationships between people, materials, and countries and consider the direction and weight of the relationship as well as relationship attributes. Links can be categorized as simple or complex. Examples of simple relationships include lending money and buying goods; meeting more than once per week to watch a movie and eat food is an example of a complex relationship. It is possible to collect data regarding complex relationships and integrate the multiple links involved in complex relationships to generate a network. However, it is often more effective to use links with a simple meaning that generate a simple network for data collection. A link might be defined simply as the existence of a relationship. When considering the directionality of the link, it is important to clearly establish the direction of the link from one node to another. It should be noted that it is possible to limit the analysis of directional data to the existence of a relationship without incorporating the directionality of the link into the analytical process.

Moreover, when links are weighted, it is important to clearly establish clear criteria for assigning weights to links. For example, links might be weighted based on criteria such as the number of transactions or transaction duration. Weighting of links enables the researcher to perform a more detailed and precise analysis, while maintaining the ability to limit the analysis of the data to the existence of a relationship without incorporating the weight of the link into the analytical process. Links might also possess attributes (e.g., the transaction initiation date or the type of transaction).

3. *Network Modeling*: The different types of networks can be efficiently expressed using a meta-matrix that defines the type of network based on the nodes and the links connecting each node. For instance, Table 4.2 presents the

Table 4.2 Meta-matrix.

Entities	People (1)	Knowledge (2)	Resources (3)	Tasks (4)
(1)	Interaction network *Who talks to, works with, reports to whom*	Knowledge network *Who knows what, expertise or skills*	Resource network *Who has access to, who can use which resource*	Assignment network *Who is assigned to task, who does what*
(2)		Information network *Connections among types of knowledge*	Resource skill needs network *Knowledge for using resource*	Task skill needs network *Knowledge needed for tasks*
(3)			Substitutes and coordinated resource network *Connections among resources*	Task resource needs network *Resources needed for tasks*
(4)				Task precedence network *Tasks related to task*

network generated by different nodes such as the people, knowledge, resources, and type of work within an organization. Communication networks within an organization can be captured by an interaction-based network between people with different positions in the organization, such as supervisors interacting with subordinates. Organizational cultures can be captured by a knowledge-based network in which individuals are associated with different types of knowledge.

The researcher can define the meta-matrix [2] cells in many ways, which can be expanded as the number and types of nodes and links increase. Furthermore, the diagonal cells of the meta-matrix exhibit a one-mode network in which the nodes have identical attributes, with the remaining cells exhibiting a two-mode network in which nodes have dissimilar attributes.

4.3.2 Establishing Network Boundaries

In social network research that investigates actors, groups composed of actors, or social phenomena, it is essential for the researcher to determine the boundaries of the analysis. Because network characteristics are dynamic and the scope of the research, which initially involves the relationship between two actors, can expand significantly, delimiting the boundaries of the network is essential. It might be difficult to establish network boundaries because the number of actors who participate in the research is extremely large and difficult to enumerate, or shifting positions within the network might make it difficult to identify group affiliations, among other issues. A network boundary is determined by the research population. Thus, to establish the network boundary, the critical issue of determining how to sample nodes and links must be addressed.

A realistic or nominal approach can be used to establish the network boundary. In a realistic approach, the network boundary is determined by the set of entities who define themselves as actors. In a nominal approach, the network boundary is based on the researcher's theoretical interests. Although the researcher adopting a nominal approach might identify the actor as a member of a group within the network, the actors themselves might not acknowledge that they are members of that group. Once the network boundary has been established, an exhaustive examination of all subjects within the network boundary is performed. Because network data typically does not exhibit a bell-shaped distribution, significant deviations might be observed in the sample. For instance, a 10-student sampling to perform a kinship network analysis of a class of 40 students might not clearly reflect the kinship structure of the entire class. Furthermore, the network structure might change depending on which students were selected. A researcher who cannot perform an exhaustive examination but is familiar with the entire population might appropriately obtain a sample from a subgroup. For example, because it might not be possible to exhaustively examine every student for a survey of the entire university student body, every student within a particular department or enrolled in a particular year might participate in the survey. When it is not possible to identify all members of the subgroup, the snowballing method can be used to identify survey subjects. The snowballing method, which is used when the extent of the population cannot be determined at the outset, begins by selecting an actor in the group to be examined and continues by using that actor to identify other actors in the group who are known to that actor. Using this method to obtain research participants requires the researcher to initially identify a node that has many links to subsequently identify neighboring nodes and use those nodes to find new neighboring nodes. If the node that is initially selected has few links, identifying other research participants is difficult, so the researcher's intuitive selection of nodes with the appropriately number of links to other nodes is critical.

Another aspect of establishing a network boundary is the choice of the network node or link as the basis for the network boundary. If the boundary basis is the node, the researcher must decide which nodes to include. If the boundary basis is the link, the research must decide which type of relationship to use and delimit the range of the relationship. Because establishing the network boundary relies on both objective and subjective researcher judgments, the researcher must use appropriate and clear standards that are consistent with extant research when establishing a network boundary.

4.3.3 Measurement Evaluation

Social network research typically focuses on the patterns exhibited by social structures. Because these social structures exhibit relatively continuous and stable patterns of interactions, research related to social networks has tended to investigate structures with relatively continuous and stable interacting patterns and has not investigated interactive networks that emerge as the result of unexpected and special circumstances. When investigating social networks, the researcher must establish measurement validity and reliability, and identify measurement errors in the network data collected [3]. Moreover, data based on actor self-reports might also affect the quality of the measurement.

1. *Measurement validity*: Measurement validity refers to the extent to which the research measure actually reflects the reality the researcher seeks to measure. The systematic failure that occurs when measurements do not accurately capture the concept the researcher wants to measure will continue to occur even if the measurements are repeated. Social network research generally assumes face validity. Therefore, for measurement items and methods to effectively reflect the actual measurement methods, all of the researchers and the research subjects must agree upon the measurement procedures. In face validity, the measurement items must seem to look as if the measurement was intended. A situation in which the researcher measures trust relationships within an organization by presenting organization members with a list of organization members and asks respondents "Within this list of people, who is the most trustworthy?" exhibits face validity. In addition to face validity, construct validity of the measurement items can be assessed. Construct validity evaluates the extent to which the operationalization of the concept is appropriate. When the concept cannot be measured directly by the researcher,

different measures that are related to the operational definition are used. In social network research, selection of the actors who participate in the research is related to identifying characteristics of the actor that exhibit construct validity.

2. *Measurement reliability*: Measurement reliability refers to the degree to which the results of multiple measurements on the same subject are identical. Reliability is assessed by test-retest comparisons of two datasets to evaluation reliability and, alternatively, by assessing the extent to which two data sets are correlated. Networks are not static and their characteristics change even over short time periods, which makes it difficult to evaluate reliability through multiple measurements. Consequently, for the respondent sample, reliability is typically evaluated based on actor responses and reaction frequencies.

3. *Measurement error*: Measurement error occurs when the measurement does not correspond to the observed concept. In network research, errors typically occur when the concept is measured or during observation. Errors in network research might occur when a list of responses is provided to the respondent because this limits the responses available to the respondents. For example, a list of preselected responses to a question such as "Select the three most trustworthy members in the organization from the following list" might or might not include the three individuals most trusted by the respondent; if the available responses do not include the most trusted individuals, respondents might identify an individual who was less trustworthy because they were forced to select a response.

4. *Measurement accuracy*: An additional problem that must be considered during the evaluation of the measurements is measurement accuracy. Because the data used in social network research are based on interactions between actors and the responses of interacting participants, it is essential that data collection processes obtain accurate information. Research experience suggests that actors might not provide accurate information for interactions that occur during exceptional circumstances but usually provide adequate information for interactions that occur during normal circumstances. Because network research tends to focus on the network structures that exhibit relatively stable interactive patterns, there is less interest in interactions during exceptional circumstances in social network studies. That does not mean that the patterns exhibited during exceptional interactions are excluded (e.g., patterns of interactions during emergency situations). However, for network research, interactions and data exhibited in general and repetitive situations typically provide more precise measurements than do data based on special and exceptional situations.

5. *Use and release of data*: Because network research is based on implicit and explicit relationships, the researcher must be ensure the protection of privacy in the use and release of the data collected. Depending on actor characteristics,

the node name should be anonymized before data analysis and a separate correspondence sheet should be constructed to ensure that the information is secure. Because network research focuses on how the network structure is formed and the types of patterns the network exhibits rather than on information identifying particular individuals or events, due caution must be exercised to maintain the individual's privacy when using or releasing data.

4.4 Acquisition of Network Data

Network data can be acquired from surveys, interviews, observations, experiments, and archival records [4].

4.4.1 Survey

When acquiring data through surveys, a name generation survey is typically used. A name generation survey allows the respondent to write a specific name or to select from a roster of names. The survey questionnaires can be classified by the existence of a roster, a limited selection range, or whether there is an evaluation of the selected subject.

1. *Roster and free recall*: Because the researcher can provide the respondent with a list from which to select or can require the respondent to write for himself or herself, the survey can be divided into a roster and a free recall survey. In the roster survey, the researcher attempts to create a complete list for the respondents' selection and makes it convenient for the respondents to provide answers; the survey is in a form that the researcher can control. However, if the respondent's choice of actor is not on the list, the results can be distorted. Conversely, free recall allows the respondent to directly enter the actor into the survey; such a technique is used when the researcher cannot predetermine the list of actors to be selected by the respondent. Free recall requires prolonged time for the respondent to recollect the actors in question, cannot distinguish between homonyms, and may include actors who are not the objects of investigation (Table 4.3).

2. *Fixed choice and free choice*: A survey that may or may not limit the number of actors who can be designated by the respondents can be divided into fixed-choice

Table 4.3 Roster and free recall surveys.

Roster Survey	Free Recall Survey
In the past month, select the person who has provided you with useful information	*In the past month, provide the names of people who have given you useful information*
☐ Heckerman, J. ☐ Lydia, S. ☐ Abia, K. ☐ Tony, M.	________ ________ ________ ________

Table 4.4 Fixed- and free-choice surveys.

Fixed-Choice Survey	Free-Choice Survey
Write the names of no more than three individuals who have provided useful information during the past month	Write the names of all of the individuals who have provided useful information during the past month

Table 4.5 Ranking and rating surveys.

Ranking Survey	Rating Survey
Select (or write) the individuals who have provided useful information during the past month and rank the individuals in the order of the usefulness of their information	Select (or write) the individuals who have provided useful information during the past month and rate the usefulness of their information on a 10-point scale
1st rank ____________	____________ ( ) score
2nd rank ____________	____________ ( ) score
3rd rank ____________	____________ ( ) score

and free-choice models. A fixed-choice survey limits the number of actors who may be designated; it has the advantage of inducing a response that can be used for network analysis, but if the respondent wants to designate more subjects than the limit, the results may become distorted. A free-choice survey enables the respondent to designate actors without limitations. This provides the respondent with freedom but may result in too many or too few actors designated, which could decrease the reliability of the survey results (Table 4.4).

3. *Ranking and rating:* Ranking and rating is a method of measuring the actor who has been designated by the respondent, where the evaluated value can be used as a weight for the links. In ranking, the designated actors are assigned a standing and assigned a comparative superiority. In rating, the designated actors are each assigned a score. When the number of subjects is not large, ranking is appropriate, but when the number of subjects becomes larger and comparative standing is difficult to determine, rating is appropriate (Table 4.5).

4.4.2 Interview, Observation, and Experiment

Network data can be acquired by a face-to-face interview or by telephone, video, online, and so on. However, there is a limit to data collection: significant time and costs are associated with interviewing, which typically is used when the network is not large and is centered on a single actor (i.e., it is an ego-centered network).

Network data acquisition through observations is a method to observe the interactions among actors and is appropriate for a small group that can interact in person. Moreover, when it is difficult for the actor to react to the interview or survey, observation may be applied to data acquisition from a joint participation network similar to an event or a club attended by the actor.

Data acquired through experiments are divided into a control group and an experimental group, and a comparative reference should be clearly defined before data collection. Furthermore, the researcher must be able to select the actor group, and interaction among the actors in a controlled laboratory environment must be used for the observation. At that time, the researcher records the interactions among the actors and reaches an understanding of the relationships among the actors through observations.

4.4.3 Existing Data

Network data can be collected from existing data, including the Web, journals, newspapers, legal documents, meeting notes within an organization, trade, and so on. From trade data between countries, we not only can understand the flow of the different product types but also can verify dependency on trade. From the academic journal data, co-author analysis, citation analysis, and keyword concurrent-emergence analysis can be performed, which can reveal the academic development situation.

1. *Social media data*: Social media is an excellent source of data for social network research, and there is an abundant amount of data scattered around us for analysis. The data available for social network analysis include blogs, social bookmarks, and SNS (social networking service), with Twitter and Facebook as the most representative examples.A blog will contain a significant amount of information, but its data will be in long-form text and the relationships among bloggers are unclear, rendering analysis difficult. Through connections among blogs, data can be formed into a one-mode network; through connections between a blog and its text, a two-mode network can be formed.

   Data from social-bookmarking sites (for example, delicious.com, digg.com, reddit.com, and google.com/bookmarks) are shared data; users save Web pages of interest and publicly share them with other users, thus creating a connection through the Web site. Bookmark-related information is an important data that can look about the bookmark user' interest and lifestyle. A two-mode network can be formed by correlating users with the bookmarking page.

   Twitter (www.twitter.com) data are rich with information in the span of 140 characters. Through Twitter, five networks can be formed, including following relationships, follower relationships, retweet (RT) relationships, hashtag (#) simultaneous-occurrence relationships, identical hashtags, and URL (Uniform Resource Locator: Web site address)-use relationships. In particular, retweets are repetitive and constitute extremely useful data for analysis. Repeated retweets show the diffusion of information and influence patterns within the network. A use relationship can form a two-mode network between the

PSY @psy_oppa - Jul 16
RT "@YouTube: One Year. 1.74 billion views and counting. Happy anniversary to @psy_oppa's "Gangnam Style. "goo.gl/q9s7J"
View conversation
Reply Retweet Favorite More

PSY @psy_oppa - Jul 12
Billboard – News – PSY Reaches 3 Billion YouTube Views
With ma man ByungHun Lee at his starring #RED2 premier
pic.twitter.com/FdWbMwSvSs

Figure 4.2 PSY's tweets.

researcher and the hashtags or URL, which can be transformed into an indirect relationship between people with identical hashtags or shared URLs. A simultaneous-occurrence relationship is a relationship between hashtags and is used when forming a hashtag network. If two hashtags are included in a tweet, their relationship can be speculated as having meaning. Twitter data include information about time and location that facilitate an understanding of when, where, and how fast information is transferred through the network. Figure 4.2 shows Twitter comments posted by the South Korean singer PSY[1] in which retweeted comments have an *RT@YouTube*. *#RED2* is a hashtag, the *@psy_oppa* is a reference to a particular researcher, and a URL is included at the end of the tweets as "goo.gl/q9s7j, billboard.com/articles/news,pic.twitter.com/FdWbMwSvSs."

Although there is pressure to open Facebook data (www.facebook.com) to the public, personal security issues have prevented full disclosure. Using Facebook data, information can be collected from the private ego networks of individual users and public pages such as fan pages. Facebook users can verify a user's friends (first-step neighbors) and friends of friends (second-step neighbors) after logging in through the Facebook app [5]. Table 4.6 shows the private ego network that can be verified in Facebook. The VARCHAR (variable character) describes the characteristics of the variable and provides the node characteristic and link within the private ego network. Of the data acquired through Facebook, the information collected via the public pages can form a two-mode network by forming a relationship using "likes," "comments," and "shares."

2. *Public and server logs data*: Public information maintained by countries or international organizations can be used to form various networks. Currently,

[1] PSY is a singer in South Korea. He is internationally known for his hit single "Gangnam Style."

Table 4.6 Ego-network data of facebook.

```
nodedef>name VARCHAR, label VARCHAR, sex VARCHAR, locale VARCHAR, agerank INT
624523815, OOO, male, ko_KR, 56 683882032, OOO, male, ko_KR, 55
818262355, OOO, male, en_US, 54 1848255940, OOO, male, en_US, 48
100000037378613, OOO, male, ko_KR, 46 100000218416480, OOO, male, ko_KR, 45
100000276848796, OOO, female, en_GB, 44

edgedef>node1 VARCHAR, node2 VARCHAR
624523815, 100001313575816 683882032, 1780775998
683882032, 100000879485010 818262355, 1780775998
818262355, 1822535999 818262355, 1848255940
818262355, 100000009170698
```

many countries, including Korea (www.data.go.kr), the United States (www.data.gov), the United Kingdom (www.gov.uk), and Australia (www.data.gov.au), have shared public information from the government sector to ensure information transparency and the right to public knowledge. Furthermore, international organizations such as the United Nations (www.un.org) and the OECD (Organization for Economic Cooperation and Development, www.oecd.org) collect statistical data from various countries.

The log files left in a company's server may also be used for social network data. Log files in e-mails and instant messengers provide information about the direction of the network data, forming a relationship between e-mail/message senders and recipients.

4.5 Data Cleansing

When the data are collected, a cleansing and preprocessing stage is required for data analysis. The collected data must be transformed into a matrix form for network analysis but, depending on the characteristics of the collected data, preliminary decisions on treating the extraction of the relationship, the directional change in the link, and the self-loop must be made. For example, in the aforementioned tweet by singer PSY, if PSY retweets comments from YouTube, there will be a link formed with in the direction from YouTube to PSY (source node: YouTube → target node: PSY). Conversely, if PSY tweets himself with hashtag #RED2, a link would be formed in the direction from PSY to #RED2 (source node: PSY → target node: #RED2).

Therefore, preliminary data processing puts the data into a format appropriate for the researcher to analyze. To obtain an analysis result that coincides with the analytical purpose, the current data must be checked for the correct format. First, it is necessary to verify whether the data have been correctly collected according to the research design and to preprocess both insincere responses and data that do not conform to the expected format. However, for an individually identifying survey, nonresponding surveys should not be excluded from the analysis because another survey respondent might have noted the nonresponding individual. However, for an individually identifying survey, a nonrespondent survey should not be excluded from the analysis because another survey respondent might have noted that nonrespondent individual. Data with a characteristic direction may have been collected, but data transformation to reflect the intended analysis can be performed if a relationship analysis without direction is needed, if analysis is needed for at least a certain number of links, if analysis is needed for particular nodes, or if a directional change in the link is needed. Data transformation is performed primarily through directional changes in the link, the weights, and the extraction of the node and links.

To explain the preconditioning of the data, export data for steel products have been used as an example. Table 4.7 shows trade data supplied by the United Nations from January to April 2014 and includes the export of iron and steel and articles of iron and steel commodities for four nations, including South Korea. The values within the matrix are the export amount (in millions of US dollars) to that country (Table 4.7A). For the export relationship matrix, the row country exports to the column country and thus, South Korea exports US$1184 million to Japan and Japan exports US$2995 million to South Korea (Table 4.7B). The EX-TOTAL in the node attributes shows the total export amount in US dollars of the identified country among the four nations within the given time period (January to April 2013) (Table 4.7C). Visual network interpretation of the export relationship shows the direction of export flow among the nations, where the links become thicker with increased export amounts among the nations.

Therefore, the export amount of the iron and steel from the United States to Japan is lower than the export amount of the commodity from Japan to the United States.

4.5.1 Extraction of the Node and Link

Depending on the researcher's intentions, a node can be extracted that satisfies a particular condition and forms a new network. Furthermore, a direct relationship between neighboring first-stage nodes and a particular node can be extracted and used in the analysis. In link extraction, particular links that satisfy a certain condition of the link attributes can be both extracted and analyzed. In link extraction, particular links that satisfy certain conditions can be extracted; in addition, researchers can reduce particular links that fall below certain conditions and apply an analysis to the data. Figure 4.3 shows the iron and steel commodity export network from Table 4.7, in which the export amount is more than US$5000 million among nations (node's attributes), and the export amount exceeds US$2500 million within the export relationship (link's attributes).

4.5.2 Merging and Separation of Data

Two matrixes with the same node can be merged into a single matrix. Connecting the same node can be accomplished through several links. When merging a link with varying weights, a merging method must be determined. When merging two or

Table 4.7 Export network of iron and steel.

A. Export Relationship Matrix

	S. Korea	*China*	*Japan*	*USA*
S. Korea		1 483	1 184	1 229
China	3 661		1 523	3 730
Japan	2 995	2 811		1 331
USA	445	732	165	

B. Node Attribute

Country	EX_TOTAL
S. Korea	4 504
China	12 423
Japan	7 519
USA	6 642

C. Visual Network

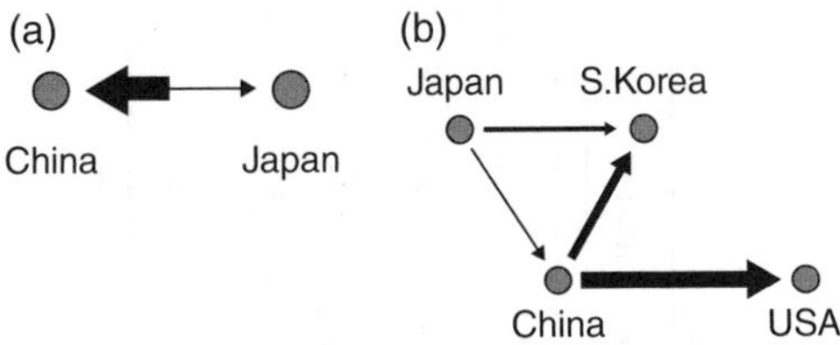

Figure 4.3 Visualization of the extracted node and link. (a) Visual network of the extracted node. Node attribute: total export amount >US$5000 million. *(b) Visual network of the extracted link.* Link attribute: export amount >US$2500 million.

morevweights, one can use one value and drop the other, using the sum, average, maximum, or minimum value. In Table 4.8, the iron and steel detailed an itemized classification (UN trade statistics HS (Harmonized Commodity Description and Coding System) classification code) of Export_72 Iron and Steel (Table 4.8A) and Export_73 Articles Iron or Steel (Table 4.8B), which can be merged by a "summation" method resulting in the iron and steel total export relationship matrix previously shown in Table 4.8C.

A weighted matrix can be split into multiple matrixes depending on the various conditions. Splitting the weighted values within a matrix depends on the conditions established by the researcher, where the particular values are transformed to be identical to a set value that is, greater than, greater than or equal to, less than, or less than or equal. Table 4.9 shows the splitting of the iron and steel export relationship between South Korea, China, Japan, and the United States (Table 4.7A) depending on the amount of trade (trade amount exceeding US$1000 million [Table 4.9A], greater than or equal to US$2000 million [Table 4.9B]). When splitting the matrix according to the trade amount, the matrix is dichotomized by 1 if the value exceeds or equals the set value or by 0 if the value is less than the set value.

In addition, to transform two matrix values with the same node into a multiplex link, the weights of various pairs can be encoded and used as the weighted value of the new link. In Table 4.10, the iron and steel export relationship matrix in Table 4.7A can be encoded like Table 4.10B and can form a multiplexed link, as shown in Table 4.10A.

4.5.3 Directional Transformation in the Link

Symmetrizing is transforming a network data with direction into a network data without direction. For example, the export relationship from Korea to the United States (Korea → USA) can be changed to an export relationship between Korea and the United States (Korea-USA). Symmetrizing ignores the direction between links and evaluates the existence of a relationship. In Table 4.11A, the nonsymmetric matrix with direction of the export network relationship is formed into a nondirectional symmetric matrix. At this time, we must determine the particular criteria on which to base the symmetric matrix, where the matrix can be formed symmetrically across the diagonal of the matrix according to the "maximum, minimum, average, summation, or multiplication," and so on.

Table 4.8 Merging of the iron and steel export network data.

A. Export_72. Iron and steel

	S. Korea	*China*	*Japan*	*USA*
S. Korea				
China				
Japan	2995			
USA				

+

B. Export_73. Articles iron or steel

	S. Korea	*China*	*Japan*	*USA*
S. Korea		1483	1184	1229
China	3661		1523	3730
Japan		2811		1331
USA	445	732	165	

=

C. Total export_iron and steel

	S. Korea	*China*	*Japan*	*USA*
S. Korea		1483	1184	1229
China	3661		1523	3730
Japan	2995	2811		1331
USA	445	732	165	

Table 4.9 Splitting of the iron and steel network data.

A. Trading amount > US$1000 million

	S. Korea	*China*	*Japan*	*USA*
S. Korea		1	1	1
China	1		1	1
Japan	1	1		1
USA	0	0	0	

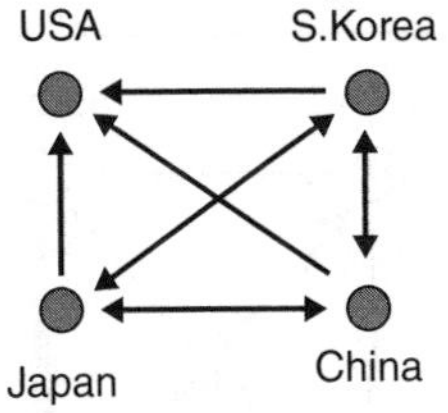

B. Trading amount ≧ US$2000 million

	S. Korea	*China*	*Japan*	*USA*
S. Korea		0	0	0
China	1		0	1
Japan	1	1		0
USA	0	0	0	

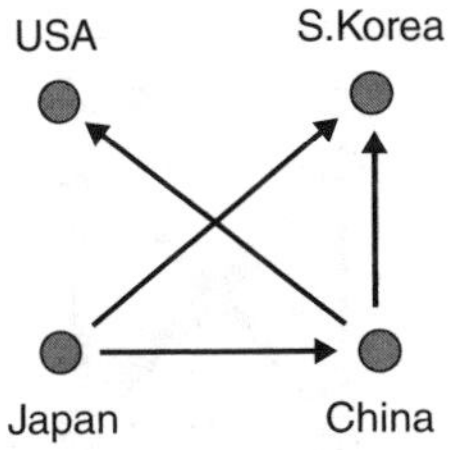

Table 4.10 Multiple links of iron and steel network data.

A. Multiple Link

	S. Korea	*China*	*Japan*	*USA*
S. Korea		1	2	3
China	4		5	6
Japan	7	8		9
USA	10	11	12	

B. Multiple Link Coding

Code	Iron and steel	Articles of iron or
0	0	0
1	0	1483
2	0	1184
3	0	1229
4	0	3661
5	0	1523
6	0	3730
7	2995	0
8	0	2811
9	0	1331
10	0	445
11	0	732
12	0	165

Table 4.11 Directional changes in the network links of the iron and steel exports.

A. Symmetrize (criteria: maximum value)

	S. Korea	*China*	*Japan*	*USA*
S. Korea		3661	2995	1229
China			2811	3730
Japan				1331
USA				

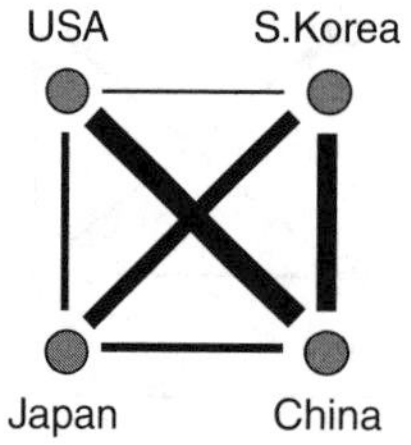

USA S.Korea Japan China

B. Transpose (matrix of import relationship)

	S. Korea	*China*	*Japan*	*USA*
S. Korea		3661	2995	445
China	1483		2811	732
Japan	1184	1523		165
USA	1229	3730	1311	

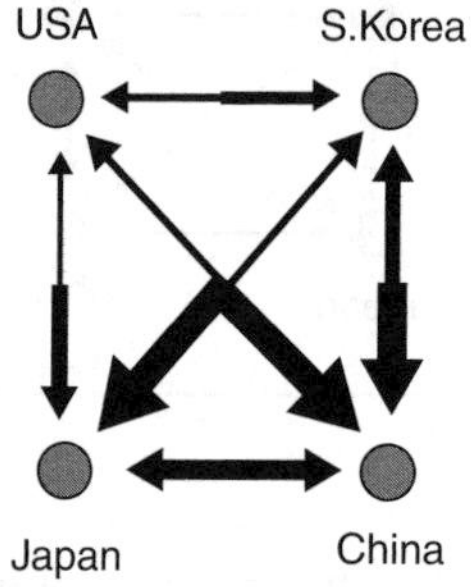

USA S.Korea Japan China

To transpose is to switch the row and columns of the matrix and form a network. Thus, the source and target nodes can be switched or the acquired data can be expressed in a manner contradictory to that of the liberal translation. From Table 4.7A, if we wish to express the iron and steel export relationship matrix in an import relationship matrix, the export relationship matrix direction can be transposed and the source node changed to the importing nation with the target node as the exporting nation. Therefore, in Table 4.11B, the first column is the importing country and the first row can be the exporting country. South Korea imports iron and steel goods worth US$3661 million from China and US$2995 million from Japan.

4.5.4 Transformation of the Weights in Links

Weight changes in the links involve methods of dichotomizing, reversing, normalizing, and recoding. To manage the self-looping, there is also a diagonal that involves changing the diagonal values in the matrix. Variation of the weights is shown by treating the export relationship matrix provided in Table 4.7A.

Dichotomizing is the most common method for changing weights by transforming a weighted complex network to a nonweighted simple network. The link weights are transformed to 0 if the value falls below the value set by the researcher and 1 if the value exceeds the set value. In Table 4.12A, the weights become 0 when the

Table 4.12 Weight transformations in links of the iron and steel export network.

A. Dichotomize

	S. Korea	*China*	*Japan*	*USA*
S. Korea		0	0	0
China	1		0	1
Japan	1	1		0
USA	0	0	0	

B. Reverse (interval)

	S. Korea	*China*	*Japan*	*USA*
S. Korea		2412	2710	2596
China	233		2372	165
Japan	900	1083		2564
USA	3450	3163	3730	

C. Reverse (ratio)

	S. Korea (%)	*China* (%)	*Japan* (%)	*USA* (%)
S. Korea		0.07	0.8	0.08
China	0.03		0.07	0.03
Japan	0.03	0.04		0.8
USA	0.22	0.14	0.61	

D. Normalize

	S. Korea	*China*	*Japan*	*USA*
S. Korea		0.38	0.30	0.32
China	0.41		0.17	0.42
Japan	0.42	0.39		0.19
USA	0.33	0.55	0.12	

E. Recoding

	S. Korea	*China*	*Japan*	*US*
S. Korea		4	3	1
China	2		3	1
Japan	2	2		1
USA	2	4	2	

F. Diagonal

	S. Korea	*China*	*Japan*	*USA*
S. Korea	1000	1483	1184	1229
China	3661	1000	1523	3730
Japan	2995	2811	1000	1331
USA	445	732	165	1000

export amount falls below US$2000 million and 1 when the export amount exceeds this set value. Reversing the link's value is used when the analysis is performed on the acquired data in a manner contradictory to the liberal translation. Reversing can be used by applying "interval, ratio." First, "interval" reverses the weights linearly. In other words, return the reversed link weighted value after excluding the chosen link weight values from the sum of the maximum and minimum values. Therefore, in Table 4.12B, from the sum of the maximum and minimum value (3895 = 3730 + 165), subtract the export amount from Korea to the United States of US$1299 million and return the reversed weight of 2596 (3895 − 1299). By using the "ratio" in the reverse method of the weights, the weighted link values are divided by the link weights where 1 was selected. Therefore, in Table 4.12C, the weights between the export amounts from Korea to the United States were 0.08% (1/1229).

Link normalization is used when comparing the matrix with different scales that measured. At this time, the values of the matrix's rows and columns are transformed to a predefined value by the researcher through normalizing with the sum, average, and maximum values. By normalizing the weights so that the sum of the column values is 1, Table 4.12D indicates the weight between the exports from Korea to the United States as 0.32.

Next, to simplify the analysis by excessively extending the range of the weighted values or to reset the definition of the values, recoding the weights can be performed. Table 4.12E is recoded as follows: values between US$0 and US$1000 million are given a 1, US$1001–2000 million are given a 2, US$2001–3000 million are given a 3, and US$3001–4000 million are given a 4.

Finally, to change the self-loop [6] (links that connect nodes to themselves) weights in the diagonal of the matrix to particular values, the diagonal handling method can be used. Depending on the researcher's analytical approach, the application of the self-loop can vary and the weights of the self-loop can be modified accordingly. The diagonal value of the matrix has been fixed at US$1000 million in Table 4.12F.

4.5.5 Transformation of the Two-Mode Network to a One-Mode Network

As previously mentioned, a two-mode network expresses the relationship between nodes with different characteristics. If the two-mode network describes a direct relationship between nodes with different characteristics, it can be transformed and expressed through an indirect relationship with nodes having characteristics identical to that of a one-mode network. In the transformation of a two-mode network (direct relationship) to a one-mode network (indirect relationship), the resemblance of the indirect relationship, which is a measure of the similarity of the connection or relationship between each node, can be measured through the assortativity index [7].

The Jaccard coefficient divides the common intersect-set value with the sum-set value of the two rows (or columns) in the dichotomized 0 and 1 matrix. Pearson correlation quantifies the linear relationship of continuous data with values ranging from −1 to +1. A close relationship between two nodes results in a value close to +1. Spearman's rho is applied when two continuous data distributions fall outside the normal distribution spectrum or when the data are measured using an ordinal scale. Generally, because the Spearman's ρ describes the relationship between two nodes regardless of linearity or nonlinearity, it is useful, but the calculation takes longer to perform and therefore is used for small data sets. Cosine similarity describes the similarity between two nodes from the established angle between the two nodes ranging from −1 to +1. If the two nodes are identical a +1 value is given, if the two nodes are completely independent a 0 is given, and if the two nodes are opposite a −1 value is given. The scalar product (or inner product, dot product) is the multiplication of two nodes without consideration of the direction and is given as a single value. The Euclidean distance obtains the distance between two nodes and divides 1 by the distance, suggesting that the two nodes are closely identical if the values are larger.

$$\textit{Jaccard coefficient} = \frac{v_{11}}{v_{01} + v_{10} + v_{11}} \quad (4.1)$$

$$\textit{Pearson's correlation} = \frac{\sum_{k=1}^{n}\left(v_{ik} - \overline{v}_i\right)\left(v_{jk} - \overline{v}_k\right)}{\sqrt{\sum_{k=1}^{n}\left(v_{ik} - \overline{v}_i\right)^2}\sqrt{\left(v_{jk} - \overline{v}_k\right)^2}} \quad (4.2)$$

$$\text{Scalar product} = \sum_{k=1}^{n} v_{ik} v_{jk} \quad (4.3)$$

$$\text{Spearman's } \rho = \frac{\sigma \sum_{k=1}^{n}\left(v_{ik} - v_{jk}\right)^2}{n\left(n^2 - 1\right)} \quad (4.4)$$

$$\text{Euclidean distance} = \frac{1}{\sqrt{\sum_{k=1}^{n}\left(v_{ik} - v_{jk}\right)^2}} \quad (4.5)$$

$$\text{Cosine similarity} = \frac{\sum_{k=1}^{n} v_{ik} v_{jk}}{\sqrt{\sum_{k=1}^{n} v_{ik}^{\ 2}}\sqrt{\sum_{k=1}^{n} v_{jk}^{\ 2}}} \quad (4.6)$$

Table 4.13 Iron and steel two-mode network matrix.

Item	*S. Korea*	*Japan*	*USA*	*China*
Iron and steel	—	2995	—	—
Articles of iron or steel	1229	1331	445	1523

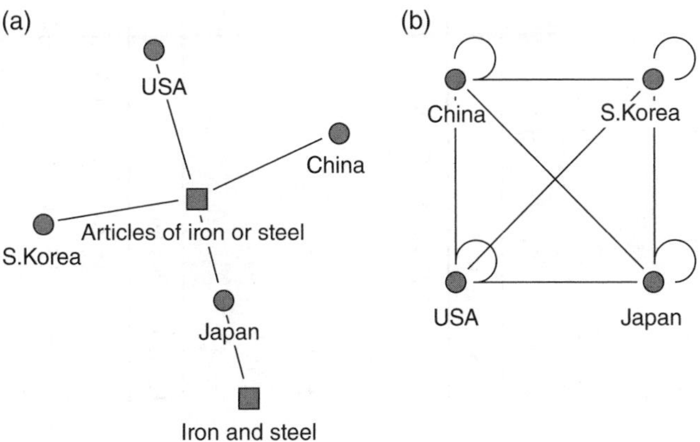

Figure 4.4 Visualization of the two-mode and one-mode networks. (a) two-mode network (export: products–countries) and (b) one-mode network (export: countries–countries).

Table 4.14 Transformation of the two-mode network to a one-mode network for iron and steel.

A. Jaccard Coefficient

	S. Korea	*China*	*Japan*	*USA*
S. Korea	1	0.5	1	1
China	0.5	1	0.5	0.5
Japan	1	0.5	1	1
USA	1	0.5	1	1

B. Pearson's Correlation

	S. Korea	*China*	*Japan*	*USA*
S. Korea	1	1	1	1
China	1	1	1	1
Japan	1	1	1	1
USA	1	1	1	1

C. Spearman's ρ

	S. Korea	*China*	*Japan*	*USA*
S. Korea	1	−1	1	1
China	−1	1	−1	−1
Japan	1	−1	1	1
USA	1	−1	1	1

D. Cosine Similarity

	S. Korea	*China*	*Japan*	*USA*
S. Korea	1	0.8	1	1
China	0.8	1	0.8	0.8
Japan	1	0.8	1	1
USA	1	0.8	1	1

E. Scalar Product

	S. Korea	*China*	*Japan*	*USA*
S. Korea	15181154	16138864	5228445	34730060
China	16138864	26126418	5558284	36921023
Japan	5228445	5558284	1800696	11961160
USA	34730060	36921023	11961160	79452265

F. Euclidean Distance

	S. Korea	*China*	*Japan*	*USA*
S. Korea		3005	2554	5017
China	3005		4100	5634
Japan	2554	4100		7572
USA	5017	5634	7572	

For the transformation of a two-mode network into a one-mode network, the aforementioned trade statistical data has been organized into a two-mode network of the product item and the export country. In Table 4.13 of the two-mode network relationship matrix, although we cannot establish which country exports which product to another country, the amount and product items exported can be obtained for each country. The transformation of the two-mode network having a direct relationship with the export product and the country into a one-mode network having an indirect relationship with the countries exporting identical items results in Figure 4.4 and Table 4.14.

References

1 Borgatti, S.P., Everett, M.G., and Johnson, J.C. (2013) *Analyzing Social Networks*, London: SAGE.

2 Carley, K.M. (2002) Computational organizational science and organizational engineering, *Simulation Practice and Theory*, **10**(5–7), 253–269.

3 Marsden, P.V. (1990) Network data and measurement, *Annual Review of Sociology*, **16**, 435–463.

4 Wasserman, S. and Faust, K. (1997) *Social Network Analysis: Methods and Application*, New York: Cambridge University Press.

5 https://apps.facebook.com/netvizz/ (You can use after the login to Facebook.)

6 Evans, J.R. and Minieka, E. (1992) *Optimization Algorithms for Networks and Graphs*, Marcel Dekker: New York.

7 Cox, T.F. and Cox, M.A.A. (2001), *Multidimensional Scaling*, NY: Chapman & Hall/CRC Press.

References

5

Position and Structure

One of the most crucial parts of network analysis is "who is the most important or the most dominant actor." This is relevant to the position of an actor in a network. Generally, the actor who is at the most essential or the most dominant position is located at a strategic point. An individual, who has high centrality, is described to have special socio-economic status. A group with a high centrality has a high survival rate showing good performance. Network analysis suggests methods of centrality analysis that includes connectivity, degree, closeness, and betweenness according to the different conditions and ranks of the individual actors. In other words, the positions of each individual actor in a network are quantitatively defined. Regarding the actor's index, we can add and compare measured outcomes within the level of a group or a whole network. Centrality analysis can be divided according to the existence of directional relations, where the analysis results can vary depending on a weighted value of relations. The measurement of directional relation is divided into in-degree and out-degree.

5.1 Position

In social network analysis, researchers are primarily interested in the "most important or most dominant" actors, an issue that is related to the position of the actors within a network. The most important or dominant player within the network is typically

Fundamentals of Big Data Network Analysis for Research and Industry, First Edition. Hyunjoung Lee and Il Sohn.

located at a strategic location in the network. Network analysis proposes various analytical methods, depending on the characteristics of the connectivity, closeness, betweenness, and so on, of the actors. Namely, network analysis is quantified as the centrality [1] that is the actor's position within the network. Indexing of the centrality can be compared by summation of the analysis results within the group and from a global perspective.

Centrality can be divided according to the existence of a direction and can vary depending on the consideration of the weight among relationships. Measurement of a directional relationship can be divided and analyzed according to the in-degree and the out-degree. An established actor will have many in-degree relationships and will be an actor selected by many other actors. A centrality's index or reputation can be indicative of importance and dominance within the network. However, if we consider the reputation of the actor in the in-degree, both the frequency of being chosen by other actors and the selection of many other actors of out-degree should be considered. Therefore, both the nondirectional and the directional relationships should be considered in the centrality analysis. For a directional relationship, the centrality analysis must consider both the in-degree and out-degree, but for the nondirectional relationship, the in-degree and out-degree will yield identical results and only a single centrality index is needed.

However, analysis of individual actors can be obtained from the summed result within the group-level analysis and the overall network analysis, which is termed centralization. That term refers to the centrality analysis of an entire network and indicates a characteristic of the actor's group or network. The connectivity ratio of the actors can be measured by subtracting the average connection from the maximum connection possible by the actor and generally results in a value between 0 and 1, where a value closer to 1 corresponds to greater centralization.

Table 5.1 shows the export and import of iron and steel from January to April 2013 among South Korea, China, Japan, the United States, and countries with more than US$10 billion in trade, where each cell indicates the import and export amount in millions of US dollars. Figure 5.1 is the visual representation of Table 5.1. The link in the outer direction is the export and the link thickness is the export amount. China exports US$37 296 million to the United States and has less than US$10 000 million in imports from the United States.

5.1.1 Degree Centrality

If the relationship between the actors has been measured without direction and weight (i.e., if the matrix is symmetrized and dichotomized), then a measurement with a defined centrality can be performed on those actors to identify the important, dominant actor. Centrality describes the maximum degree of centrality, closeness, betweenness, and so on, of an act.

A simple definition of an actor's centrality can be defined by that actor's activity by identifying the most connections between other actors within a network [1a]. Therefore, the maximum number of an actor's connections within a network is "Total number of nodes–1." An actor with a high level of activity can have a high centrality

Table 5.1 Major trading countries of iron and steel matrix.

		Out link (export) →								
In link (import) →		S. Korea	China	Japan	USA	Brazil	Canada	Mexico	Singapore	Thailand
	S. Korea		14 831	22 823	28 725					
	China	36 613		15 227	37 296				12 257	
	Japan	63 107	28 114		27 989					19 641
	USA						45 999	29 782		
	Brazil				10 851					
	Canada				30 789					
	Mexico				18 369					
	Singapore									
	Thailand									

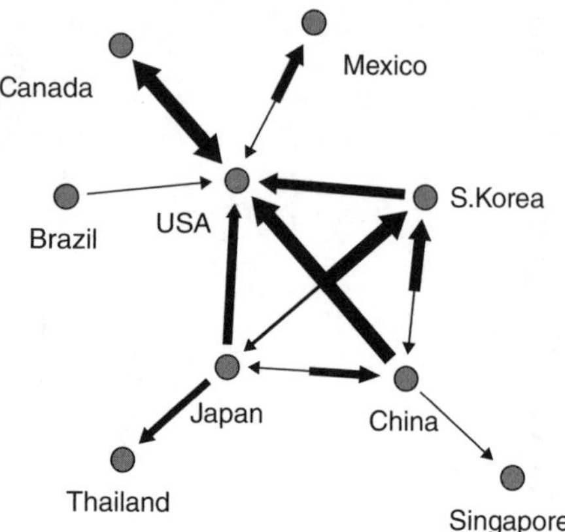

Figure 5.1 Visual representation of iron and steel trade.

index and because actors interact, all actors can have the same centrality index. The degree of centrality focuses on direct and neighboring relationships and dominance or activity follows from how many connections exist among the actors.

5.1.1.1 Nondirectional Relationship

The number of an actor's connections with other actors is an important measurement index. Therefore, the individual centrality of an actor can represent the node's connectivity, $d(n_i)$, and degree centrality is the total sum of the connection between the nodes. A standardized centrality can be obtained through Equation 5.1 and can be used to compare the size of the network with other networks with different sizes. $C_D(n_i)$ is the degree centrality of the node i and g is the total number of nodes.

$$C_D(n_i) = d(n_i)/(g-1) \tag{5.1}$$

For an actor, a high degree centrality indicates the actor's high level of activity within the network. The degree of centrality is focused on identifying the high-profile actor within the network analysis. When an actor is has a vast number of connections to other actors, that actor will be at the center of the network and other actors will expect him or her to lead in disseminating information within the network using his or her numerous network relationships. Conversely, actors with a low degree of centrality who are located far from the core of the network may be considered as unimportant, low-activity actors. If an actor has absolutely no relationship with other actors, that actor can be excluded from the network and have no end effect on the analysis of the relationships within the network.

If the trade relationship matrix of iron and steel is transformed to a matrix without direction and weight, Table 5.2 will result, with cells having a value of 1 for existing trade amounts; the empty cells will coincide with nonexisting trade amounts. Table 5.3 contains the degree of centrality of the individual nodes from Table 5.2 and shows the United States to have the highest degree of centrality. This implies that the United States has more trading countries within the network than any other country (Figure 5.2).

Table 5.2 Non-directional trade relationship matrix.

	S. Korea	China	Japan	USA	Brazil	Canada	Mexico	Singapore	Thailand
S. Korea		1	1	1					
China	1		1	1				1	
Japan	1	1		1					1
USA	1	1	1		1	1	1		
Brazil				1					
Canada				1					
Mexico				1					
Singapore		1							
Thailand			1						

Table 5.3 Analysis of the degree centrality for the non-directional relationship.

	Degree centrality	Ego size	# of links	# of possible links	Ego density
S. Korea	0.375	3	6	6	1
China	0.500	4	7	10	0.700
Japan	0.500	4	7	10	0.700
USA	0.750	6	9	21	0.429
Brazil	0.125	2	1	1	—
Canada	0.125	2	1	1	—
Mexico	0.125	2	1	1	—
Singapore	0.125	2	1	1	—
Thailand	0.125	2	1	1	—
Mean	0.306	Number of nodes	9	Density	0.306
Standard devition	0.221				
Minimum	0.125				
Maximum	0.750				
Degree centralization	0.071				

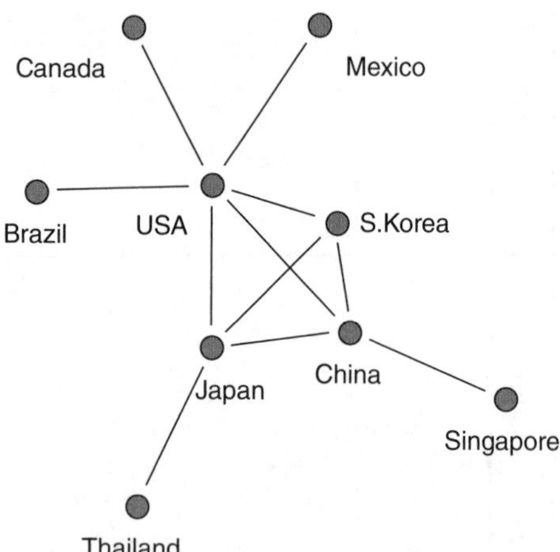

Figure 5.2 Visualization of the non-directional trade relationship.

With respect to the degree centrality, individual nodes' ego density can be examined. Nodes' ego density in a nondirectional relationship can be determined from the ratio of the number of links among individual nodes in an ego network to the maximum number of links. If we assume a nondirectional relationship, the ego density of Korea and the United States is 100% (6/6) and 42.86% (9/21), respectively.

A network's centrality tendency is a group-level centrality and indicates how links between actors focus on a particular actor, which can be verified by the centralization value. Centralization allows a quantitative analysis of the changes and range in the index of individual actors and can be calculated from the summation of the actors' connectivity, as expressed in Equation 5.2. C_D is the centralization and $C_D(n^*)$ is the maximum centrality of the network. The centralization of the steel product trade-relationship network resulted in a value of 0.0714 (=Σ[(0.750 − $0.375_{\text{S.Korea}}$) … (0.750 − 0.125_{Thailand})]/[(9 − 1)(9 − 2)]).

$$\overline{C_D} = \frac{\sum_{i=1}^{g}\left[C_D(n_i) - C_D(n_i)\right]}{\left[(g-1)(g-2)\right]} \tag{5.2}$$

The density of the group is the average degree within the group and a major index representing the group, which is predominantly used to measure the group's cohesiveness. If the connectivity of the individual actors does not vary, the density tends to decrease as the size of the group increases. If the centralization value is an index to describe a focal connection on a particular actor or to examine a network's centering trend, density is used to describe the actors' connections to one another in the network and is an average degree index of the actors. Therefore, group density adds the actors' connectivity and divides by the total number of nodes, as shown in Equation 5.3.

$$D_{non-direction} = \frac{\sum_{i=1}^{g} C_D(n_i)}{g} \tag{5.3}$$

5.1.1.2 Directional Relationship

The calculation of degree centrality for a directional relationship may appear to be easy, but separately calculating in and out connectivity can complicate matters. Essentially, a relationship with direction is based on the actor's choice and differs from the measurement of the degree centrality with a nondirectional relationship. When calculating degree centrality, in-degree centrality is based on connections in the inward direction (Equation 5.4) and out-degree centrality is based on connections in the outward direction (Equation 5.5).

$$C_{inD}(n_i) = \frac{ind(n_i)}{g-1} \tag{5.4}$$

$$C_{outD}(n_i) = \frac{outd(n_i)}{g-1} \tag{5.5}$$

Although the steel product direction has direction, there are no weights, and the degree of centrality analysis for the matrix can be shown by transforming the matrix in Table 5.2 to that of Table 5.4.

Table 5.4 Trade relationship matrix with direction.

		Out link (export) →								
In link (import) →		S. Korea	China	Japan	USA	Brazil	Canada	Mexico	Singapore	Thailand
	S. Korea		1	1	1					
	China	1		1	1				1	
	Japan	1	1		1					1
	USA						1	1		
	Brazil				1					
	Canada				1					
	Mexico				1					
	Singapore									
	Thailand									

The degree of centrality analysis of a matrix with direction can be classified by an out-degree of centrality and an in-degree of centrality, as in Table 5.5. From the results, the United States – with the highest degree of centrality in a nondirectional relationship – has a high in-degree of centrality at 0.750 but a low out-degree of centrality of 0.25. Thus, the United States imports steel products from various countries within the network, including China, Japan, Canada, Korea, Brazil, and Mexico, but primarily exports to Canada and Mexico. It should be noted that this is an analysis of export and import relationships of more than US$1 billion (Figure 5.3).

The degree of centrality analysis of a matrix with direction can be classified by an out-degree of centrality and an in-degree of centrality, as whom in Table 5.6. From the results, the United States with the highest degree of centrality in a nondirectional relationship has a high in-degree of centrality at 0.750 but has a low out-degree centrality of 0.25. Thus, the United States imports steel products from various countries within the network including China, Japan, Canada, Korea, Brazil, and Mexico, but mostly exports to only Canada and Mexico. It should be noted that this is an analysis of the export and import relationship with more than US$1 billion.

In a directional relationship, the density of the ego network considering the direction can be obtained from the ratio of the connected links of inward and outward relationships to the maximum total number of connected links. The density of the nondirectional relationship of Korea and the United States is 100% and 42.86%, but the density of a directional relationship for South Korea is 75% (9/12) and the United States is 33% (14/42), resulting in a lower density considering the direction. The directional relationship of steel products results in an in-degree centralization Equation 5.6 of 0.0848 ($=\Sigma[(0.750-0.250_{\text{S.Korea}})$ … $(0.750-0.125_{\text{Thailand}})]/[(9-1)(9-2)]$) and an out-degree centralization Equation 5.7 of 0.0446 ($=\Sigma[(0.500-0.375_{\text{S.Korea}})$ … $(0.500-0.000_{\text{Thailand}})]/[(9-1)(9-2)]$).

$$C_{inD} = \frac{\sum_{i=1}^{g}\left[C_{inD}\left(n^{*}\right)-C_{inD}\left(n_{i}\right)\right]}{\left[(g-1)(g-2)\right]} \tag{5.6}$$

$$C_{outD} = \frac{\sum_{i=1}^{g}\left[C_{outD}\left(n^{*}\right)-C_{outD}\left(n_{i}\right)\right]}{\left[(g-1)(g-2)\right]} \tag{5.7}$$

The density of the entire steel product network can be estimated by dividing the average inward and outward degree of centrality with the total node numbers, as shown in Equation 5.8.

$$\overline{C_{in-outD}} = \frac{\sum_{i=1}^{g} C_{inD-outD}\left(n_{i}\right)}{g} \tag{5.8}$$

Table 5.5 Trade relationship matrix with direction.

In link (import) →	Out link (export) →								
	S. Korea	China	Japan	USA	Brazil	Canada	Mexico	Singapore	Thailand
S. Korea		1	1	1					
China	1		1	1				1	
Japan	1	1		1					1
USA						1	1		
Brazil				1					
Canada				1					
Mexico				1					
Singapore									
Thailand									

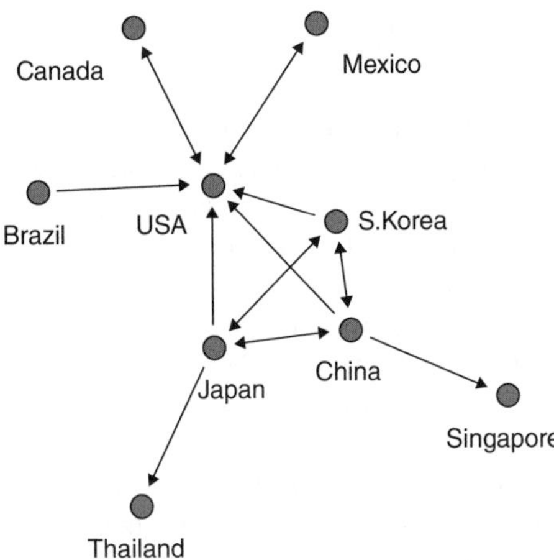

Figure 5.3 Visualization of the trade relationship with direction.

Table 5.6 Analysis of the degree of centrality for the directional relationship.

	Degree centrality		Ego size	# of links	# of possible links	Ego density
	In	Out				
S. Korea	0.250	0.375	3	9	12	0.750
China	0.250	0.500	4	10	20	0.500
Japan	0.250	0.500	4	10	20	0.500
USA	0.750	0.250	6	14	42	0.330
Brazil	0.000	0.125	2	1	2	0.500
Canada	0.125	0.125	2	2	2	1.000
Mexico	0.125	0.125	2	2	2	1.000
Singapore	0.125	0.000	2	1	2	0.500
Thailand	0.125	0.000	2	1	2	0.500
Mean	0.222	0.222	# of nodes	9	Density	0.221
Standard deviation	0.202	0.184				
Minimum	0.000	0.000				
Maximum	0.750	0.500				
Degree centralization	0.084	.045				

5.1.2 Closeness Centrality

The second concept in the centrality of the actor is the closeness centrality, which based on the distance between the actors. Closeness centrality is a measured index that focuses on the distance of the actor from other actors within the network and determines an actor to have higher centrality if the actor is located where interactions can occur rapidly [1]. In terms of a communication relation, higher centrality suggests an independence from other actors in receiving information. Therefore, an actor with a high degree of closeness centrality would be in an efficient position to exchange information from other actors. Furthermore, when a problem occurs within the network, the selection of problem-solving actors, who have short communication distances within the network, can provide a more efficient solution. As a result, the closeness centrality is focused on the economic aspects.

With respect to the closeness centrality, the node that has the fewest connections with other nodes would have higher centrality and can be measured by the minimum distance. If a node in the network is far from other nodes, the closeness centrality will decrease, which requires more connections to connect with other nodes. On the other hand, a node with the minimum number of steps to connect with other nodes can interact with other nodes rapidly having less dependence from other nodes, resulting in higher closeness centrality.

In the measurement of the centrality of the actor, the closeness centrality indicates how close the actor is with other actors of the network in terms of distance. The actors' closeness is the distance of the diameter of the network; as the diameter increases, the closeness centrality of the actor decreases. The closeness centrality of the node "*i*" is the reciprocal of the total distance to other nodes within the total network. Therefore, measurement of the closeness centrality has significance within connected networks and, depending on the total number of nodes, the maximum value of the closeness centrality can be determined. The minimum of the closeness centrality is the distance to itself, which is 0. In case the sizes of the network are different, direct comparison of the closeness centrality between the networks may be difficult and thus require normalization with (total node number−1). The normalized closeness centrality is between 0 and 1, which can be considered to be the reciprocal of the average distance between the actor "*i*" (node "*i*") and other actors (other nodes). This defined centrality considers both the directly connected relationship and the indirectly connected relationships, which can be calculated by Equation 5.9. In the equation, $C_C(n_i)$ is the closeness centrality of node "*i*," and $d(n_i, n_j)$ is the distance between node "*i*" and "*j*," which is normalized by dividing the minimized reachable distance $(g-1)$ resulting in the standard index.

$$C_C\left(n_i\right)=\frac{g-1}{\sum_{j=1}^{g} d\left(n_i,n_j\right)} \tag{5.9}$$

Closeness centralization is one of the indexes for the entire network that can be obtained similarly by identifying the degree centralization using the closeness centrality value. However, assuming the distance between all the actors is 1, the calculated maximum value would be $[(g-2)\ (g-1)]/(2g-3)$. Here, if one actor selects another actor, the maximum distance that can be obtained is $(g-1)$ and if the selected actor is to select other actors the maximum distance would be $(g-2)$. C_C is the centralization of the network, $C_C(n^*)$ is the measured maximum closeness centrality, and $C_C(n_i)$ is the value of the closeness centrality of the node "i."

$$C_C = \frac{\sum_{i=1}^{g}\left[C_C\left(n^*\right)-C_C\left(n_i\right)\right]}{\left[(g-2)(g-1)\right]/(2g-3)} \tag{5.10}$$

For the closeness centrality analysis of the steel product trade relation matrix that has no direction and weighted value, the United States with the highest degree centrality also had the shortest distance between other countries, indicating that the US node to be at the center of the network in terms of closeness. Brazil, Canada, Mexico, Singapore, and Thailand had identical degree centrality values, but Brazil, Canada, and Mexico, which has trade relations between the United States having the shortest distance, were found to have a higher closeness centrality. Even the closeness centralization was 0.588, which was higher than degree centralization. Although steel trade is not concentrated toward a particular country, the connected distance in the entire trade relation seems to be unevenly distributed and concentrated toward a particular country in terms of distance. Thus, the United States has the shortest distance to other countries (nodes) in the steel product entire trade relation and is in a position to expand or affect other countries in the shortest time compared with other countries.

The closeness centrality defined by the distance between two actors can also be applied and measured to relationships with direction. For relations with direction, the distance between the actors n_i and n_j cannot be assumed to be the same for the distance between n_j and n_i. In other words, because the $d(n_i, n_j)$ is not the same for $d(n_j, n_i)$, the closeness centrality of n_i must take into account the inner distance n_i and the outer distance J_i within the network Equation 5.11. In terms of the information accessibility, a higher inner closeness centrality suggests higher accessibility of related information no matter where the information originated. A higher external closeness centrality indicates a higher transmission capability of information. In the import export trade relation, a higher inner closeness centrality suggests a higher expandability of the import trade relation and a higher outer closeness centrality suggests indicates a higher expandability of the export trade relation (Table 5.7).

$$C_C\left(n_i\right) = \frac{J_i\left(g-1\right)}{\left[\sum_{j=1}^{g} d\left(n_i,n_j\right)/J_i\right]} \tag{5.11}$$

Table 5.7 The results of the closeness centrality analysis depending on the existence of direction.

	Closeness centrality			Distance		
	Non-direction	Direction		Non-direction	Direction	
		In	Out		In	Out
S. Korea	0.615	0.143	0.400	13	56	20
China	0.667	0.143	0.421	12	56	19
Japan	0.667	0.143	0.421	12	56	19
USA	0.800	0.333	0.143	10	24	56
Brazil	0.471	0.111	0.160	17	72	50
Canada	0.471	0.276	0.140	17	29	57
Mexico	0.471	0.276	0.140	17	29	57
Singapore	0.421	0.160	0.111	19	50	72
Thailand	0.421	0.160	0.111	19	50	72
Mean	0.556	0.194	0.228			
Standard deviation	0.127	0.079	0.141			
Minimum	0.421	0.111	0.111			
Maximum	0.800	0.333	0.421			
Closeness centralization	0.588	0.336	0.466			

5.1.3 Betweenness Centrality

The betweenness centrality is based on the actor's location within the network [1,2]. Interactions between non-adjacent actors are possible through an actor existing between the two actors. In fact, the go-between actor of non-adjacent actors can not only act as a conduit between the actors but also is at a position for control. An actor that is located at the geodesic position of actors can be assumed to have a high betweenness centrality. This actor has control of the connection and flow of information within the network and thus has information control power in terms of communication. An actor with high betweenness centrality can chose to pass on information or not to other actors within the network. Therefore, if an actor with high betweenness centrality is removed from the network, the connection, and communication within the network could be disrupted.

There exist several geodesic connections between two different actors within the network. Let's assume the weight factor is identical and the interactions occur through the geodesic distance between the paths of n_j to n_k. g_{jk} is the number of geodesic connections between n_j and n_k. g_{jk} is the number of geodesic connections between n_j and n_k. If the number of geodesic connections is identical between two nodes, the probability of a path to be selected would be equal and the probability of ni to appear in the interactions would be simply $1/g_{jk}$*100 (%). If there are several geodesic connections between n_j and n_k that n_i appear, the probability that the path will pass n_i would increase. Therefore, if the number of geodesic path between two actors that contain n_i is $g_{jk}(n_i)$, the betweenness centrality of n_i, which is $C_B(n_i)$, can be defined by $g_{jk}(n_i)/g_{jk}$. At that time, the minimum value of n_i is 0 because it may not appear in the geodesic path and the maximum value is the pair of actors that does not include n_i, which is $(g-1)$ $(g-2)/2$. Therefore, if the aforementioned betweenness centrality value is normalized with respect to the maximum value that follows the geodesic path containing n_i, the betweenness centrality value can be ascertained according to Equation 5.12. In other words, the denominator is used to normalize the comparison index by dividing the numerator with the maximum value that the numerator can obtain.

$$C_B(n_i) = \frac{\sum_j^g \sum_k^g \frac{g_{jk}(n_i)}{g_{jk}}}{\left[(g-1)(g-2)/2\right]} \tag{5.12}$$

The betweenness centralization is obtained by comparison of the largest betweenness value of $C_B(n^*)$ within the network and by normalizing with the maximum betweenness centrality value resulting in the betweenness centralization Equation 5.13.

$$C_B = \frac{2\sum_{i=1}^g \left[C_B(n^*) - C_B(n_i)\right]}{\left[(g-1)^2(g-2)\right]} \tag{5.13}$$

An analysis of the betweenness centrality of steel products trade relations as a matrix, USA (0.179) was verified to have the highest betweenness centrality (Table 5.8). Others such as China and Japan also had a high betweenness centrality compared to other nodes. Therefore, if USA is removed, the cluster becomes disconnected and there will be significant increase in the number of steps to reach other nodes within the network. In other words, if the USA was to be removed, there would be a great deal of difficulty for Mexico, Canada, Brazil to maintain trade, because the USA is at the center of the trade relations. In particular, Canada, which is highly dependent on other nodes, can experience significant hardships. Dependency measures the reliance on a particular node, when transferring information or products to other nodes. In addition, if China and Japan does not participate in the trade, Singapore and Thailand can run into problems with steel product trading. This can be translated to a well-connected trade relation of steel products amongst the trade participants. Figure 5.4 shows the visualization of a bigger node with higher betweenness centrality.

5.1.4 Prestige Centrality

The prestige centrality is based on a weighted value of the importance of the other actor. Namely, the prestige centrality utilizes the fact that the single connection with a highly influential actor can increase ones' influence than several connections with less influential actors [3]. If the degree centrality considered all connected actors

Table 5.8 Results of betweenness centrality and centralization.

	Betweenness centrality	Dependency
S. Korea	0.000	0
China	0.036	0
Japan	0.036	0
USA	0.179	0
Brazil	0.000	0
Canada	0.000	5
Mexico	0.000	5
Singapore	0.000	2
Thailand	0.000	2
Mean	0.028	0.194
Standard deviation	0.055	0.876
Minimum	0	0
Maximum	0.179	5
Betweenness centralization	0.170	

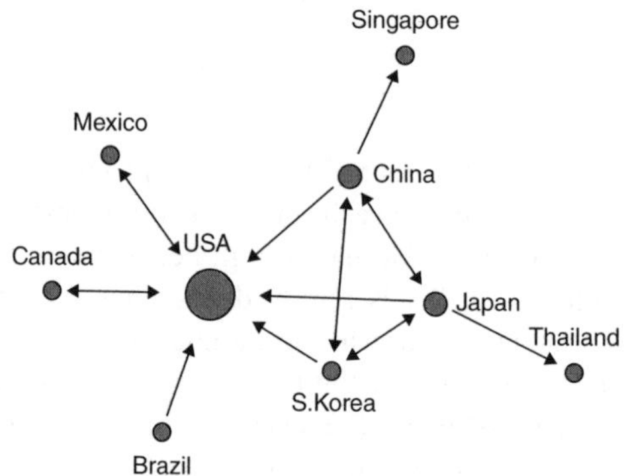

Figure 5.4 Visualization of betweenness centrality.

equally, the prestige centrality is a weighted degree centrality that assigns a weighted value to the neighboring actors.

The prestige of the actor n_i is increased as the number of correspondences with other actors with higher prestige is present. Of course, this interpretation can be conceptualized by the number of contact that the actor has with other high profile influential actors. Therefore, the prestige centrality considers both the central influence of the actor with others and the influence of other actors that is connected to that actor (Equation 5.14).

$$C_P(n_i)(\alpha,\beta)=\sum_{i}^{g}(\alpha+\beta p_j)Z_{ji} \tag{5.14}$$

In the equation to evaluate the prestige centrality C_P, Z_{ji} is the observed direct relationships of the g×g matrix, α, β is a random value set by the researcher. α is a constant to normalize the centrality index and β describes the degree of interactions. If the impact of the other actor is a positive and complementing relationship β would be positive and if the other actor is a negative and competitive relationship β would be set to a negative value. Theoretically, under normal circumstances, α would be 0 and β would be 1. More specifically, in the calculation of the prestige centrality value of the relationship between n_i and n_j, the centrality of n_i does not only rely on the centrality of n_j but the centrality of n_j will also be affected by n_i. Therefore, if n_j provided a centrality value to n_i in the first step, then in the second step will receive part of the centrality that was reflected back to n_j. This received back centrality is the reflected centrality and is the centrality value of n_i that was only related to the centrality value received from n_j termed the derived centrality. Therefore, the reflected centrality and derived centrality can be assumed to be the degree of interactions between n_i and n_j.

The results of the prestige centrality analysis of the steel product trade relations matrix shows S. Korea to have smaller neighborhoods compared to the USA, but the neighborhoods of the USA including Mexico, Canada, Brazil does not have other neighbors unlike S. Korea, where the neighbors have other neighbors and considering the indirect connections there would be a larger chain reaction resulting in the highest prestige centrality (Table 5.9).

Next, we'll discuss some of the methods to measuring the prestige centrality. First, Page-rank [4] is a method used to determine the order of the Web page found in the Internet search engine Google. The order of the Web page through this method

Table 5.9 Results of prestige centrality.

	Eigenvector centrality	Reflected part	Derived part	Constant part
S. Korea	0.515	0.094	0.252	0.170
China	0.433	0.047	0.216	0.170
Japan	0.503	0.083	0.249	0.170
USA	0.484	0.055	0.259	0.170
Brazil	0.044	–0.004	–0.122	0.170
Canada	0.187	0.007	0.009	0.170
Mexico	0.121	–0.003	–0.046	0.170
Singapore	0.044	–0.004	–0.122	0.170
Thailand	0.083	–0.005	–0.083	0.170
Mean	0.268			
Standard deviation	0.198			
Minimum	0.044			
Maximum	0.515			

is based on the fact that important sites receives connections from other important sites and the importance of a site depends on how many links has been received from other important sites.

Power [5] is the case where a negative β is given for the calculation of the prestige centrality. The centrality of a neighbor gives a negative effect on the centrality of the actor and thus if connected to a node with high prestige can actually lower its bargaining power. If the neighboring node has a lower prestige, the influence of the node to the neighboring node will increase.

The centrality analysis through Katz considers the strength of the relationship and also the ripple effect of the indirect relations. Katz [6] looks at not only the direct connections between neighboring nodes, but also the connections of the neighboring nodes with other nodes. In other words, beyond the simple primary neighboring connections, the influence of the second, tertiary, and nth neighbor indirect connections are also considered in the measurement of the centrality.

In HITS (Hypertext Induced Topic Selection) [7], the search engine Clever developed by IBM incorporates the hyperlink structure amongst the Web pages describing the topic of interest to identify the order. The basic idea of this method is assuming that a good hub will send links to an authority and if it is indeed a higher authority will receive the link from the good hub. Therefore, the hub points for each node will be proportional to the sum of all out-neighbor authority values and the authority value of each node will be proportional to the sum of the in-neighbors hub value resulting in a circulating calculation.

If we look at the results of the analysis of the steel product trade relations matrix, USA has high values in the Page Rank, Power and in-neighbors centrality score within the Katz centrality, and the authority score of the HITS. Japan had a high score in the Power and out-neighbors centrality of the Katz centrality. This result suggests a high ripple effect of the USA regarding import relations, but Japan would have a larger impact on the export relations compared to other countries (Table 5.10).

5.1.5 Broker

The broker identified in the network analysis allows flexibility between actors through various social interactions within the relationship structure [8]. In order to verify the role of the broker, the preliminary classification of the subordinate group within the network must be identified and depending upon where the actor stands amongst the subordinate group the broker can be divided into five types. Generally, the broker is at an important position within the group or between the groups and is an actor that has a certain high centrality and is divided into different types depending on the role of each actor within the group (Figure 5.5).

A coordinator is a mediating actor between actors within an identical group and receives a link from a node and transfers that link to another node. Therefore, an actor within the group that has high in-degree and out-degree connectivity. A representative is an actor that represents the entire group and receives links from the actors within the group and transfers those links to the actor of another group. The gatekeeper

Table 5.10 Results of page-rank, power, Katz centrality, and HITS.

	Page-rank centrality	Power centrality		Katz centrality		HITS	
		In	Out	In	Out	Authority	Hub
S. Korea	0.030	1.487	0.982	0.658	1.234	0.357	0.474
China	0.032	0.640	1.500	0.310	1.591	0.335	0.540
Japan	0.032	0.567	2.054	0.294	2.161	0.335	0.540
USA	0.293	2.296	1.121	1.085	0.782	0.764	0.000
Brazil	0.017	0.000	0.161	0.000	0.147	0.000	0.253
Canada	0.141	0.686	0.456	0.487	0.418	0.000	0.253
Mexico	0.141	0.444	0.272	0.315	0.250	0.000	0.253
Singapore	0.023	0.183	0.000	0.082	0.000	0.179	0.000
Thailand	0.023	0.293	0.000	0.129	0.000	0.179	0.000
Mean	0.082	0.733	0.727	0.373	0.732	0.239	0.257
Standard deviation	0.088	0.680	0.686	0.316	0.729	0.233	0.212
Minimum	0.017	0.000	0.000	0.000	0.000	0.000	0.000
Maximum	0.293	2.296	2.054	1.085	2.161	0.764	0.540

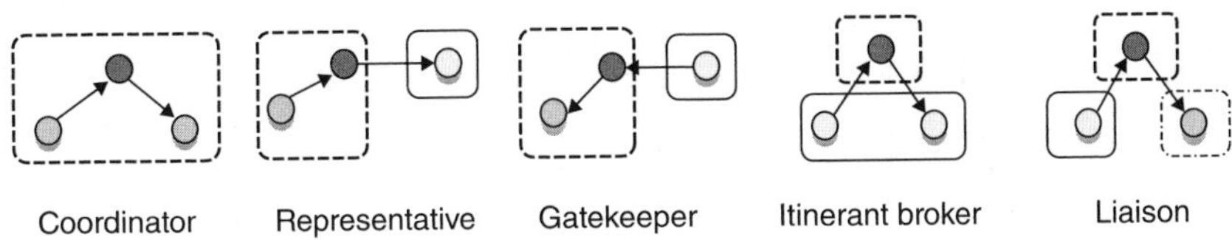

Figure 5.5 Type of broker.

is an actor that is in a position to accept a link from another group and transfer that link to other actors within its group. The itinerant broker is located in a different group and connects actors within the same group and often called the consultant. A liaison connects actors within different groups receiving links and transferring the links within and beyond its own group.

Broker analysis allows the identification of the individual actor's role within the network depending upon the actor's location, but like the degree centrality considers only direct relationships and is a non-essential measurement method.

In the steel product trade relations, countries set the region with a variable to allow grouping and performed a broker analysis. That resulted in China and Japan to behave as coordinators and the USA to behave as a representative, gatekeeper, iterant broker, and liaison. USA in particular acts as a gatekeeper, where it imports significantly from countries in other regions and exports large amounts to countries within identical regions (Table 5.11).

Table 5.11 Results of broker analysis.

	Partition value	Coordinator	Representative	Gatekeeper	Itinerant	Liaison	Total
S. Korea	Asia	0	0	0	0	0	0
China	Asia	2	0	0	0	0	2
Japan	Asia	2	0	0	0	0	2
USA	North America	0	1	5	1	3	10
Brazil	South America	0	0	0	0	0	0
Canada	North America	0	0	0	0	0	0
Mexico	South America	0	0	0	0	0	0
Singapore	Asia	0	0	0	0	0	0
Thailand	Asia	0	0	0	0	0	0
Mean		0.444	0.111	0.556	0.111	0.333	1.556
Standard deviation		0.831	0.314	1.571	0.314	0.943	3.095
Minimum		0	0	0	0	0	0
Maximum		2	1	5	1	3	10

5.2 Cohesive Subgroup

Cohesive subgroup analysis is an analysis method that determines the network structure by grouping actors that are intimately connected with one another [9]. By dividing a huge network into several subgroups, the network structure can be expressed more simply and the characteristics of the network can not only be understood much easier, but the relationship amongst the actors within the subgroup and the relationship between the subgroups can be identified more clearly and precisely.

The general procedure for a cohesive subgroup analysis is first identifying the closely connected group of actors within the network that are continuously connected using the component analysis. Next for each component instead of the links between the groups focus on increasing the number of links within the group and perform a community analysis distinguishing the sub groups and allow a more elaborate identification of the subgroups. Through this analysis procedure, the cohesive subgroups within the network can be more effectively understood. In addition, the Clique analysis allows the comprehension of the subgroups that are perfectly connected with all the actors and K-core analysis allows the discovery of the group of nodes that have a minimum of k number and more of connections.

5.2.1 Component

Component is a subgroup with a connection system having continuous links amongst the nodes and the component analysis is an analysis method to identify the cohesive subgroup through the connection possibility of nodes [10]. For instance, two nodes that are connected by a direct or indirect path is considered to fall within a single component. The component is the largest range to distinguish groups within the cohesive subgroup analysis and is applied at the initial stages of the analysis. Only connected nodes are included in a single component and because there is no connected links between components, an analysis to identify the connected degree and geodesic path within a component does not affect the analysis index.

A strong component must have a path that connects two nodes and considering the direction of the link the path can be from A to B or B to A in that strong component. A weak component does not have direction and is defined only by the existence of a connection path between A and B, which suggests a more tempered connection than a strong component. Component analysis considers only the possibility of node connections and weights of links have no meaning. A bi-component is a component with a connected node of more than two independent paths without a repetitive node in the middle (Figure 5.6).

In translating the analysis results of the component analysis, caution should be taken in the number and size of the component. If the entire network is composed of a single component, the relevant network is considered to be structured so that information flow is relatively smooth. On the other hand, if the entire network is composed of two similar sized components, the network is composed of two disconnected subgroups and information transfer is cut off resulting in severed communication to the other subgroup. Also, a network composed of a giant component and several small

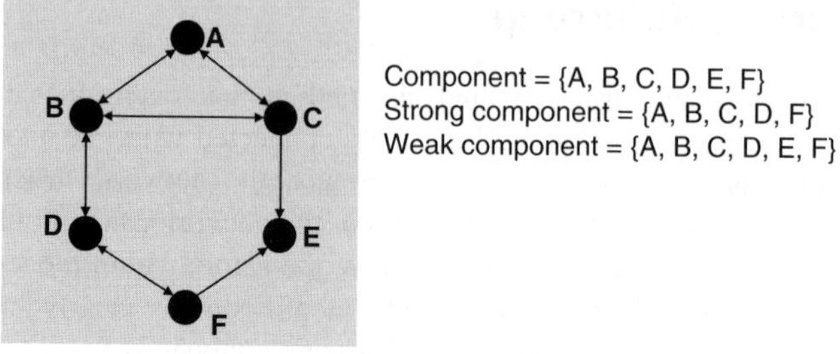

Figure 5.6 (Strong vs. weak) component.

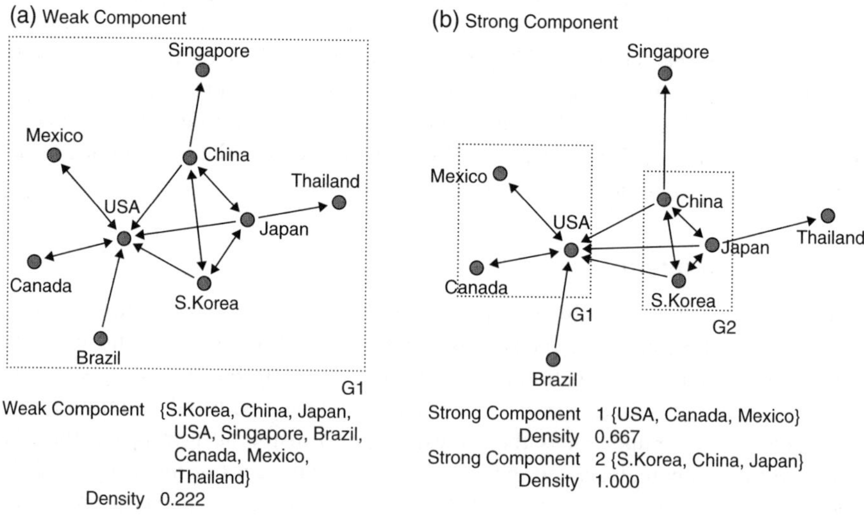

Figure 5.7 Results of component analysis. (a) Weak component and (b) strong component.

components translates to information that is not transferred to several alienated groups or actors within the network (Figure 5.7).

The component analysis of the steel product trade relations matrix resulted in weak components with no directions including all nine countries of S. Korea, China, Japan, USA, and so on, and two strong components with direction. Component 1 contained USA, Canada, Mexico and component 2 contained S. Korea, China, and Japan.

5.2.2 Community

Community [11] analysis is an analysis method that identifies cohesive subgroups by setting the number of links within the group to be higher than the links between groups. The analysis is based on the likelihood of links with high betweenness centrality in the entire network to be links not within the group but links that extend beyond the group.

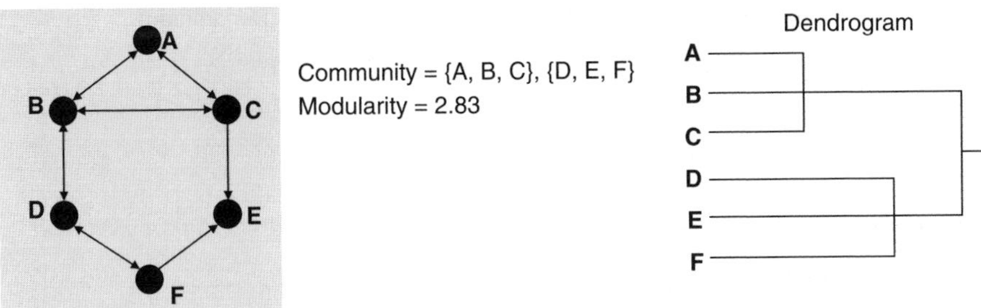

Figure 5.8 Community.

Therefore, in the community analysis the links are ordered according to the betweenness centrality, where the pair of nodes corresponding to the link with the lowest value is included into the group sequentially resulting in the identification of the cohesive subgroup. In the actual procedure, the betweenness centrality is calculated for all of the links and the link with the highest value is removed which is repeated until no links are left and when the last link is left the pair of nodes is sequentially included into the cohesive subgroup. Before the analysis, the network must be dichotomized and symmetrized.

The number of cohesive subgroups can be determined by the modularity, which describes the informative ability of the cohesive subgroup. The cohesive subgroup number can be determined by the point of sudden change in the modularity from increasing to decreasing trend. In the random network, the modularity is defined by an appreciable difference in the community structure from the community structure of the present network. In other words, it is an index that describes how many links exist and how well the nodes form a single unique community. The community analysis in NetMiner results in a dendrogram showing the hierarchical structure within the group and depending on the researcher's propensity can distinguish the group accordingly at a certain subjective step resulting in the number of cohesive subgroups (Figures 5.8).

The community analysis of steel product trade relations matrix showed five distinct communities. S. Korea, China, Japan to be cohesive subgroup 1, USA, Mexico, Canada to be cohesive subgroup 2, Brazil, Singapore, and Thailand to be subgroup 3, 4, and 5 (Figure 5.9).

5.2.3 Clique

Clique analysis is based on cohesiveness, where all of the nodes within the group have links that are directly connected having a density of 1 with a group of perfect connection [12]. Due to the stringent condition of all nodes to have perfect connections, Clique is actually difficult to find and have a characteristic of having repetitive nodes within several Cliques. For example, within a clique of five nodes, there can simultaneously be a clique with three nodes and a clique with four nodes. Due to this, when performing a clique analysis usually the maximal concept is applied, where the largest clique that includes the relevant nodes is addressed. Because repetition of nodes within the Clique

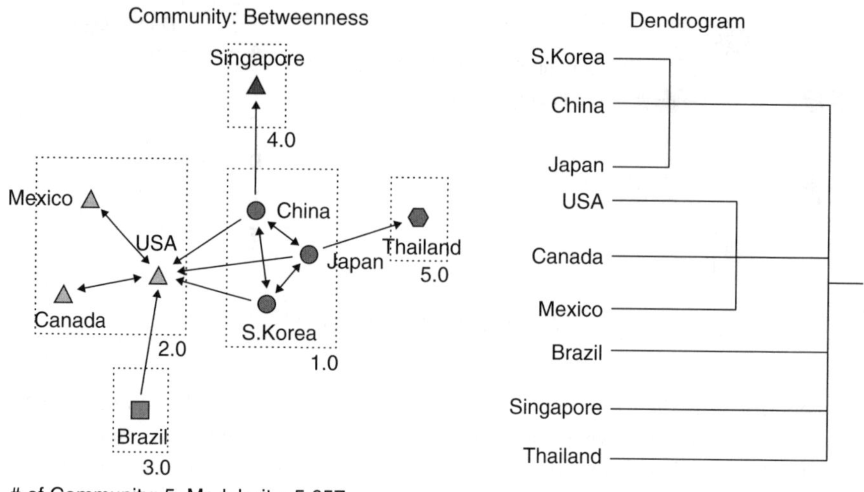

Figure 5.9 Results of community analysis.

analysis is allowed, identification of relevant nodes to the particular clique can be done similar to the 2-mode network allowing additional analysis.

To relax the stringent conditions of the clique, the n-clique, n-clan, and the k-plex that eases the connectivity degree can be applied.

1. *n-clique* [1b,12]: The clique is a set of nodes that are connected by a distance 1 and n-clique is a set of directly or indirectly connected nodes with distance of more than or equal to 2. Here the n stands for the distance between the nodes and the n-clique describes the complete connection at a distance of at least n. Thus, if n is 1, 1-clique is identical to the clique and if n is 3 the 3-clique is a cohesive subgroup where all the nodes are connected to each other within three steps.

2. *n-clan* [13]: n-clan is a set of nodes within the n-clique that has no external node connections. Therefore, the n-clan must have a maximum path (diameter: the maximum distance between the geodesic paths of two nodes) within the network to be less than or equal to n, n-clan. Moreover, because it can only be applied to networks without direction or weights, before the analysis is performed the subject network much be dichotomized and symmetrized.

3. *k-plex* [14]: Based on the degree, the k-plex, which eases the conditions of the clique, is valid when the connection degree of all the nodes is equal to or greater than n−k (n is nodes, k is connected degree). Therefore, a network with six nodes and a 2-plex reference describes a set of nodes that have a connection degree of 4 (= 6−2) or more. 1-plex describes a set of nodes with connection degree of 5 (= 6−1) or more, which is a clique. k-plex is used to distinguish a cohesive subgroup using a more relaxed condition. Figure 5.10 shows the clique, n-clique, n-clan, and k-plex. In a network composed of

six nodes, n and k is given both a two and a minimum of three nodes is included within a particular subgroup.

5.2.4 k-Core

Within a network, there exist various types of nodes, where the nodes may have several relationships or a single relationship. The relationship of nodes is useful in identifying the cohesiveness of the component. k-core is a method to identify only the nodes that have k or more connections [15]. Thus, a higher k value can assume that the nodes within the subgroups have a stronger degree of connectivity. For example, in the aforementioned Figure 5.10, extraction of the three-core nodes will exclude the nodes A, D, E, F having a degree of connectivity of 2 with only B and C left, which has a connection with three nodes.

Figure 5.11 shows the clique, n-clique, n-clan, k-plex, k-core analysis of the steel product trade relation matrix.

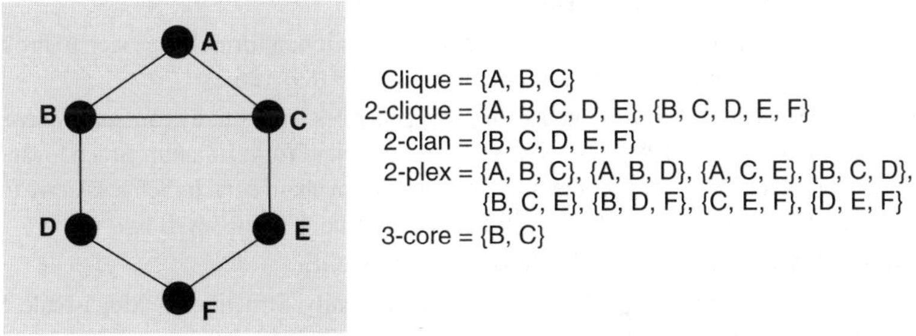

Figure 5.10 Clique, n-clique, n-clan, k-plex, and k-core.

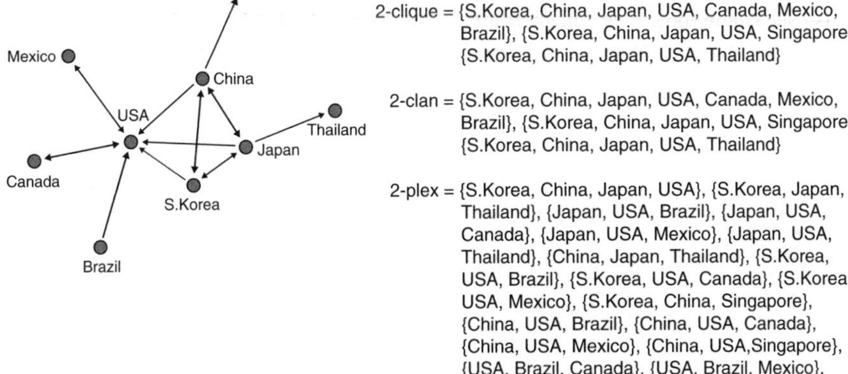

Figure 5.11 Results of clique, n-clique, n-clan, k-plex, and k-core.

References

1 (a) Freeman, LC. (1979) Centrality in social networks: I. Conceptual clarification, *Social Networks*, **1**, 215-239; (b) Wasserman, S. and Faust, K. (1997), *Social Network Analysis: Methods and Application*, New York: Cambridge University Press.

2 Brandes, U. (2001) A faster algorithm for betweenness centrality, *Journal of Mathematical Sociology*, **25**(2), 163–177.

3 Bonacich, P. (1972) Factoring and weighting approaches to status scores and clique identification, *Journal of Mathematical Sociology*, **2**. 113–120.

4 Brin, S. and Page, L. (1998) The anatomy of a large-scale hypertextual Web search engine, *Computer Networks and ISDN Systems*, **30**, 107–117.

5 Bonacich, P. (1987) Power and centrality: a family of measures, *American Journal of Sociology*, **92**(5), 1170–1182.

6 Katz, L. (1953) A new status index derived from sociometric analysis, *Psychometrika*, **18**(1), 39–43.

7 Kleinberg, J.M. (1998) Authoritative sources in a hyperlinked environment. Proceeding of the ACM-SIAM Symposium on Discrete Algorithms.

8 Gould, J. and Fernandez, J. (1989) Structures of mediation: a formal approach to brokerage in transaction networks, *Sociological Methodology*, **19**, 89–126.

9 (a) Burt, R.S. (1984) Network items and the general social survey, *Social Networks*, **6**, 293-340; (b) Collins, R. (1988), *Theoretical Sociology*, New York: Harcourt Brace Jovanovich; (c) Erickson, B. (1978) Some problems of inference from chain data, In Schuessler, K.F. (ed.), *Sociological Methodology, 1979*, 276–302, San Francisco, CA: Jossey-Bass.

10 Scott, J. (2000) *Social Network Analysis*, London: SAGE.

11 Wakita, K. and Tsurumi, T. (2007) Finding Community Structure in Mega-scale Social Networks, cs.CY/0702048, http://arxiv.org/abs/cs.CY/0702048v1 (accessed 22 May 2015).

12 Bock, R.D., and Husain, S.Z. (1950) An adaptation of Holzinger's B-coefficients for the analysis of sociometric data, *Sociometry*, **13**, 146–153.

13 Mokken, R.J. (1979) Cliques, clubs and clans, *Quality and Quantity*, **13**, 161–173.

14 Seidman, S. and Foster, B. (1978) A note on the potential for genuine cross-fertilization between anthropology and mathematics, *Social Networks*, **1**, 65–72.

15 Seidman, S. (1983) Network structure and minimum degree, *Social Networks*, **5**, 269–287.

6

Connectivity and Role

In network analysis, it is important to find out the structural characteristics of how groups are divided and interconnected. There are some features showing the structural characteristics of a network. This allows the determination of whether the entire system is split into many groups or overlapping exists among groups, or how the sizes of groups are distributed. For instance, if there is no overlap among groups and there is a system composed of completely separated groups, conflicts and confrontations will be severe and new innovations will be difficult to accept by all of the members. Members in identical groups share common thoughts, behave similarly, and provide an identity that coincides with the group attributes. Some methods of network analysis were developed to split up members in a group depending on the existence of a relationship. The method to divide subgroups depends on how a subgroup is defined. For example, should a subgroup have a mutually reachable channel or can a subgroup just have a unilaterally reachable channel? Or should we regard groups connected with indirect relations as an identical subgroup? Subgroups can be divided according to these standards.

Fundamentals of Big Data Network Analysis for Research and Industry, First Edition. Hyunjoung Lee and Il Sohn.

6.1 Connection Analysis

6.1.1 Connectivity

Connectivity [1] analysis is used to identify the vulnerability of the network connection, and because the analysis occurs through the links between the nodes, the connectivity analysis can be approached on the basis of the node, which is the node connectivity, or on the basis of the links, which is the link connectivity. If between two nodes one of the nodes or a link is removed and the connection path is severed, then the connection between the two nodes cannot be considered to be strong. Thus, a disconnection between two nodes with respect to the number of nodes and links measures the connectivity; the larger value of the connectivity would describe a strong connection. If the component number increases with the removal of a node, the removed node would be called the cut-point or the cut-node, and if the component numbers increase with the removal of a link, the link would be called the bridge. Because the node connectivity is unrelated to the direction of the link, the network should be symmetrized during preprocessing. Because the link connectivity is unrelated to the weights and a single link is considered a single step, the network should be dichotomized during preprocessing.

The route here is the continuation of the node and links, which is the graph expressing the node-link-node-link sequence. Route is distinguished between walk, trail, path, where walk is a route with repetitive passing of nodes and links. In walk, a closed walk is where the starting and finishing nodes are identical, and a cycle is where the node and link appear only once and the start and finish nodes are identical. The trail is a case where the same node can be passed multiple times in an identical route but cannot pass links multiple times. A path is a route where nodes and links cannot be passed multiple times, and the distance is the number of links in a path. The shortest path is a path with the fewer number of links. Thus, the shortest path is the fastest path between random nodes. In certain cases, the weights of the links can be considered the strength of the relationship and a link with higher weights can be assumed to have two nodes, which are closer, resulting in the shortest path (Figure 6.1).

Table 6.1 and Figure 6.2 show the results of the connectivity analysis in terms of the node and links of the steel product trade relations matrix. Node connectivity [2] analyzes the node connectivity weakness within the network. The connectivity values of the node are the minimum number of nodes to remove in order for two nodes to be disconnected. Table 6.1 shows that to disconnect the connection between S. Korea and China, three nodes need to be removed, but for S. Korea and Brazil, only one node can disconnect the connection. Link connectivity [1] is the minimum number of links to remove to disconnect two nodes. The removal of the link between two nodes eliminates a node pair (bridges) and one node increasing the number of components, which is shown in Figure 6.2 with the removal of the component with a node (cut-points).

The analysis result of the shortest path [3] between two node connections without consideration of the direction showed the shortest path between S. Korea and USA to be 1 and that between Singapore and Brazil to be 3. In the nine nodes that comprise

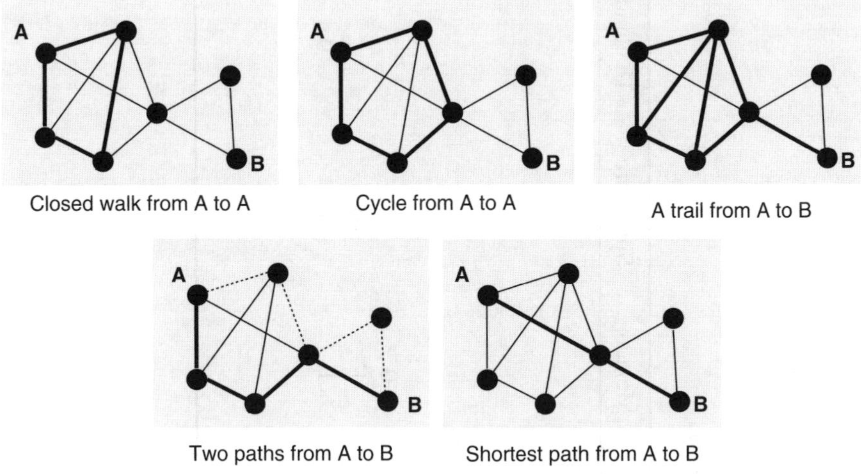

Figure 6.1 Walk, trail, path.

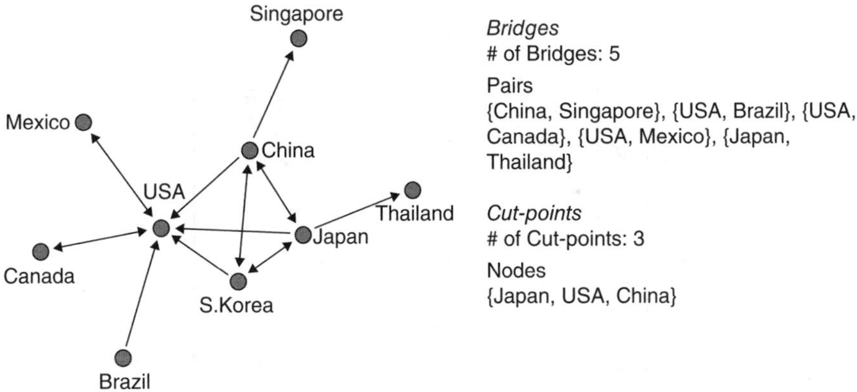

Figure 6.2 Results of link connectivity.

the entire set of nodes, the average geodesic distance is 1.889, and because all nodes are reachable, the number of reachable nodes is the entire node subtracted by itself, resulting in eight nodes (Table 6.2).

6.1.2 Reciprocity

Reciprocity is one method to identify the network structure, which is possible by analyzing the dyad relationship of possible links between two nodes. The dyad [4] relationship can be divided into a mutual dyad, where a mutual relationship is established; an asymmetric dyad, where a unilateral relationship is established; or a null dyad, where there is no relationship (Figure 6.3).

Table 6.1 Results of node connectivity.

	S. Korea	China	Japan	USA	Brazil	Canada	Mexico	Singapore	Thailand
S. Korea	0								
China	3	0							
Japan	3	3	0						
USA	3	3	3	0					
Brazil	1	1	1	1	0				
Canada	1	1	1	1	1	0			
Mexico	1	1	1	1	1	1	0		
Singapore	1	1	1	1	1	1	1	0	
Thailand	1	1	1	1	1	1	1	1	0
Mean		1.333			Minimum		1		
Standard deviation		0.745			Maximum		3		

Table 6.2 Results of shortest path.

	S. Korea	China	Japan	USA	Brazil	Canada	Mexico	Singapore	Thailand
S. Korea	0								
China	1	0							
Japan	1	1	0						
USA	1	1	1	0					
Brazil	2	2	2	1	0				
Canada	2	2	2	1	2	0			
Mexico	2	2	2	1	2	2	0		
Singapore	2	1	2	2	3	3	3	0	
Thailand	2	2	1	2	3	3	3	3	0

	Geodesic Distance	No. of Reachable Nodes
Mean	1.889	8
Standard deviation	0.698	0
Minimum	1	8
Maximum	3	8

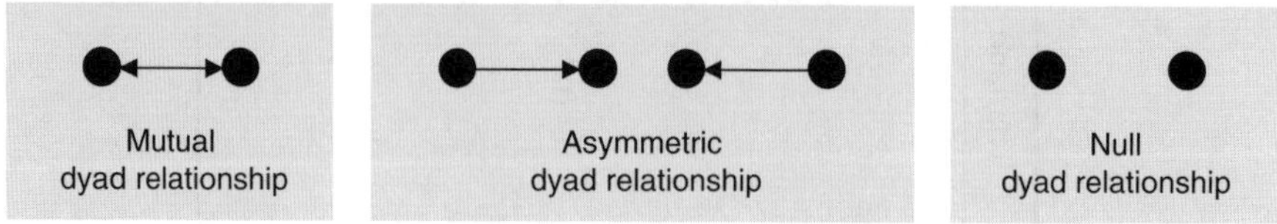

Figure 6.3 Type of dyad relationship.

The dyad relationship analysis between nodes of the whole network identifies the number of mutual, asymmetric, and null dyad relationship between pairs of nodes resulting in an organized table termed the dyad census. Through the dyad census, the degree of mutual relationship between each node can be identified. Namely, if there are numerous mutual dyad relationships within the network, the mutual relationship is dominant, if there are numerous asymmetric dyad relationships, the relationship can be considered to be one-sided, and if there are numerous null dyad relationships, the relationships can be considered to have many disconnected relationships.

Excluding the case of the dyad relationship with no relationship, reciprocity is measured by identifying the ratio of the mutual relationship existing within the dyad relationship. Therefore, a single value is obtained for the whole network, and with this value, the network characteristic of having a strong unilateral or bilateral relationship can be determined.

By realizing the type of reciprocity in the node pair of the steel product trade relations (Figure 6.2), the mutual dyad relationship was five (S. Korea–Japan, S. Korea–China, China–Japan, USA–Canada, USA–Mexico), the asymmetric dyad relationship was six (S. Korea–USA, Japan–USA, Japan–Thailand, China–Singapore, China–USA, USA–Brazil), and the null dyad relationship was found to be 25.

6.1.3 Transitivity

Transitivity [5] is used to identify the form of the triad relationship, where if a link between nodes i and j and nodes j and k exists, the ratio of the link between i to k is determined. Generally in a triad relationship, depending on the type of link, there are 16 different types, and for each form, there exists a name with three numbers and one letter alphabet. The three numbers are the number of mutual, asymmetric, and null dyad relationships of the mutual relationship, and the alphabet describes the link pattern in the triad relationship of up, down, cycle, and transitive [6] (Figure 6.4).

Like the dyad census, all of the triad relationship in the whole network is specified within the 16 types and can be organized into a table termed triad census (Figure 6.5). The 16 triad relationships can be divided into the transitive, intransitive, mixed relationship [7].

The analysis of the transitivity from the triad census of the node regarding steel product trade relations (Figure 6.2) is provided in Table 6.3. In other words, similar to

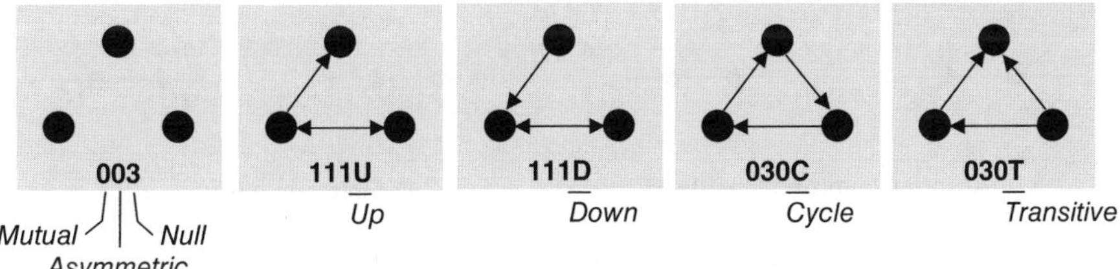

Figure 6.4 Type of triad relationship.

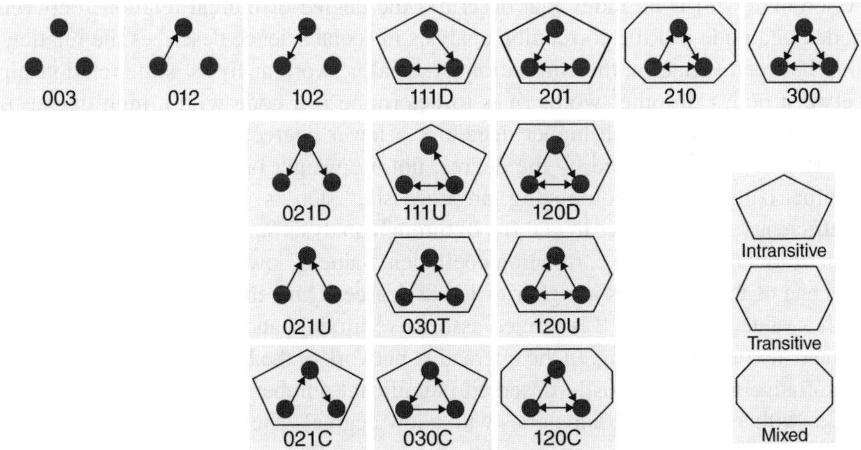

Figure 6.5 Triad isomorphism classes.

Table 6.3 Results of triad relationship.

Type of Triad Relationship	No. of Observed Relationship	Type of Triad Relationship	No. of Observed Relationship
003	33	030T	0
012	14	030C	0
102	15	201	1
021D	2	120D	0
021U	3	120U	3
021C	0	120C	0
111D	8	210	0
111U	4	300	1

the dyad relationship, the triad relationship shows 33 without a relationship (003 type), 3 nodes with a mutual relationship (300 type) represents 1 (S.Korea-China-Japan), and 1 is 120 type of triad relationships, which has only 2 nodes with a mutual relationship of the three nodes (Mexico–USA–Canada).

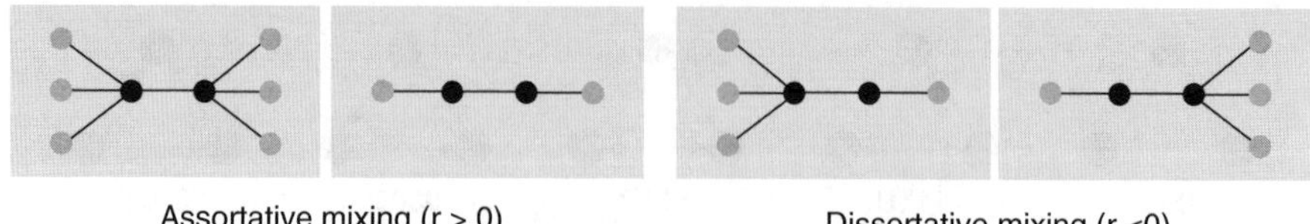

Figure 6.6 Assortative relationship.

6.1.4 Assortativity

Assortativity [8] is an index that describes the degree of mutual relations between node i and node j. If the correlation analysis in social science describes the relationship between variables, the correlation in social network analysis is the relationship between nodes. In other words, it is to determine if a node with a high degree is connected to a node with higher degree or a lower degree. Therefore, because the assortativity is determined by the degree, not the weight or direction of the link, a symmetrizing and dichotomizing preprocessing step is required. A correlation coefficient value of higher than 0 ($r>0$) through analysis suggests both nodes have a high or low degree and a correlation coefficient value of lower than 0 ($r<0$) suggests that one of the nodes has a higher or lower degree. Thus, the correlation coefficient with a value higher than 0 is termed assortative mixing, and a value lower than 0 is termed dissortative mixing. In the interacting network of the Internet or the protein the dissortative mixing is mostly observed (significant number of connections between nodes with a high degree and nodes with a low degree). The assortativity of the steel product trade relation matrix was found to be –0.592 and showed a dissortative mixing relationship (Figure 6.6).

6.1.5 Network Properties

Thus, before the initiation of the analysis, it is recommended to looking into the following index of the whole network [9]. Observation of the network properties in the steel product trade relations resulted in number of nodes to be 9, number of links to be 16, density of 0.222, average degree of 1.778, number of weak component to be 1, number of strong components to be 5, and inclusiveness of 1 (Table 6.4 and Figure 6.7).

6.2 Role

The role analysis provides an index that bundles the group of actors with similar patterns of relationships between actors within the network and through the connection structure between groups resulting in the effective identification of the role of actors within the complex network. Thus, the analysis follows the basic assumptions of the network, where the location depends on the relationship within the network and the role is dependent on the location. Furthermore, because the nodes are assumed to have a defined location and role, the role analysis should always result in all nodes belonging to a single group. Role analysis is often compared with similarity,

Table 6.4 Index of network properties.

Index	Description
Number of nodes	Number of nodes existing in the whole network
Number of links	Number of links existing in the whole network
Density	Ratio of the actual connected links to the total possible links in the whole network
Average degree	Average degree of the nodes
Number of (weak or strong) components	Number of cohesive subgroups existing in the whole network
Inclusiveness	Ratio of the number of connected nodes except for the isolated nodes to the entire node numbers

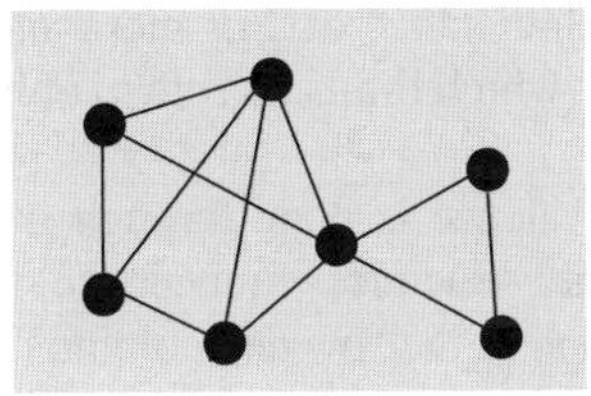

Number of nodes	7	Average degree	1.571
Number of links	11	Number of components	1
Density	0.524	Inclusiveness	1

Figure 6.7 Network properties.

where the similarity defines the typically similarity of the individual attributes and the role analysis looks at the similarity of the relationship pattern. In other words, the location similarity within the network.

6.2.1 Structural Equivalence

Structural equivalence groups actors according to similar social status and describes the relationship between the groups providing information on actors with relatively similar relationships within the network [10]. Thus, regardless of a relationship existing between two actors, the structural equivalence is defined by the type of relationship formed by each actor with other actors. Even without a direct connection, actors with more or less similar roles within the network are considered to have identical social status it terms of structure. For example, similar to Figure 6.8 nodes B and C receives a link from A and nodes D, E, and F send links. Here, nodes E and F receive links from nodes B and C, but node D also sends node G a link, which distinguishes the particular node. Thus, in the present network, nodes B and C and nodes E and F have similar relationship patterns, which could be identified to be at identical locations structurally.

Structural equivalence shares the same neighbor and the same relationship method, which provides indirect proof of the similarity between two nodes. Namely, two random nodes with connections to an identical node with the same relationship pattern (direction of link) can be determined to have equivalence.

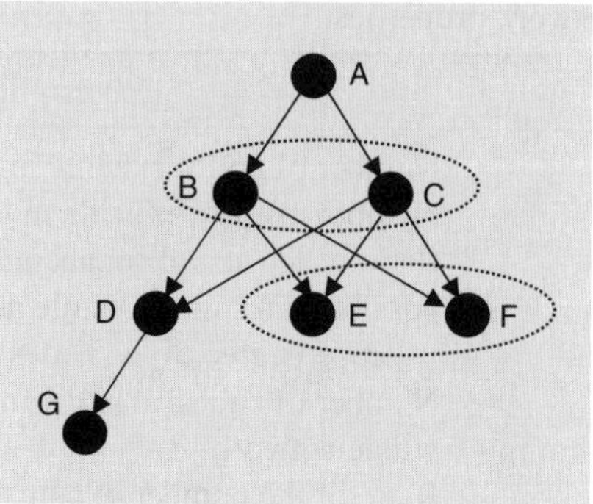

Figure 6.8 Structural equivalence.

However, structural equivalence is not an analysis with distance of 2 or more and is an analysis of direct connections between neighbors, which limits its role to only a localized region.

Generally, the measurement of the structural equivalence is done through the Euclidean distance and correlation coefficient. If the structural equivalence is measured through the Euclidean distance, the comparison of the row and column of the nodes in the matrix will yield an in-degree and out-degree measurement. At this time, if two random nodes are not equally located structurally the Euclidean distance is greater than 0 and if the two nodes are equally located structurally the row and column of the node will result in the same in-degree and out-degree value resulting in a Euclidean distance of 0. For example, if the node i and j is connected to k (out-degree) and k is also connected to node i and j (in-degree), the Euclidean distance of node *i* and *j* is 0 ($Sd_{ij}=0$) and the two nodes are at identical positions.

$$Sd_{ij} = \sqrt{\sum_{k=1}^{g}\left[\left(Z_{ik} - Z_{jk}\right)^2 + \left(Z_{ki} + Z_{kj}\right)^2\right]} \tag{6.1}$$

If the structural equivalence is measured through the correlation coefficient and the random node *i* and *j* is equally spaced perfectly, a value of +1 ($r_{ij}=1$) will be obtained and a value of 0 ($r_{ij}=0$) will result for non–equally spaced locations of the random nodes. The correlation coefficient can be calculated using Equation 6.2, where $\bar{Z}_{i\cdot}$ and $\bar{Z}_{j\cdot}$ are the average of row i and row j and $\bar{Z}_{\cdot i}$ and $\bar{Z}_{\cdot j}$ are the average of column *i* and column *j*.

$$r_{ij} = \frac{\sum\left(Z_{ik} - \bar{Z}_{i\cdot}\right)\left(Z_{jk} - \bar{Z}_{j\cdot}\right) + \sum\left(Z_{ki} - \bar{Z}_{\cdot i}\right)\left(Z_{kj} - \bar{Z}_{\cdot j}\right)}{\sqrt{\sum\left(Z_{jk} - \bar{Z}_{i\cdot}\right)^2 + \left(Z_{jk} - \bar{Z}_{j\cdot}\right)^2}\sqrt{\sum\left(Z_{ki} - \bar{Z}_{\cdot i}\right)^2 + \left(Z_{kj} - \bar{Z}_{\cdot j}\right)^2}} \tag{6.2}$$

In the measurement of the structural equivalence using the Euclidean distance and the correlation coefficient, the derived value from the two indicators may not always coincide. For the measurement through the correlation coefficient if equal spacing is observed a value of +1 will result, but for measurement by the Euclidean distance due to the difference in the mean and variance, the value will not result in a perfectly equal spacing of +1 even though the identical nodes were measured. Therefore, if the focus was on the relationship pattern between two nodes, the structural equivalence analysis using the Euclidean distance would be helpful.

In addition, considering the characteristic of the network documents is expressed in mostly a binary documentation, the structural equivalence can also be measured using the similarity and dissimilarity index. The representative measurement methods is the simple matching, Jaccard, Russel, and Rao. Simple matching is expressed as a ratio, where the number of existing links corresponding to two random nodes in the matrix consisting of the binary data is taken as the numerator and the total link number is taken as the denominator. Jaccard coefficient is the measurement that excludes the unconformable link from the numerator and the denominator from the simple matching. This is to consider the possibility of the absence of conformable links due to the larger size of the network, as the sheer size of the network may make the formation of links difficult. Thus, including the measurements with the absent conformable links may distort the measured values and is excluded from the analysis. Russell and Rao is a measurement that excludes the absent conformable link value from the numerator.

From the structural equivalence analysis through the Euclidean distance and verification of the profile matrix [11] on the steel product trade relations, Mexico and Canada were found to have a structurally equivalent relationship in both import and export relationship, whereas S. Korea, China, and Japan were found to be structurally equivalent in the import relationship, as shown in Table 6.5. Canada, Mexico, and Brazil were found to be structurally equivalent in the export relationship and Singapore and Thailand were found to be structurally equivalent in the export relationship. According to the profile matrix, if each node was found to have structural equivalence the value would be close to 0, and if structural equivalence was not observed than the value would become larger. The structurally equivalent relationship can also be verified by the dendrogram shown in Figure 6.9.

6.2.2 Automorphic Equivalence

Although the structural equivalence and automorphic equivalence have similarities in measuring the role of the node in the network, there is a distinct difference [7]. For example, if the relationship form of node i and j connected to other nodes is identical, node i and j will have structural equivalence. If the relationship pattern is similar to Figure 6.10, even if the node is not identical there is automorphic equivalence. Namely, B and C cannot be assumed to have structural equivalence, but has a similar relationship pattern that can be considered to have automorphic equivalence. In addition, D, E, F, and C can also be considered to be automorphically equivalent nodes. Therefore, automorphic equivalence can be considered an analysis that locates the nodes that have identical values of the network analysis index including degree, reachable node, and centrality.

Table 6.5 Results of structural equivalence.

In direction (import relationship)→		Out direction (export relationship) →								
		S. Korea	China	Japan	USA	Brazil	Canada	Mexico	Singapore	Thailand
	S. Korea	0.000	1.000	1.000	2.000	1.414	1.414	1.414	1.732	1.732
	China	0.000	0.000	1.414	2.236	1.732	1.732	1.732	1.732	2.000
	Japan	0.000	0.000	0.000	2.236	1.732	1.732	1.732	2.000	1.732
	USA	1.732	1.732	1.732	0.000	1.414	1.000	1.000	1.414	1.414
	Brazil	1.414	1.414	1.414	2.236	0.000	0.000	0.000	1.000	1.000
	Canada	1.732	1.732	1.732	2.236	1.000	0.000	0.000	1.000	1.000
	Mexico	1.732	1.732	1.732	2.236	1.000	0.000	0.000	1.000	1.000
	Singapore	1.000	1.414	1.000	2.236	1.000	1.414	1.414	0.000	0.000
	Thailand	1.000	1.000	1.414	2.236	1.000	1.414	1.414	1.414	0.000

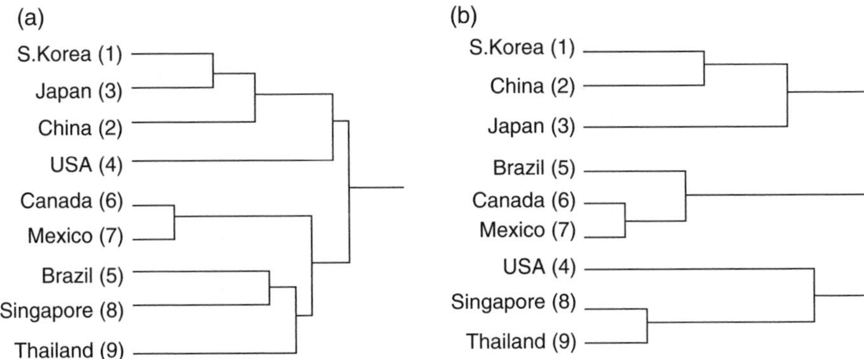

Figure 6.9 Dendrogram of structural equivalence. (a) Import relationship dendrogram and (b) export relationship dendrogram.

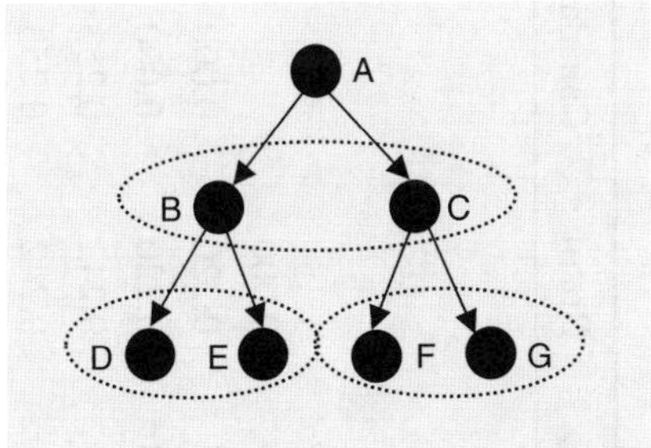

Figure 6.10 Automorphic equivalence.

6.2.3 Role Equivalence

Role equivalence is used to find equivalence groups that have smaller number than the structural equivalence [12]. For example, if country A and country B exports to certain countries D, E, and F, let's assume country A has more export trading to country D and country B has more export trading to country F. Here, country A and country B is not equivalent for structural equivalence, but considering these two countries have a higher export trading to one country shows equivalence. In other words, the structural location maybe different in the type of relationship, but has similarity in the fact that the two countries have a larger export trade to one other country (Table 6.6).

Role equivalence does not require a condition of identical node, but is measured by the similarity of the relationship pattern and the equivalence is calculated from the distribution of the triad relationship. Thus, find the total of the different patterns in the triad relationship between a random node and other node and compare the distribution of the triad relationship to measure the role equivalence. If the network size is g, the number of the triad relationship between the ego or focal node with

Table 6.6 Results of role equivalence.

	S. Korea	China	Japan	USA	Brazil	Canada	Mexico	Singapore	Thailand
S. Korea	0.000								
China	0.202	0.000							
Japan	0.202	0.000	0.000						
USA	0.551	0.503	0.503	0.000					
Brazil	0.401	0.487	0.487	0.709	0.000				
Canada	0.391	0.500	0.500	0.698	0.220	0.000			
Mexico	0.391	0.500	0.500	0.698	0.220	0.000	0.000		
Singapore	0.429	0.505	0.505	0.621	0.242	0.253	0.253	0.000	
Thailand	0.429	0.505	0.505	0.621	0.242	0.253	0.253	0.000	0.000

other nodes would be $(g-1)(g-2)/2$. The 36 different possible types of triad relationships is shown in Figure 6.5. If the node i and node j is equally distributed between the 36 types of triad relationships, the distance of the role equivalence would be 0 ($Rd_{ij}=0$) and if unequally distributed than the value would be closer to 1. Here P is the number of t type relationship of node i from the 36 types of triad relationships.

$$Rd_{ij} = \sqrt{\sum_{t=1}^{36}\left(P_{it} - P_{jt}\right)^2} \tag{6.3}$$

In role equivalence, the equivalence can be determined through identifying the role relationship even though the detailed structural relationship can be different. Thus, after dichotomizing the network matrix of the analysis subject, if the Euclidean distance calculations is close to 0, it can be assumed to be role equivalent. If the value is close to 1, then it could be assumed to be not role equivalent. From the analysis of the steel product trade relations matrix, Canada and Mexico, China and Japan, and Singapore and Thailand were found to be perfectly role equivalent. On the other hand, Brazil was found to have structural equivalence but did not have role equivalence. Brazil had structural equivalence with Canada and Mexico, where the countries all exported to USA, but Brazil did not import, unlike Canada and Mexico.

6.2.4 Regular Equivalence

Regular equivalence can be considered the most relaxed definition compared to all other equivalences. Two nodes are considered as regular equivalences, when two random nodes have similar relationships with other nodes. If node i and node k have a relationship and a node j and node l have a similar type of relationship, node i and node j are considered to be regularly equivalent. For example, as shown in Figure 6.11, if B, C, and D are team leaders and E, F, G, H, and I are team members, B, C, and D form regularly equivalent groups and F, G, H, and I also form regularly equivalent groups (Table 6.7).

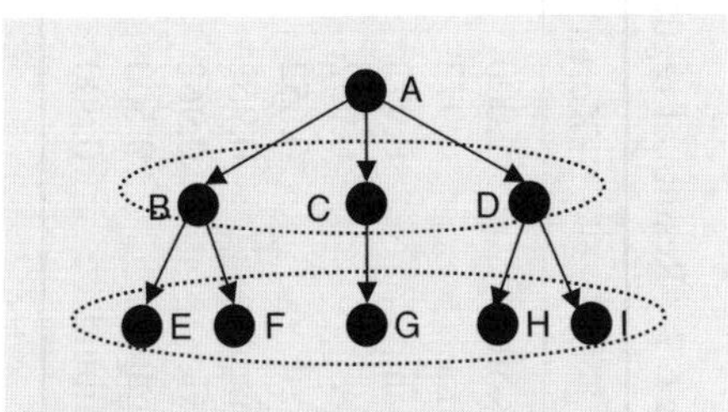

Figure 6.11 Regular equivalence.

Table 6.7 Results of regular equivalence.

	S. Korea	China	Japan	USA	Brazil	Canada	Mexico	Singapore	Thailand
S. Korea	1.000								
China	0.973	1.000							
Japan	0.973	1.000	1.000						
USA	0.952	0.945	0.945	1.000					
Brazil	0.652	0.669	0.669	0.311	1.000				
Canada	0.962	0.946	0.946	0.882	0.667	1.000			
Mexico	0.962	0.946	0.946	0.882	0.667	1.000	1.000		
Singapore	0.500	0.426	0.426	0.734	0.000	0.637	0.637	1.000	
Thailand	0.500	0.426	0.426	0.734	0.000	0.637	0.637	1.000	1.000

Regularly equivalence looks at the existence a two node group connection, where the team leader and team member form a relationship and is not focused on a particular relationship between a specific team leader and a specific team member. This approach method is important because it provides a method for determining the social status from the existing connection type within the network. Regular equivalence stipulates the social status and attempts to understand the interactions through the social status and instead of relying on the attributes of the nodes itself, discovers the behavior of the connection type within the network resulting in a defined social status. Regular equivalence starts from input of the data and the generation of the similarity matrix, where the degree of similarity or dissimilarity is provided. This matrix is expressed by the measurement of the correlation coefficient or the Euclidean distance. This matrix forms a cluster matrix and is the basis for classification of identical social status using the REGGE [13] or CatRE [14] method, which can then be visualized by a hierarchical cluster diagram, dendrogram, multidimensional scaling, and so on. REGGE is typically used for data with direction, where a mathematical algorithm or graphical representation can be used and has merits in that results can be obtained through various methods. CatRE is obtained through clustered variables and must include clustered variables. Depending on the level of the cluster, the Hierarchical cluster diagram shows hierarchical positions of the node groups. Dendrogram shows the grouping of nodes with identical roles dependent on the cluster level. Multidimensional scaling determines the coordinates between the distances of the nodes using the similarity matrix and is a method to assist in the classification of the nodes.

Regular equivalence can be established with the relationship between actors with similar roles, and using the REGGE of data with direction, the regular equivalence analysis of steel product trade relations matrix was performed. Values close to 1 in the matrix were identified to be regularly equivalent. and values close to 1 were identified to be not equivalent. China and Japan, Canada and Mexico, Singapore, and Thailand was found to be regularly equivalent, while Brazil and Singapore, Thailand was found to be not equivalent.

SimRank [15] has similar principles to the eigenvector centrality, where the similarity between two nodes is calculated from the similarity average between neighborhoods. Therefore, similar values between nodes to the reference value of a selected two nodes are considered to be equivalent. SimRank score is calculated from a node pair and if a dampening parameter is provided the whole network measurement can be performed. (SimRank score of each steps = dampening parameter × sum of neighborhoods score for node pairs). SimRank starts from pairs of nodes with identical values and is continuously calculated resulting in new values at each step. (SimRank score of each steps = dampening parameter × sum of neighborhoods score for node pairs) (Table 6.8).

SimRank score ranges from 0 to 1 and a value closer to 1 result in two nodes having equivalence. The dampening parameter for the SimRank is 0.8. Using the SimRank score of the export relationship, Brazil, Canada, and Mexico are found to have equivalence with all exporting to USA and in terms of the

Table 6.8 Results of SimRank.

		Out direction (export relationship) →								
In direction (import relationship)→		S. Korea	China	Japan	USA	Brazil	Canada	Mexico	Singapore	Thailand
	S. Korea	1.000	0.188	0.188	0.107	0.316	0.316	0.316	0.000	0.000
	China	0.392	1.000	0.142	0.093	0.240	0.240	0.240	0.000	0.000
	Japan	0.392	0.392	1.000	0.093	0.240	0.240	0.240	0.000	0.000
	USA	0.247	0.247	0.247	1.000	0.000	0.000	0.000	0.000	0.000
	Brazil	0.000	0.000	0.000	0.000	1.000	0.800	0.800	0.000	0.000
	Canada	0.149	0.149	0.149	0.089	0.000	1.000	0.800	0.000	0.000
	Mexico	0.149	0.149	0.149	0.089	0.000	0.800	1.000	0.000	0.000
	Singapore	0.528	0.256	0.528	0.247	0.000	0.149	0.149	1.000	0.000
	Thailand	0.528	0.528	0.256	0.247	0.000	0.149	0.149	0.256	1.000

import relationship, Mexico, and Canada is found to have equivalence with both importing from USA.

A favorable position within the network increases competitiveness and not only increase productivity can obtain high quality information. In addition, nodes located at similar positions within the network can form closer bonds and allow easier communication but may also form a competitive relationship from the identification of substitutions. Therefore, by identifying the position of each nodes within the network and strategically using the positions effectively, a more effective competitive edge can be established.

6.2.5 Block Modeling

To identify the existence of a connection between the nodes located at specific locations with other nodes at different positions, a block model can be formed [7]. In the block model, the nodes are grouped and a new relationship is formed between the groups. In more detail, the block model is based on the multirelationship and instead of focusing on the information of the individual nodes attempts to identify the relationship between the groups. In the aforementioned connection relationship between nodes, if the nodes are grouped into similarities of the pattern, block modeling is a summary of the connection relationship between groups and the relationship pattern among the various groups.

For block modeling, first the matrix of the individual nodes must be transformed into groupings of nodes with the same attribute. Here the same attribute is the attribute of the nodes. To identify the relationship between groups, the density with each group must be obtained. For example, calculate the density of group 1 and group 2 and calculate the links between the nodes of group 1 and group 2, which allow the identification of the inner and exterior connection of the groups. By realizing the connection between groups, the image matrix of relationship between groups can be completed after dichotomizing with respect to the cut-off point. An image matrix is a schematic of the connection between groups and the connections within the group, which can be a scaled-down graph of the existence of connections between groups. By block modeling the complex network can be simplified and the relationship pattern can be intuitively identified.

In the division shown in Figure 6.12, A is the division leader, B, C, and D are the team leaders, E, F, G, H, and I are the team members. B, E, and F are in Team 1, C and G are in Team 2, and D, H, and I are in Team 3. The block model of the division can be expressed as Figure 6.12.

The block modeling of the steel product trade relation matrix according to the location of the countries results in Asia exporting to North America and North America importing and exporting to South America. Block modeling simplifies the relationship of the nodes into blocks of nodes with similar attributes allowing an intuitive observation of the network relationship in a simpler form. Even in the steel product trade relations, the trade between countries can be identified to relationship of the regions from relationship of the trade (Figure 6.13).

(a)

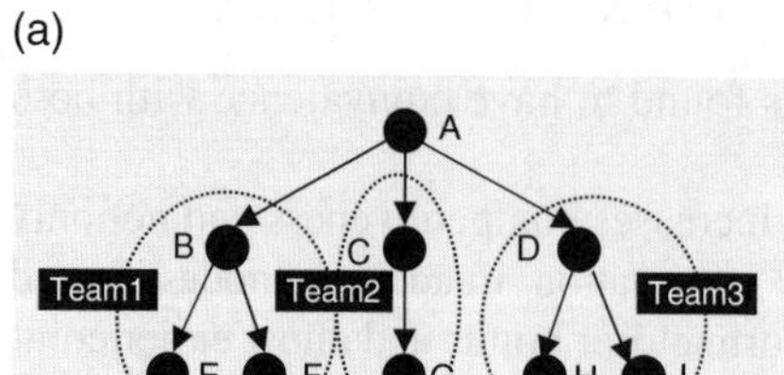

(b)

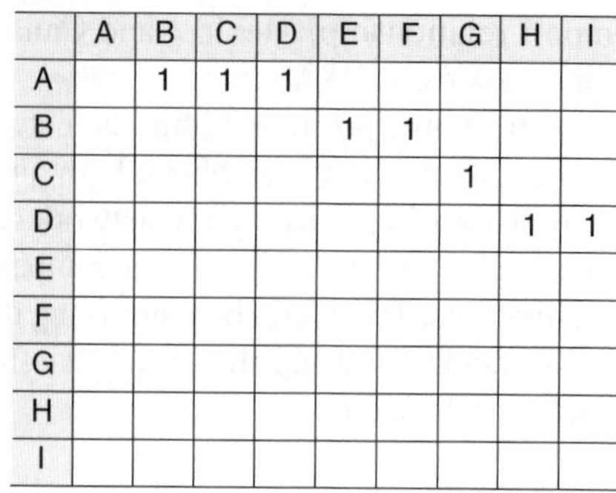

	A	B	C	D	E	F	G	H	I
A		1	1	1					
B					1	1			
C							1		
D								1	1
E									
F									
G									
H									
I									

(c)

	A	B	C	D	E	F	G	H	I
0	1	0	0	0	0	0	0	0	0
1	0	1	0	0	1	1	0	0	0
2	0	0	1	0	0	0	1	0	0
3	0	0	0	1	0	0	0	1	1

(d)

	0	1	2	3
0	0	1	1	1
1	0	1	0	0
2	0	0	1	0
3	0	0	0	1

(e)

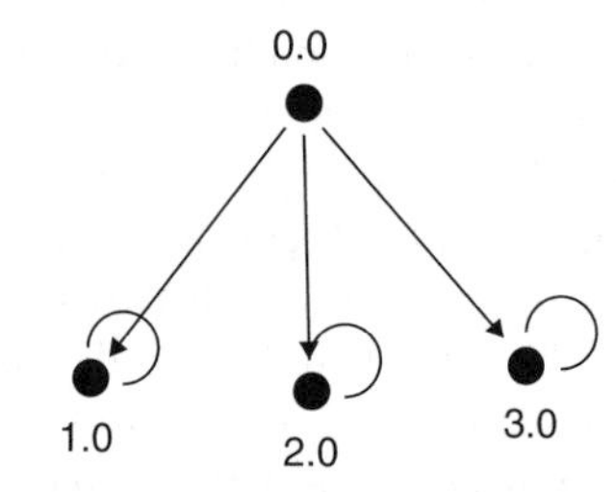

Figure 6.12 Block modeling. (a) Visualization of network, (b) matrix (node by node), (c) block-node affiliation matrix (node by group), (d) block image matrix (group by group), and (e) visualization of block image matrix.

(a)

	S.Korea	China	Japan	USA	Brazil	Canada	Mexico	Singapore	Thailand
Asia	1	1	1	0	0	0	0	1	1
North America	0	0	0	1	0	1	0	0	0
South America	0	0	0	0	1	0	1	0	0

(b)

	Asia	North America	South America
Asia	1	1	0
North America	0	1	1
South America	0	1	0

(c)

Asia
South America
North America

Figure 6.13 Results of block modeling. (a) Block-node affiliation matrix (node by group), (b) block image matrix (group by group), and (c) visualization of block image matrix.

References

1 Harary, F. (1969) *Graph Theory*, Addison-Wesley, Reading, MA.

2 Even, S. (1979) *Graph Algorithms*, Computer Science Press, Rockville, MD.

3 Floyd, R.W. (1962) Algorithm 97: shortest path, *Communications of the ACM*, **5**(6), 345.

4 Roberts Jr, J.M. (2000) Simple methods for simulating sociomatrices with given marginal totals, *Social Networks*, **22**(3), 273–283.

5 Holland, P.W., and Leinhardt, S. (1970) A method for detecting structure in sociometric data, *American Journal of Sociology*, **70**, 492–513.

6 Frank, O. and Harary, F. (1982) Cluster inference by using transitivity indices in empirical graphs, *Journal of the American Statistical Association*, **77**, 835–840.

7 Wasserman, S. and Faust, K. (1997) *Social Network Analysis: Methods and Application*, New York: Cambridge University Press.

8 Newman, M.E.J. (2002) Assortative mixing in networks, *Physical Review Letters*, **89**, 208701.

9 Scott, J. (2000) *Social Network Analysis*, London: SAGE.

10 Burt, R.S. (1976) Position in network, *Social Forces*, **55**, 93–122.

11 Lorrain, F. and White, H.C. (1971) Structural equivalence of individuals in social networks, *Journal of Mathematical Sociology*, **1**, 49–80.

12 Winship, C. and Mandel, M. (1983) Roles and Positions: a critique and extension of the blockmodeling approach. In: Leinhardt, S. (Ed.), *Sociological Methodology 1983–1984*, San Francisco, CA: Jossey-Bass, 314–344.

13 (a) White, D.W. and Reitz, K.P. (1983) Graph semigraph homomorphism on network relations, *Social Networks*, **5**, 193–234; (b) White, D.W. and Reitz, K.P. (1985) *Measuring Role Distance: Structural and Relational Equivalence*, University of California, Irvine, CA.

14 (a) Everett, M.G. and Borgatti, S.P. (1993) Two algorithms for computing regular equivalence, *Social Networks*, **15**, 361–376; (b) Everett, M.G. and Borgatti, S.P. (1993) Extract colorations of graphs and digraphs, *Social Networks*, **18**, 319–331.

15 (a) Jeh, G. and Widom, J. (2002) SimRank: a measure of structural-context similarity, In *Proceedings of the 8th ACM SIGKDD (Association for Computing Machinery's Special Interest Group on Knowledge Discovery and Data Mining) international conference on Knowledge discovery and data mining*, 538–543, NY: ACM Press; (b) Jeh, G. and Widom, J. (2003) Scaling Personalized Web Search, In *Proceedings of the 12th international conference on World Wide Web*, 271–279, NY: ACM Press.

7

Data Structure in NetMiner

The data structure in NetMiner [1] is composed of a data set with several data items that is used as the basic unit for analysis, and through this data set, all analysis and visualization are performed. Within the data items, there is the main node set, sub node set, one-mode network, and two-mode network. The results of the analysis using the data set are termed the process log. The minimum unit for analysis work within NetMiner is a workfile and the process log and data set is included in the workfile. Several workfiles are managed through one project and the basic data file for NetMiner is managed as a project, which is saved with a filename extension of nmf (NetMiner File).

7.1 Sample Data

NetMiner has already been introduced in Chapter 2: Basic Program for Analyzing Networks. Here, a detailed tutorial of network analysis with sample data provided in NetMiner will be explained. The sample data in NetMiner are available in the folder of the installed NetMiner program, and if the researcher chooses the installed folder to be the root path, the sample data would exist in the *C:\Program Files\Cyram\NetMiner\SampleData*. The sample data discussed here would be *01. Org_Net_Tiny1*, *02.Org_Net_Tiny2*, and *03.Org_Net_Tiny3*.

Fundamentals of Big Data Network Analysis for Research and Industry, First Edition. Hyunjoung Lee and Il Sohn.

7.1.1 01.Org_Net_Tiny1

In the main node set, there are 22 imaginary employees with information on the labels and attributes including a one-mode network having personal help, work interact, work help, know personally, personal friends relationship of employees. In the sub node set, information on the employee's affiliation with clubs, interest items, and purchased commodities is available in three sub node set with each sub node set having a two-mode network (Table 7.1).

7.1.2 02.Org_Net_Tiny2

For the main node set, there are 39 imaginary employees with labels and attributes, which include a one-mode network having cooperation and friendship relationships, knowledge exchange relationships, trust, and influence relationships. In the sub node set, a two-mode network composed of club memberships, hobbies, and an evaluation of 10 movies from employees is available (Table 7.2).

Table 7.1 Nodeset and network of 01.Org_Net_Tiny1.

01. Main node set	Node Label	Employee's name	
	Attributes	Education, Gender, Job-Ranking, Department, Duration, Age	
02. one-mode network	00. Edge List	Personal Help, Work Interact, Work Help	
	01. Matrix	Know Personally	
	02. Linked List	Personal Friends	
03. Sub node set	Clubs	Node Label	Club1, Club2, Club3
		Attributes	Club's name, Manger, Meeting Day, Meeting Time, Members
	Interest Items	Node Label	Move, Monetary, Sports, Health, Music
		Attributes	Category (with friends, alone)
	Commodities	Node Label	Rice, Skirt, Pencil, TV, Audio, PC, MP3 Player, Pants, Book, Apple
		Attributes	Mart (Mart 1, 2, 3)
03. two-mode network	00. Edge List	Purchase (0.5 is the product of wish list)	
	01. Matrix	Interested In (interested hobby)	
	02. Linked List	Club Affiliation (joined clubs)	

Table 7.2 Nodeset and network of 01.Org_Net_Tiny2.

01. Main node set	Node Label	Employee's name	
	Attributes	Team, Section, Gender, Education, Position, Duration, Name, Age	
02. one-mode network	00. Edge List	Cooperation, Friendship, Knowledge	
	01. Matrix	Trust	
	02. Linked List	Influence	
03. Sub node set	Clubs	Node Label	Club A ~ G, I, K, L ~ S
		Attributes	Building, Room
	Interests	Node Label	Move, Fishkeeping, Drawing, Pottery, Books, Animation, Cooking, Music, Chess, Blogging, Military, Astronomy, Rafting, Skiing, Dancing, Basketball, Football
		Attributes	
	Movie Titles	Node Label	The Godfather, Casablanca, Schindler's List, Pulp Fiction, Star Wars, Psycho, Citizen Kane, Memento, Fight Club, The Matrix
		Attributes	Director, researcher Rating, Category (Drama, War, Thriller etc.), Company
03. two-mode network	00. Edge List	Movie Score	
	01. Matrix	Interest with coworkers, Interest with friends	
	02. Linked List	Club Affiliation	

7.1.3 03.Org_Net_Tiny3

In the main node set, information on the labels and attributes of 100 imaginary employees is available with five one-mode network including the source of advice and influence on the employees, to whom the employee reports, to whom the employee

Table 7.3 Nodeset and network of 01.Org_Net_Tiny3.

01. Main node set	Node Label	Employee's name	
	Attributes	Team, Gender, Performance Level, Position, Job Satisfaction, Name, Age, Organization Satisfaction, Department	
02. one-mode network	00. Edge List	Advice From, Influence From, Report To, Talk About Innovative idea With, Talk About Personal Issue With	
03. Sub node set	Issues	Node Label	Issue 1–4
		Attributes	Importance, Subject, Proposed Date, Proposer
03. two-mode network	00. Edge List	Interested In	

speaks to obtain innovative ideas, and to whom the employees talks for personal issues within the network. In addition, there is sample data with information on the interests of the employees within one sub node set of a two-mode network (Table 7.3).

7.2 Main Concept

7.2.1 Data Structure

The data structure in NetMiner is composed of a data set with several data items that is used as the basic unit for analysis, and through this data set, all analysis and visualization are performed. Within the data items, there is the main node set, sub node set, one-mode network, and two-mode network. The results of the analysis using the data set are termed the process log.

The minimum unit for analysis work within NetMiner is a workfile, and the process log and data set are included in the workfile. Several workfiles are managed through one project, and the basic data file for NetMiner is managed as a project, which is saved with a filename extension of nmf. The organized hierarchical structure is provided in Figure 7.1.

1. *Dataset:* In NetMiner, the node set with the one-mode network is the main node set and the node set with the two-mode network is the sub node set. One data set will have one main node set with several sub node set. Therefore, to distinguish the main and sub node set, a red check mark is indicated.

2. *Attribute data:* Attributes exist in not only nodes but also links. Node attributes are the attributes of each node, and the link attributes are the attribute assigned to the link itself. The attribute data of the node and link can be effectively used by extracting information from a particular node or link and performing

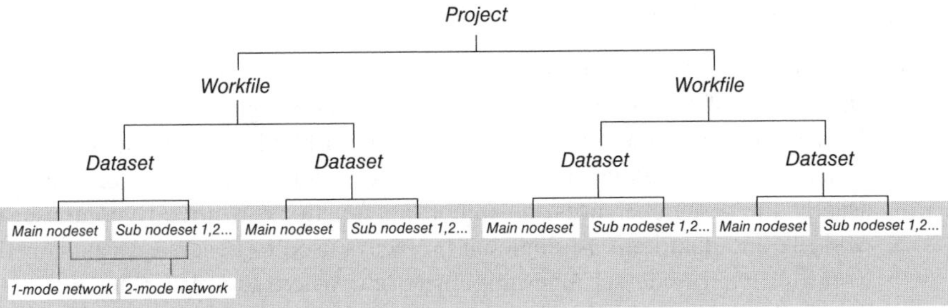

Figure 7.1 Hierarchical structure of NetMiner data.

Project
Current Workfile
DataSet ProcessLog
02.Org_Net_Tiny2
Employees [39 * 8]
Trust [69 * 0]
knowledge [84 * 3]
Influence [74 * 0]
Cooperation [59 *
Friendship [63 * 0]
Clubs [17 * 2]

Employees

		1	2	3	4
		Team	Section	Gender	Education
1	CY001	"Sales"	"Sales Branch"	"female"	'4YR College'
2	CY109	"Sales"	"Sales Support"	"male"	'4YR College'
3	CY137	"Sales"	"Sales Branch"	"male"	'4
4	CY008	"HR"	"Personnel"	"male"	st
5	CY013	"Department Manager"	artment Manager"	"male"	ctor's degree'
6	CY032	"Finance"	"Accuounting"	"male"	'4YR College'
7	CY053	"HR"	'Labor Relations"	"male"	'4YR College'

Node attribute

Project
Current Workfile
DataSet ProcessLog
02.Org_Net_Tiny2
Employees [39 * 8]
Trust [69 * 0]
knowledge [84 * 3]
Influence [74 * 0]
Cooperation [59 *
Friendship [63 * 0]
Clubs [17 * 2]

Employees knowledge

	1	2	3	4	5	6
	Source	Target	Weight	Category	Meeting Time	Feedback Score
1	CY110	CY078	3.0	"Decision Making"	15:00:00.000	2.8
2	CY229	CY109	2.0	"Decision Making"	17:30:00.000	3.2
3	CY131	CY100	5.0	"Trivial Issues"	17:30:00.000	3.9
4	CY130	CY078	3.0	"Decision Making"	15:00:00.000	4.7
5	CY145	CY057	1.0	"Trivial Issues"	15:00:00.000	
6	CY171	CY229	3.0	"Trivial Issues"	17:30:00.000	3.2
7	CY193	CY032	5.0	"Decision Making"	15:00:00.000	4.7

Link attribute

Figure 7.2 Attribute of node and link.

additional analysis or assigning different colors or sizes within the network map according to the attributes in the visualization output (Figure 7.2).

3. *Workfile:* The basic units of data sets and process logs for analysis and visualization in NetMiner are termed the workfile. The process log is composed of the sessions, which contain information on the results of the analysis and visualization; the query sets, which contain the extraction conditions of particular nodes and links; and the selections, which contain information on the particular nodes selected for the network map.

4. *Project:* In other words, even though the node set within the workfile is different, similar data can be managed under one project. If a module with a different main node set is executed, a new workfile will automatically be created. For reference, next to each data item an example of a series of numbers will be assigned such as [39*8], which would correspond to 39 nodes and 8 node attributes for a node set and 39 links and 8 link attributes for a link set.

7.2.2 Creating Data

1. *Creating a project:* Generating a project can be initiated by selection from the Main Menu of *File > New > Project,* and then choosing the project type from the screen. Two project types exist including a blank project and singleton project. The blank project is used to generate a project without a workfile and usually the researcher uses the importing functions to directly compose a workfile and data item. A singleton project is used to generate an unnamed workfile, main node set, one-mode network, where the researcher directly inserts the data within the NetMiner program. Figure 7.3 is the screenshot of the data management area, when the researcher selects a blank or singleton project.

2. *Creating a workfile:* The workfile is the basic unit for analysis and visualization containing the data set and process log, where the workfile must be first generated to carry out the actual analysis. Workfiles are created through selection of the *File > New > Workfile* dropdown menu sequentially and a workfile name can be established. The created workfile shown in Figure 7.4 can be verified in the current workfile (❶) and workfile tree (❷). After creation of the workfile, the data items of the main node set, one-mode network, two-mode network can be directly made or imported from other sources.

3. *Creating a data item:* The data items within the current workfile describes the main node set, sub node set, one-mode network, two-mode network. Creation of the data items can be accomplished using the *Data > Create New Item*

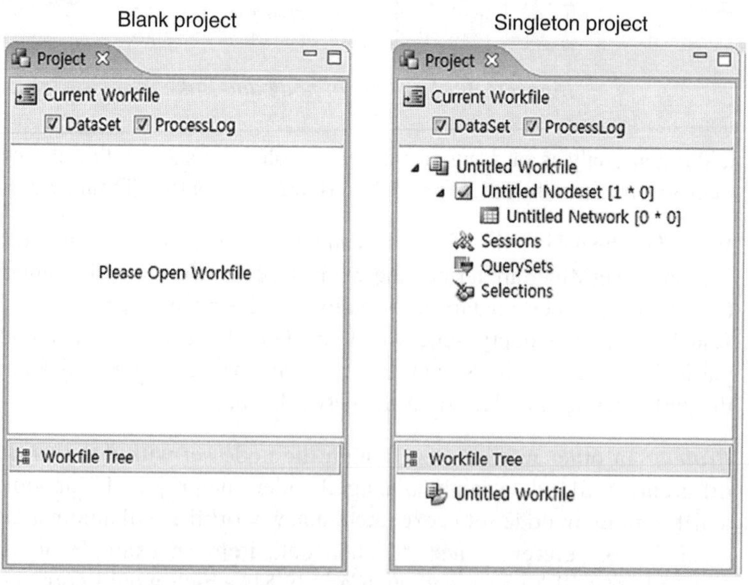

Figure 7.3 New project type.

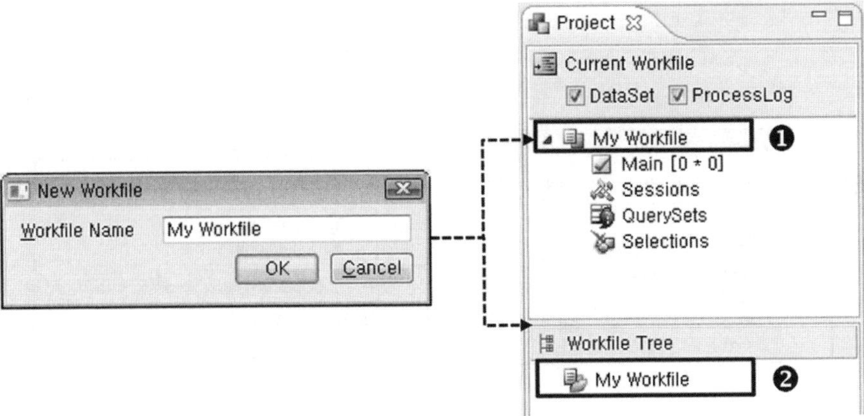

Figure 7.4 Workfile.

dropdown menu. one-mode network can be created by using the *Data > Create new Item > one-mode Network*. For example, as shown in Figure 7.5a, let's create a one-mode network data labeled "My one-mode Network Data" (Figure 7.5a❶). When configuring the name of the one-mode network, there are options below the dialog box to determine if the researcher will create a network with direction (undirected relation) or allow multiple links. Here they are not selected. After creating a one-mode network, "My one-mode Network Data" will be added to the current workfile (Figure 7.5a❷).

Before the creation of the two-mode network, the sub node set can be created by selecting the *Data > Create New Item > Sub Nodeset* dropdown menu. Similar to Figure 7.5b, "My subNodeset" can be created and verified within the sub node set of the current workfile. When the sub node set is generated, the two-mode network can be created (*Data > Create New Item > two-mode Network*). Here, "My two-mode Network Data" can be generated by selecting the previously created sub node set, as shown in Figure 7.5c.

7.2.3 Inserting Data

After the data items have been created, the researcher can directly add the nodes and links and the attributes. To insert the nodes or node attributes within the node set, the node set within the current workfile must be double clicked to activate the data editing area. After clicking the mouse right button in the column of the data editing area within the active window, users can select the *Insert Node* from the menu (Figure 7.6a❶). Here, if five nodes are added in "My node" (Figure 7.6a❷), five new nodes can be seen to be generated in the data editing area (Figure 7.6a❸). To add node attributes, the mouse right button can be pressed in the row of the data editing area, where users can select the *Insert Attribute* within the menu (Figure 7.6b❶). Here, if the attribute type within the "My attribute" is selected as a number (Figure 7.6b❷) and added,

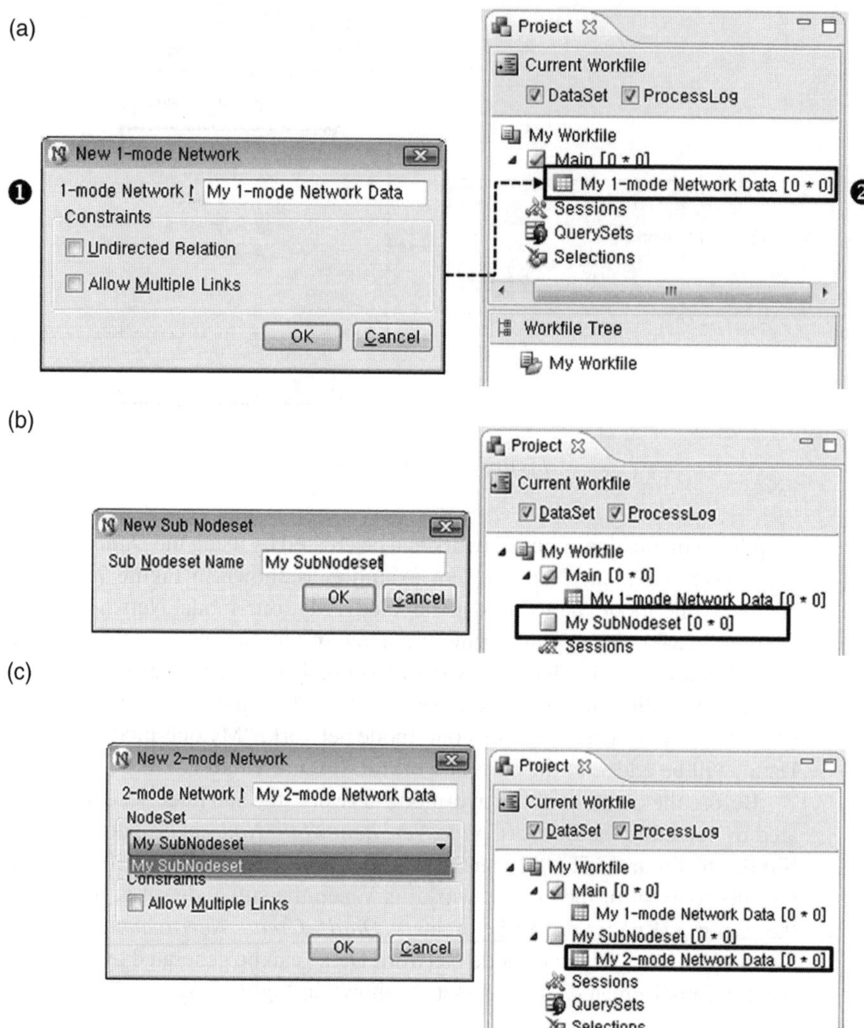

Figure 7.5 Create the network and node set. (a) Create new 1-mode network, (b) create new sub nodeset, and (c) create new 2-monde network.

a system missing value corresponding to "–999 999" will be generated as the node attribute and verified (Figure 7.6b❸). The researcher can then personally insert the attribute data in the form of a number. An attribute type of either a number, text, date time (YYYY-MM-DD 00:00:00), or time can be selected (00:00:00).

To add a link or a link attribute, the one-mode network or two-mode network must be selected within the current workfile by clicking and activating the data editing area. For the addition of a link, the researcher can directly insert the link weights within each cell from the [matrix] tab or by clicking the mouse right button on the

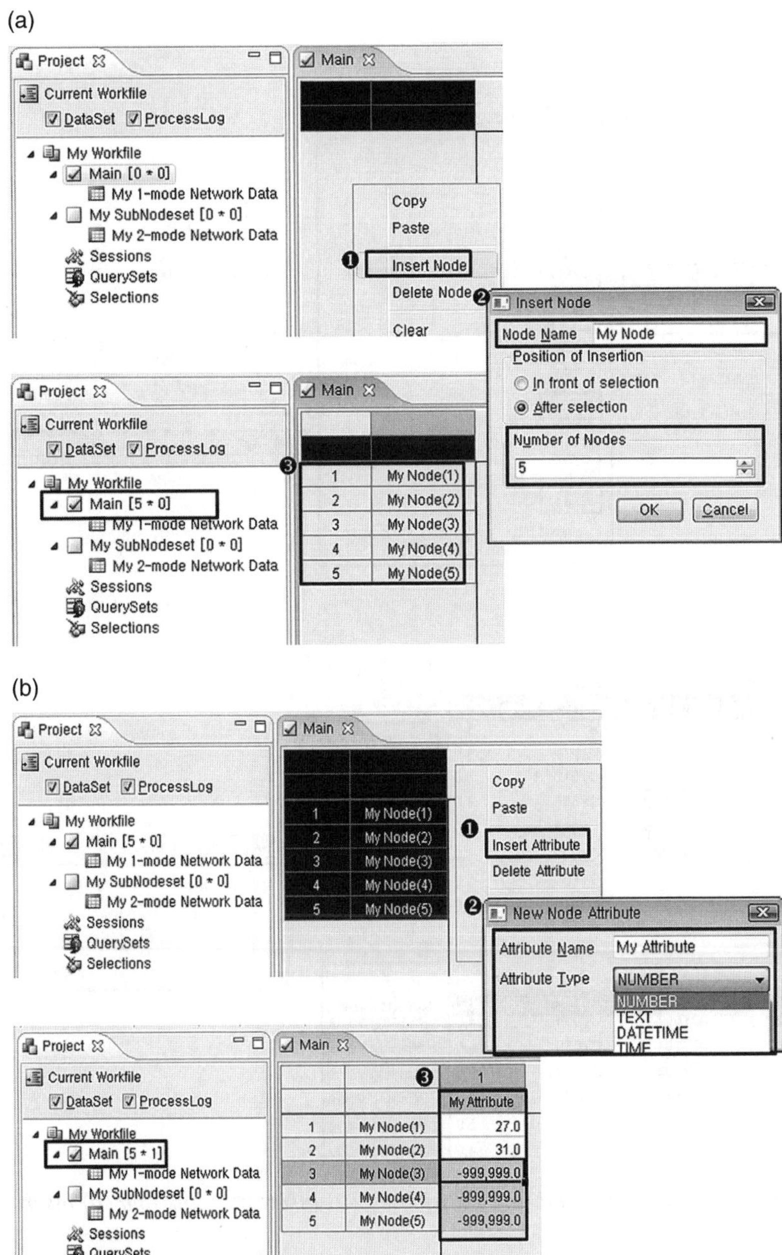

Figure 7.6 Insert nodes and node's attributes. (a) Insert new node and (b) insert new node attribute.

(a)

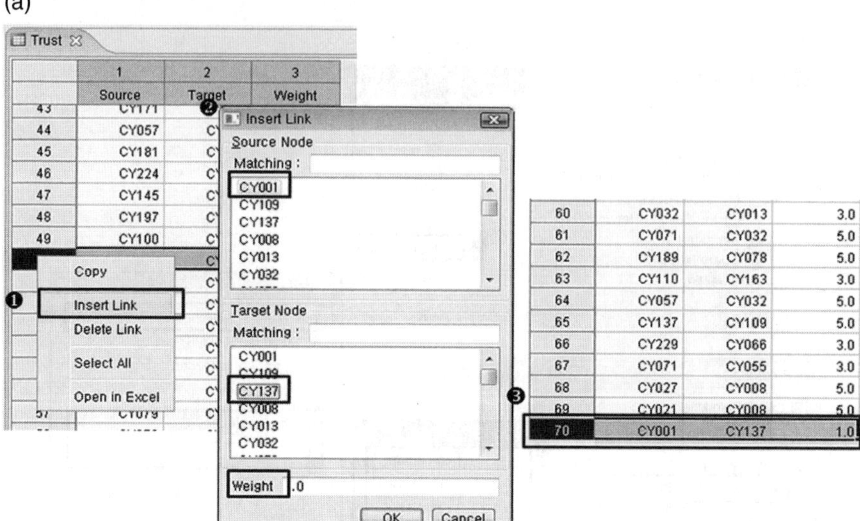

(b)

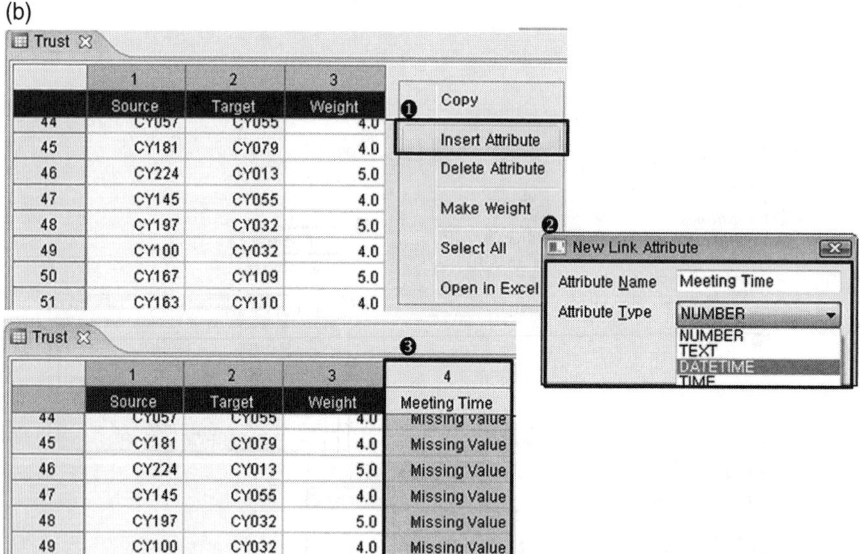

Figure 7.7 Insert links and link's attributes. (a) Insert new link and (b) insert new link attribute.

column of the [link list] tab and select the *Insert Link* from the menu (Figure 7.7a❶). Moving from the [matrix] and [link list] tabs can be done by clicking the respective tabs within the data editing area. After selecting the *Insert Link* the dialog box allows the addition of links by selection of the source and target nodes and by inserting the weights of the links (Figure 7.7a❷), the link and link weights are added (Figure 7.7a❸).

Link attributes can be added from the [link list] tab and clicking the mouse right button and using the *Insert Attribute* from the menu (Figure 7.7b❶). Here, the link attributes are "Meeting time" and the data type is date and time (Figure 7.7b❷) resulting in the additions of the link attribute (Figure 7.7b❸).

7.2.4 Importing Data

Data can be imported by using the mouse right button in the main menu screen. In the main menu, *File > Import* can be selected or data items can be retrieved by *Data > Import Data item.* In NetMiner, data files of type as Text (csv, txt), Excel (xls, xlsx), NetMiner3 previous version files (ntf), UCINET files (dl), Pajeck files (net, vec), StOCNET files (data, txt), GML files (gml) can be utilized. Here, the typical Text files and Excel files used will be explained in detail.

To import the text and excel files, the researcher can select *File > Import > Excel File (Text File).* The dialog box for the text and excel files are almost identical with the import excel file having an additional combo box to select excel sheets (Figure 7.8).

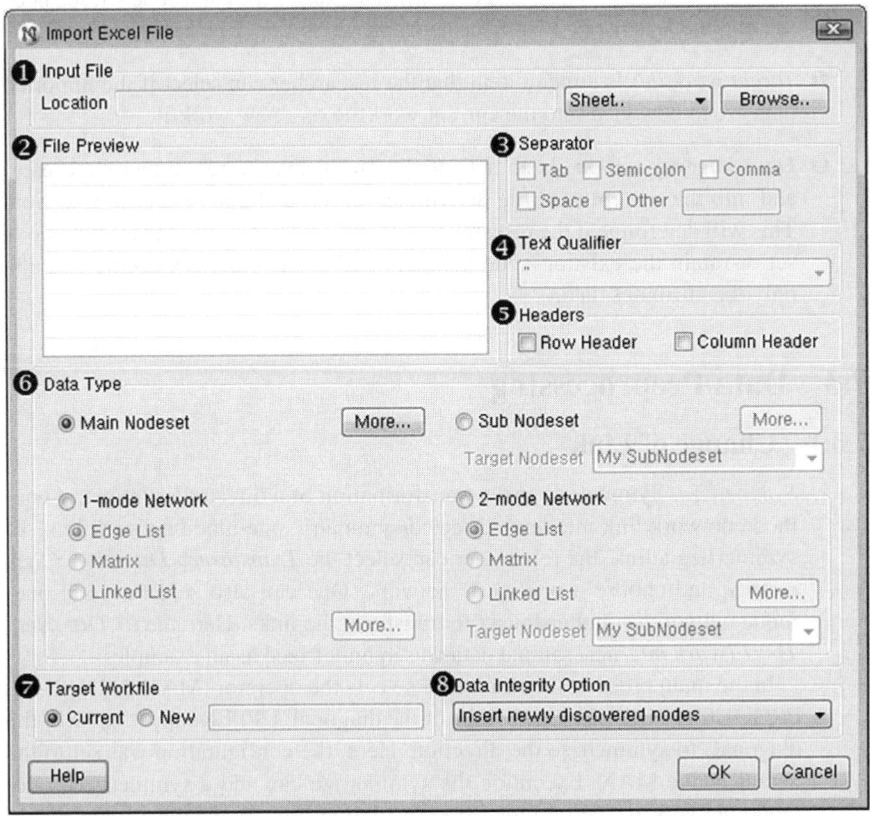

Figure 7.8 Data import.

❶ *Input file:* Menu to select the imported files. For an excel file, the researcher must select the sheet to import within the combo box.

❷ *File preview:* Is a menu item to preview the data form to be imported.

❸ *Separator:* Is a menu item, which becomes active when importing text files and provides a choice to the researcher as an option of the type of separator to use to distinguish the data columns. The selected separator choice will be reflected in the File Preview.

❹ *Text qualifier:* Is a menu item that will be activated when importing text files, where the researcher can select a particular column can be classified as a text. For example, if the quotation marks are selected, the data within the quotation marks will be identified as a text.

❺ *Headers:* This will be selected if there are headers within the row and column of the importing data.

❻ *Data type:* Depending on the type of data, the researcher can select the network type (Edge List, Matrix, Linked List) when importing the main node set, sub node set, one-mode network, two-mode network.

❼ *Target workfile:* Is a menu item that the researcher can select if the imported data are to be added into the current workfile or a new workfile.

❽ *Data integrity option:* Is an activated menu when the researcher chooses to add into the current workfile determined in the ❼ Target Workfile selection. This will determine if the researcher will add new nodes into the existing node set or retain the existing node numbers within the current workfile and add only the attributes data.

7.3 Data Preprocessing

7.3.1 Change of Link

1. *Symmetrize*: Symmetrize is the transformation of a directed/asymmetric one-mode network link into an undirected/symmetric one-mode network link. To symmetrize a link, the researcher can select the *Transform > Direction > Sym metrize* and choose a one-mode network. One can also select several one-mode networks simultaneously to transform the links. Here the *01.Org_Net_ Tiny1 (work interact)* sample data was symmetrized as an example.

   In the main process, the researcher selects the operator (MAX, MIN, SUM, PRODUCT, LOWER: lower value of the diagonal, UPPER: upper value of the diagonal) to symmetrize the direction. Here, the configuration was set to the default value MAX. Executing the symmetrize can add a symmetrized one-mode network in the current workfile (dialog box: *Add Transformed Data*) (Figure 7.9).

Before the symmetrize

Project | work interact

Current Workfile
☑ DataSet ☑ ProcessLog

- 01.Org_Net_Tiny1
  - Employee [22 * 6]
    - work interact [89 * 0]
    - personal friend [63 * 0]
    - personal help [63 * 0]
    - personal knows [24 * 0]
    - work help [66 * 0]

		1	2	3	4	5
		John	Thomas	Anna	James	Peter
1	John					
2	Thomas					
3	Anna	3.0				
4	James	2.0				
5	Peter					
6	Mary					
7	Michael	3.0				

After the symmetrize

Project | [T] Symmetrized(work interact)

Current Workfile
☑ DataSet ☑ ProcessLog

- 01.Org_Net_Tiny1
  - Employee [22 * 6]
    - work interact [89 * 0]
    - personal friend [63 * 0]
    - personal help [63 * 0]
    - personal knows [24 * 0]
    - work help [66 * 0]
    - [T] Symmetrized(work interact) [65 * 0]

		1	2	3	4	5
		John	Thomas	Anna	James	Peter
1	John			3.0	2.0	
2	Thomas					
3	Anna	3.0				
4	James	2.0				
5	Peter					
6	Mary					
7	Michael	3.0			3.0	
8	David	4.0	5.0			

Figure 7.9 Symmetrize.

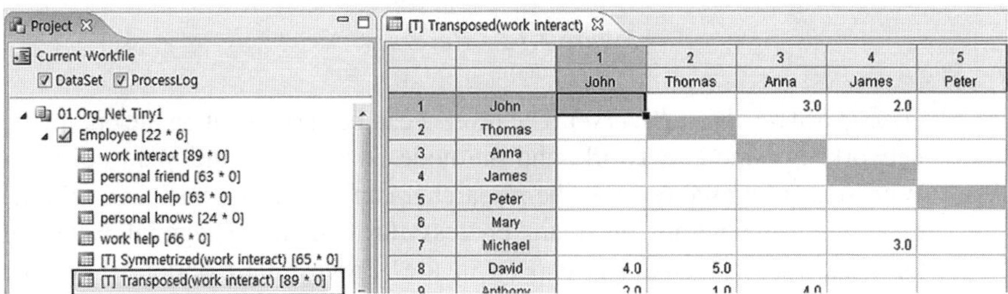

Figure 7.10 Transpose.

2. *Transpose*: Changing the direction of the one-mode network is the transpose function by selecting *Transform > Direction > Transpose.* Similar to symmetrize, the results of the transpose can be added to the current workfile (Figure 7.10).

3. *Dichotomize*: Depending on the operator, the weighted value can be transformed to an unweighted binary data (*Transform > Value > Dichotomize*). To dichotomize, the researcher will select the operator (>, >=, =, <, <=, !=) to transform into the binary within the main process and determine the value for the operation of the transformation. For example, if the operator is "!=" with a value of "0," any value of the X_{ij} not equal to 0 will be 1 and the rest will be 0 (Figure 7.11).

4. *Reverse*: For data with a weighted value, the link weight transformation termed reverse will switch the maximum weight to the minimum weight

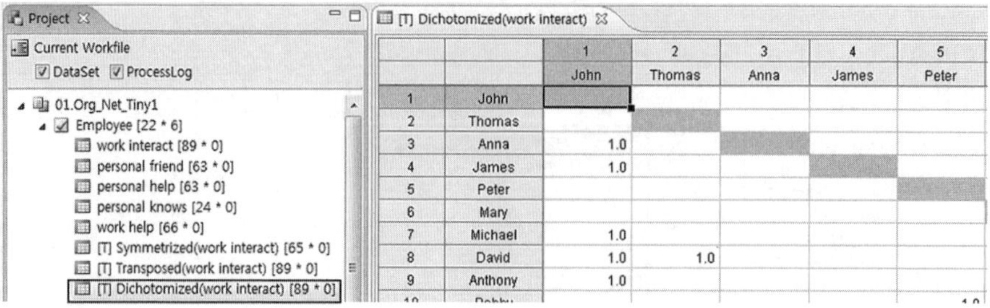

Figure 7.11 Dichotomize.

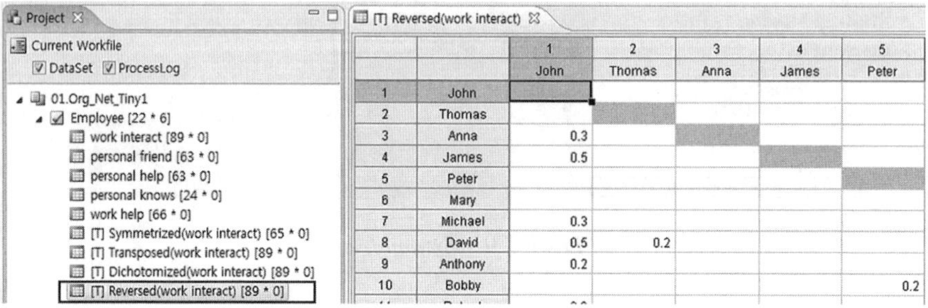

Figure 7.12 Reverse.

(*Transform > Value > Reverse*). The reverse can be carried out on the one-mode network, two-mode network, and the node attributes of the main node set. When executing the reverse, the researcher can select to ignore or retain the diagonal value within the main process through the [Diagonal Handling Option] and if [Include] is chosen in the [Process 0.0] option, 0 will be reversed to another value, otherwise the value will be retained. In addition, through the [Method] option the weighted value can be modified during the reverse by selecting (Interval, Ration, and Fixed Decay). Here, choosing the [Fixed Decay] will reverse the value to less than the input β value (β can have values less than 1). Here the reverse results using the Diagonal Ignore option and the Ratio option in the Method on the *01.Org_Net_Tiny1 (work interact)* is shown in Figure 7.12.

5. *Normalize*: To normalize data is to compare various data through a common reference. Normalize can be executed by *Transform > Value > Normalize*, where the researcher sequentially selects [Diagonal Handling Option], [Dimension], [Stop Condition], [Criterion] option in the main process. In the [Dimension] option depending on the [Criterion], rows and columns are selected to normalize and in the [Stop Condition] the number of iteration for normalization and the delta value is designated. When the rows and columns are selected in the [Dimension] option the [Stop Condition] will be activated, where the researcher will insert the delta value and values lower than the delta value will stop the

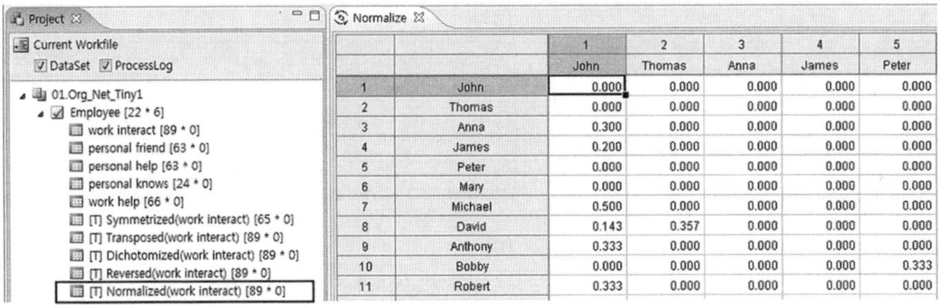

Project
Current Workfile
DataSet ProcessLog
01.Org_Net_Tiny1
Employee [22 * 6]
work interact [89 * 0]
personal friend [63 * 0]
personal help [63 * 0]
personal knows [24 * 0]
work help [66 * 0]
[T] Symmetrized(work interact) [65 * 0]
[T] Transposed(work interact) [89 * 0]
[T] Dichotomized(work interact) [89 * 0]
[T] Reversed(work interact) [89 * 0]
[T] Normalized(work interact) [89 * 0]

Normalize

		1	2	3	4	5
		John	Thomas	Anna	James	Peter
1	John	0.000	0.000	0.000	0.000	0.000
2	Thomas	0.000	0.000	0.000	0.000	0.000
3	Anna	0.300	0.000	0.000	0.000	0.000
4	James	0.200	0.000	0.000	0.000	0.000
5	Peter	0.000	0.000	0.000	0.000	0.000
6	Mary	0.000	0.000	0.000	0.000	0.000
7	Michael	0.500	0.000	0.000	0.000	0.000
8	David	0.143	0.357	0.000	0.000	0.000
9	Anthony	0.333	0.000	0.000	0.000	0.000
10	Bobby	0.000	0.000	0.000	0.000	0.333
11	Robert	0.333	0.000	0.000	0.000	0.000

Figure 7.13 Normalize.

normalize process. In the *01.Org_Net_Tiny1 (work interact),* the [Diagonal Handling Option] was Ignore, the [Dimension] was Rows, and the [Criterion] was sum, which resulted in the normalized outcome shown in Figure 7.13.

6. *Recode*: If the *Transform > Value > Recode* is executed, it is possible to transform values within a certain range to another value. For the node attribute in the *01.Org_Net_Tiny1* main node set, the Age column (Figure 7.14a) is recoded with a value of 1 for ages between 21 and 30, 2 for ages between 31 and 40, and 3 for ages between 41 and 50 (Figure 7.14b,c). The results of the recode added within the main node set Recoded (Age) (Figure 7.14d).

7. *Missing variable*: If there are missing variables, a particular value can be inserted by *Transform > Value > Missing.*

8. *Self-loop*: The diagonal value can be replaced with a particular value or a value in the node attribute (*Transform > Value > Diagonal*). Here, the diagonal value of 0 in the *01.Org_Net_Tiny1 (work interact)* has been replaced with a value of 1 (Figure 7.15).

7.3.2 Extraction and Reordering of the Node and Link

1. *Node and link*: The node or link can be extracted from the displayed window when *Transform > Query* is selected (Figure 7.16a). First, by selecting the node set or linkset to extract in the QuerySet Status (❶), the Query (❷) Target is activated and the condition for extraction can be set in the Query box (❸) below. Here, the *Employee* in the main node set of *01.Org_Net_Tiny1* extracts nodes, which have only the female gender by setting a condition of "Gender" == "Female." The operator for the extraction condition is shown in Table 7.1. After setting the extraction condition, the researcher can verify the number of nodes extracted by using the [Try] button and after applying the conditions through the [Apply] button, the [Run] button is executed to extract the nodes. After extracting the node or link, the main node set is changed and a newly workfile is created, which can be verified by the new workfile in the workfile tree (Figure 7.16b).

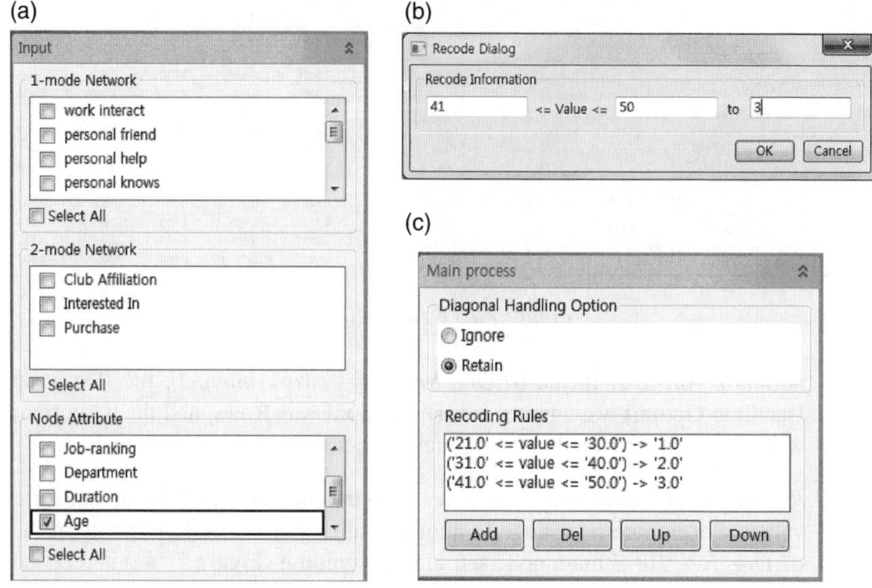

(d)

		1	2	3	4	5	6	7
		Education	Gender	Job-ranking	Department	Duration	Age	Recoded(Age)
1	John	"Master Degree"	"Male"	1.0	"Finance"	21.0	45.0	3.0
2	Thomas	"Bachelor Degree"	"Male"	5.0	"Marketing"	8.0	35.0	2.0
3	Anna	"HS Graduate"	"Female"	7.0	"Marketing"	0.5	27.0	1.0
4	James	"Bachelor Degree"	"Male"	5.0	"Marketing"	9.0	37.0	2.0
5	Peter	"Bachelor Degree"	"Male"	7.0	"Sales"	3.0	28.0	1.0
6	Mary	"Bachelor Degree"	"Female"	7.0	"Sales"	2.0	26.0	1.0
7	Michael	"Bachelor Degree"	"Male"	6.0	"Marketing"	5.0	29.0	1.0
8	David	"Bachelor Degree"	"Male"	3.0	"Marketing"	13.0	36.0	2.0
9	Anthony	"Bachelor Degree"	"Male"	4.0	"Marketing"	13.0	35.0	2.0
10	Bobby	"Bachelor Degree"	"Male"	7.0	"Sales"	2.0	25.0	1.0
11	Robert	"Doctoral Degree"	"Male"	2.0	"Marketing"	15.0	41.0	3.0
12	Susan	"Master Degree"	"Female"	5.0	"Marketing"	8.0	34.0	2.0
13	Steven	"Bachelor Degree"	"Male"	4.0	"Sales"	12.0	38.0	2.0
14	Charles	"Doctoral Degree"	"Male"	5.0	"Marketing"	10.0	33.0	2.0
15	Ashley	"Master Degree"	"Female"	7.0	"Marketing"	4.0	30.0	1.0
16	Richard	"Bachelor Degree"	"Male"	7.0	"Marketing"	1.0	30.0	1.0
17	Jessica	"Doctoral Degree"	"Female"	2.0	"Sales"	16.0	42.0	3.0
18	Elizabeth	"2YR College"	"Female"	3.0	"Marketing"	13.0	43.0	3.0
19	Laura	"HS Graduate"	"Female"	7.0	"Sales"	3.0	24.0	1.0
20	Jennifer	"Master Degree"	"Female"	6.0	"Sales"	5.0	31.0	2.0
21	Jackson	"Bachelor Degree"	"Male"	6.0	"Sales"	6.0	28.0	1.0
22	Julia	"Bachelor Degree"	"Female"	6.0	"Sales"	7.0	33.0	2.0

Figure 7.14 Recode. (a) Input variable, (b) dialog box for recode, (c) recoding rules, and (d) output of recoding.

2. *Neighbor node*: The number and density of the neighbor node can be verified with the direction (in, out, both) selection. Because identifying the neighbor node considers only the distance regardless of the weight of the link, the researcher must perform a dichotomize operation first (*Transform > Nodeset > Ego Network*).

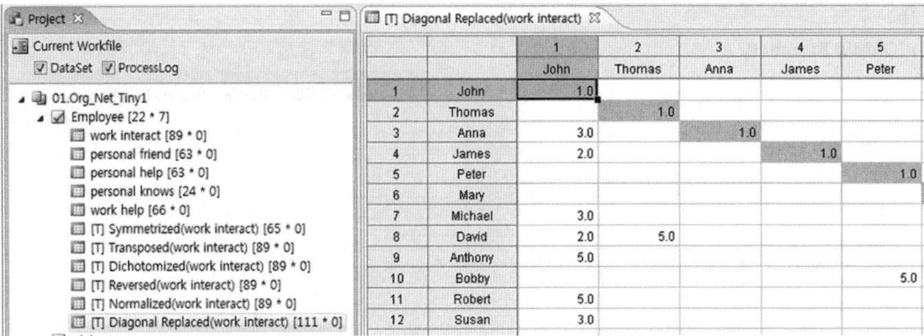

Figure 7.15 Self-loop.

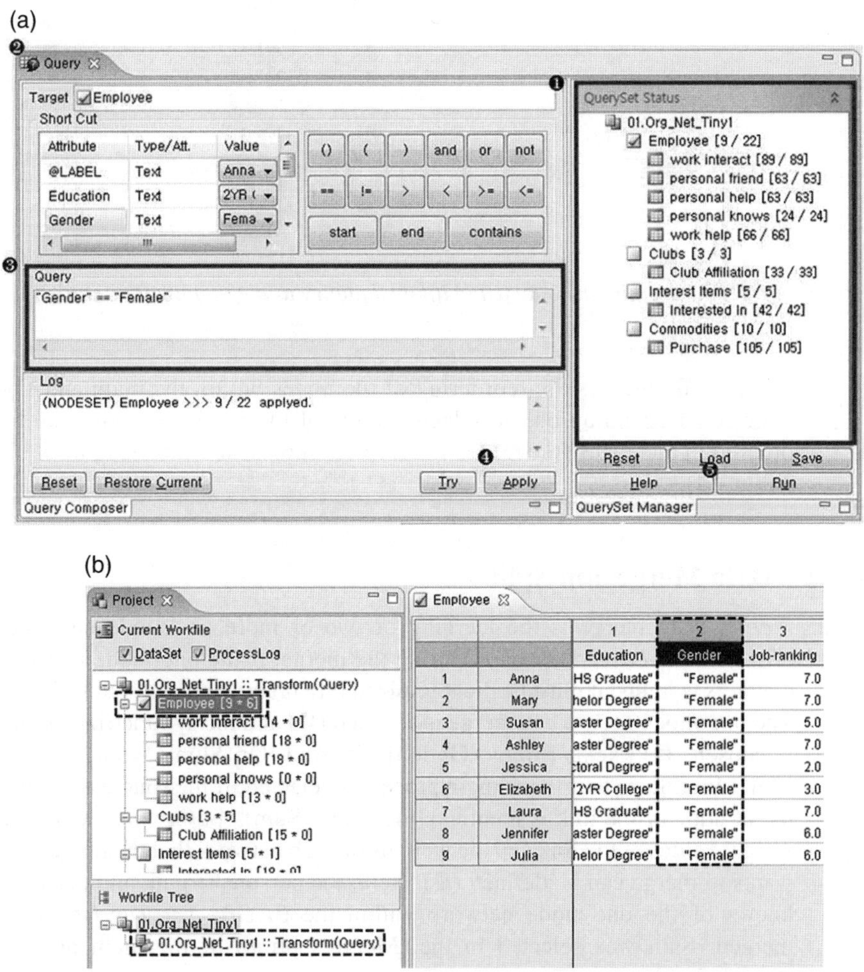

(a)

(b)

Figure 7.16 Extraction of node and link. (a) QuerySet and (b) new workfile.

(a)

- **Output Summary**

DISTRIBUTION OF EGONET MEASURES

MEASURES	VALUE	
	SIZE	DENSITY
MEAN	5.909	0.623
STD.DEV.	2.109	0.179
MIN.	3	0.333
MAX.	12	1

(b)

		1	2
		Size	Density
1	John	12	0.348485
2	Thomas	6	0.600000
3	Anna	4	0.333333
4	James	4	0.666667
5	Peter	3	1.000000
6	Mary	5	0.800000
7	Michael	5	0.700000
8	David	9	0.583333
9	Anthony	9	0.500000
10	Bobby	5	0.700000
11	Robert	7	0.523810
12	Susan	8	0.500000
13	Steven	3	1.000000
14	Charles	5	0.700000
15	Ashley	6	0.533333
16	Richard	5	0.800000
17	Jessica	5	0.400000
18	Elizabeth	7	0.571429
19	Laura	4	0.833333
20	Jennifer	5	0.600000
21	Jackson	7	0.476190
22	Julia	6	0.533333

Figure 7.17 Neighbor node. (a) Output summary and ego network details.

3. *Reorder*: Reorder is the reordering of the nodes within the main and sub node set. Depending on the selected value of the attribute, nodes can be ordered in increasing order (*Transform > Nodeset > Reorder*) (Figure 7.17, Table 7.4).

7.3.3 Data Merge and Split

1. *Merge*: Data merge is the merging of two or more one-mode networks (*Transform > Layer > Merge*). During the merge, if the one-mode network contains weights, it must be dichotomized into binary data without weights. The one-mode network to merge is selected (❶) and the symmetrize option is chosen (❷). Next, [Merge Option] (❸, And, Or, Sum, Average, Max, Min, Liner Sum) within the main process is selected. If the source node and target node of the link is identical, the [Liner Sum] option will add all the weight values of the link and the weights of each network that the researcher wants to merge can be defined (❺). Here, the personal friend and personal knows of the one-mode network within the *01.Org_Net_Tiny1* will be merged. Sum was selected in the [Merge Option] of the main process (Figure 7.18)

Table 7.4 Operator for extraction.

Operator	Description	Example	
and	*Extract a variable (value) with A and B value included*	"Gender" == "Female" and "Team" == "HR"	*Gender must be Female and in the HR team*
or	*Extract a variable (value) with A or B value included*	"Gender" == "Female" or "Team" == "HR"	*Gender must be either a Female or in the HR team*
not	*Extract a variable excluding a particular variable*	not "Team" == "HR"	*Besides the HR team*
==	*Extract only variables with a particular value*	"Gender" == "Female"	*Only those values where the gender is female*
!=	*Extract variables not having a particular value*	"Team" != "HR"	*All teams besides the HR team*
>	*Extract variable greater than a particular value*	"Age" > 30.0	*Above age 30*
<	*Extract variable less than a particular value*	"Age" < 30.0	*Below age 30*
>=	*Extract variable greater than or equal to a particular value*	"Age" >= 30.0	*Above or equal to 30*
<=	*Extract variable less than or equal to a particular value*	"Age" <= 30.0	*Below or equal to 30*
start	*Extract a variable with a particular starting text*	"Gender" start "Fem"	*Gender that starts with Fem*
end	*Extract a variable with a particular ending text*	"Gender" end "male"	*Gender that ends with male*
contains	*Extract a variable that contains particular texts*	"Gender" contains "male"	*male is included within the gender*
toupper	*Transforms the text within the parenthesis to capitals*	"Gender" == toupper("female")	*toupper("female") is considered to be equal to FEMALE*
tolower	*Transforms the text within the parenthesis to lower letters*	"Gender" == tolower("MALE")	*tolower("MALE") is considered to be equal to male*
top	*Extract n number with the highest attribute value*	"Duration" top 5	*Top 5 service years*
bottom	*Extract n number with the lowest attribute value*	"Duration" bottom 5	*Bottom 5 service years*

(a)

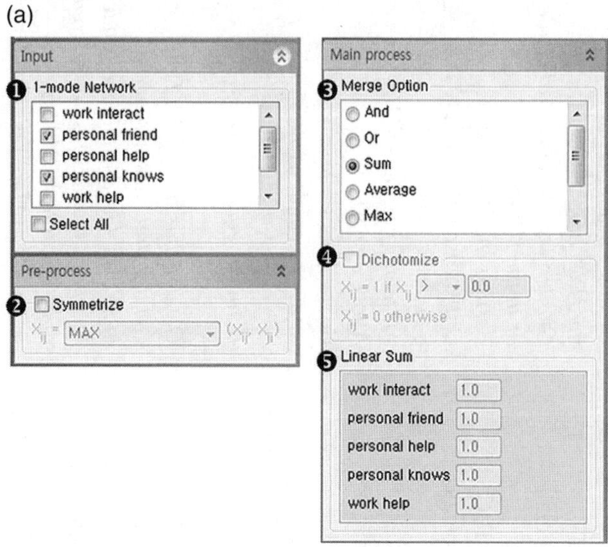

(b)

personal friend

		1	2	3
		John	Thomas	Anna
1	John			
2	Thomas			
3	Anna			
4	James			
5	Peter			
6	Mary			
7	Michael			

personal knows

		1	2	3
		John	Thomas	Anna
1	John		1.0	
2	Thomas	1.0		
3	Anna			
4	James			
5	Peter			
6	Mary			
7	Michael	1.0		

(c)

Project

Current Workfile

DataSet ProcessLog

- 01.Org_Net_Tiny1
  - Employee [22 * 6]
    - work interact [89 * 0]
    - personal friend [63 * 0]
    - personal help [63 * 0]
    - personal knows [24 * 0]
    - work help [66 * 0]
    - [T] Result [81 * 0]

[T] Result

		1	2	3
		John	Thomas	Anna
1	John		1.0	
2	Thomas	1.0		
3	Anna			
4	James			
5	Peter			
6	Mary			
7	Michael	1.0		

Figure 7.18 Merge. (a) Main process for merge, (b) one-mode networks before the merge, and (c) one-mode network after the merge.

(a)

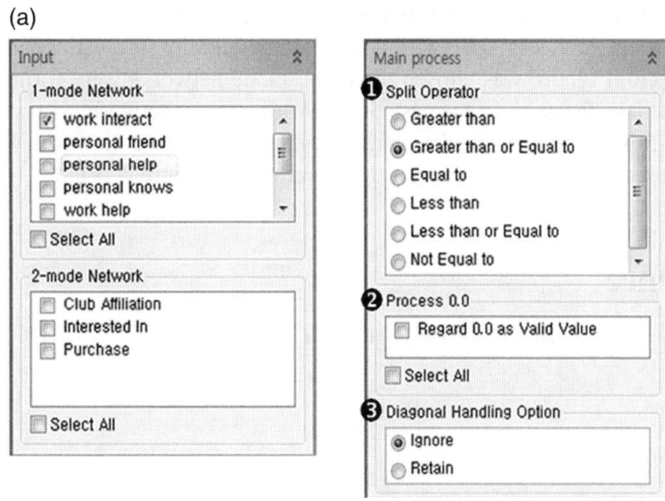

(b)

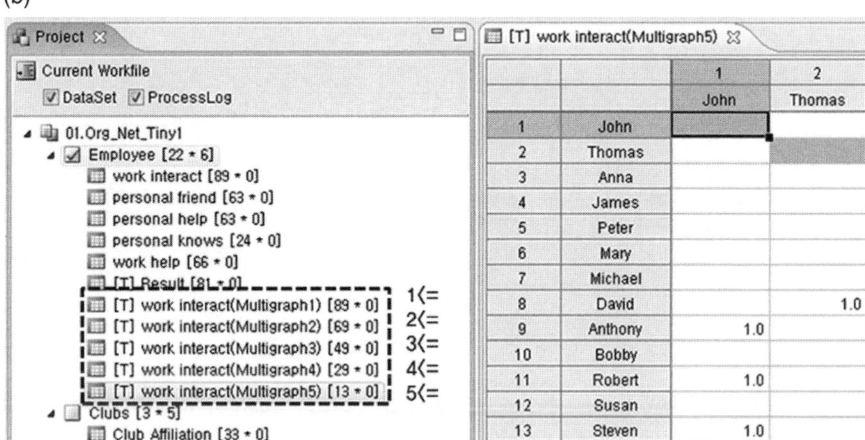

Figure 7.19 Split. (a) Main process for split and (b) one-mode networks after the split.

2. *Split*: A weighted matrix can be divided into several binary matrix (*Transform > Layer > Split*). In other words, below a particular weight a value of 0 and above a particular weight a value of 1 is given to create several matrixes, where the researcher can decide on the split operator to change the input data into a binary format for each reference condition. To split, a one-mode network or two-mode network must first be selected and the [Split Operator] (Greater than, Greater than or Equal to, Equal to, Less than, Less than or Equal to, Not Equal to) must be chosen within the main process (❶). Next, the researcher must decide to execute the split on values of 0 in the matrix of the [Process 0.0] (❷).Here, split is performed on the *work interact*

of the *01.Org_Net_Tiny1*. In the [Split Operator] Greater than or Equal to was chosen, [Process 0.0] was not selected, and for the [Diagonal Handling Option] Ignore was chosen. Five one-mode networks were formed from the result of the split. In the case of the Work interact network, a maximum value of 5 was obtained for the weighted value, where five networks were created with a value that was greater than or equal to (Figure 7.19).

Reference

1 Cyram (2015). NetMiner v4.2.1.140729 Seoul: Cyram Inc.

8

Network Analysis Using NetMiner

A detailed tutorial of network analysis with sample data provided in NetMiner will be explained.

8.1 Centrality and Cohesive Subgroup

8.1.1 Centrality

1. *Degree*: If there are two nodes with a link to one another, the two nodes are adjacent to each other. The degree is measured by the number of adjacent nodes to a single separate node. The degree is an analysis method to determine the number of neighbors of each node (*Analyze > Neighbor > Degree)*. During the analysis, one can select in the main process either the # of link or Sum of weight from the [Measure] option. The default set-up defines the # of link as the number of links of the individual nodes and is used to measure the degree, which is the general method of measuring the degree. However, if the researcher believes the weight of the link is more important than the existence of a link, the analysis can apply the weight on the link through the Sum of weight option.

Fundamentals of Big Data Network Analysis for Research and Industry, First Edition. Hyunjoung Lee and Il Sohn.

(a)

NETWORK DENSITY
0.193

DISTRIBUTION OF DEGREE

MEASURES	VALUE	
	In-Degree	Out-Degree
SUM	89	89
MEAN	4.045	4.045
STD.DEV.	2.884	0.976
MIN.	0	2
MAX.	10	5
# OF ISOLATE		0
# OF PENDANT		0
INCLUSIVENESS(%)		100%

NUMBER OF NODE TYPE

Isolate	Transmitter	Receiver	Carrier	Ordinary
0	3	0	0	19

(b)

	In-Degree	Out-Degree
John	10	5
Thomas	4	4
Anna	1	4
James	0	4
Peter	2	3
Mary	5	4
Michael	4	3
David	9	4

(c)

	Node Type
John	Ordinary
Thomas	Ordinary
Anna	Ordinary
James	Transmitter
Peter	Ordinary
Mary	Ordinary
Michael	Ordinary
David	Ordinary

Figure 8.1 Degree. (a) [R]Main, (b) [T]Degree, and (c) [T]Node Type.

From the degree analysis results, the density of the whole network, the number of nodes with respect to the node type, # of pendent (the number of nodes that are connected to only one node), inclusiveness (%) (the percentage of isolated nodes in the total number of nodes) is presented in the [R]Main. In the [T]Node Type, each node is identified to a particular node type, where in NetMiner there are a total of five distinct types including isolate(in link=0, out link=0), transmitter(in link=0, out link>0), receiver(in link>0, out link=0), carrier(in link=1, out link=1), ordinary(node not characteristic of the other four types) (Figure 8.1).

Spring map, which is provided in addition to the analysis results, is basically formed from the Kamada and Kawai algorithm and to change the algorithm the researcher selects the [Display] tab in the process control panel and selects the layout algorithm. The width length of the node expressed in the spring map shows the in-degree and the height length is the out-degree. The color of the node is differentiated by the node type and the in-degree and out-degree value is indicated next to the node name (e.g., Richard is the transmitter with an in-degree of 0 and an out-degree of 5 in the spring map) (Figure 8.2).

2. *Degree centrality*: Through the *Analyze > Centrality > Degree,* the analysis result of the *work interact* degree centrality in the one-mode network shows the [R]Main, [T]Degree Centrality Vector, [M]Spring, [M]Concentric. In the [M]Main, the distribution of degree centrality scores and network degree centralization index is provided (Figure 8.3a). The results of the centralization can be verified within the [M]Concentric. If the centrality if focused on a single node, the centralization is focused on the whole network and thus can determine if the flow of the network is concentrated to a single node. In other

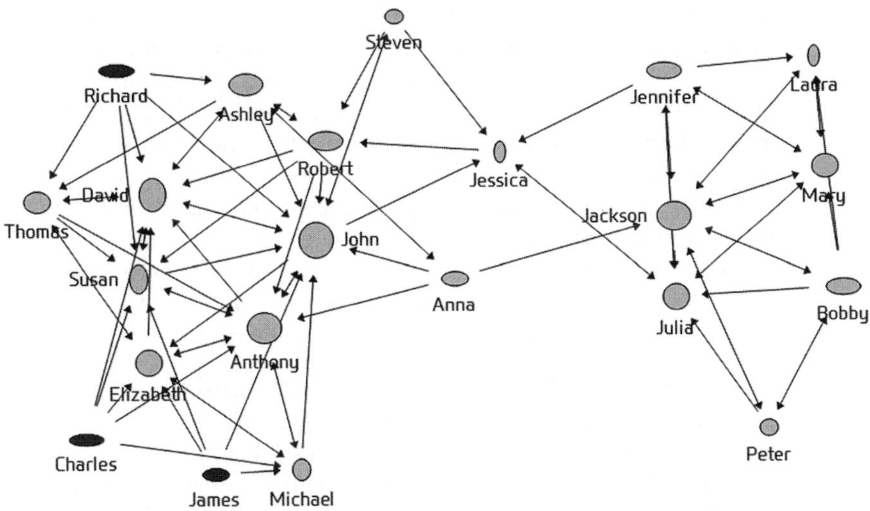

Figure 8.2 [M]Spring map of degree.

(a)

DISTRIBUTION OF DEGREE CENTRALITY SCORES

MEASURES	VALUE	
	In-Degree Centrality	Out-Degree Centrality
MEAN	0.193	0.193
STD.DEV.	0.137	0.046
MIN.	0	0.095
MAX.	0.476	0.238

NETWORK DEGREE CENTRALIZATION INDEX
29.705% (IN), 4.762% (OUT)

(b)

	1	2
	In-Degree Centrality	Out-Degree Centrality
John	0.476190	0.238095
Thomas	0.190476	0.190476
Anna	0.047619	0.190476
James	0.000000	0.190476
Peter	0.095238	0.142857
Mary	0.238095	0.190476
Michael	0.190476	0.142857
David	0.428571	0.190476
Anthony	0.380952	0.238095
Bobby	0.095238	0.238095

(c) (d)

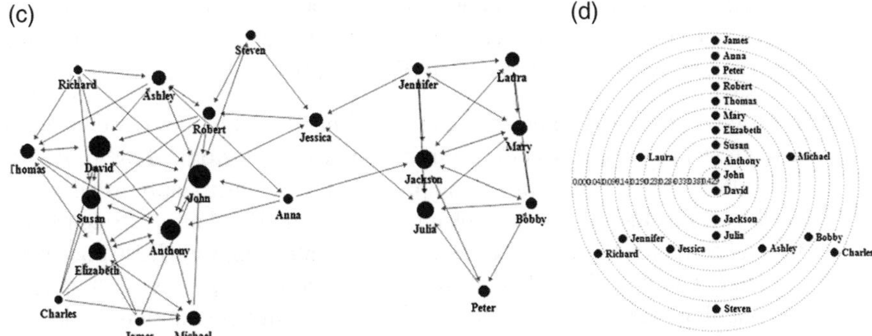

Figure 8.3 Degree centrality. (a) [R]Main, (b) [T]Degree centrality vector, (c) [M]Spring (node size: in degree centrality), and (d) [M]Concentric.

words, if a few nodes exist within the inner concentric the centralization is comparatively high and if most of the nodes within the concentric the centralization can be assumed to be low (Figure 8.3d).In the result of the degree centrality, the centrality value of each node specified in the [T]Degree Centrality Vector can be added as a node attribute (Figure 8.3b, *Mouse right button > Add To Workfile > Node Attribute*). The visualization result of the degree centrality provided as the [M]Spring map is the map according to the Kamada and Kawai algorithm, where the node size becomes larger as the centrality value becomes larger (Figure 8.3c). In the [Inspect] tab located below the process control panel, the in or out degree centrality can be selected and the node size can be varied according to the node direction.

3. *Closeness centrality*: The closeness centrality of the network, which is based on the geodesic distance between the nodes, can be analyze by the *Analyze > Centrality > Closeness.* Through the preprocess, the one-mode network, which takes priority in the analysis, is dichotomized and in the main process the [Ignore Unreachable] can be selected from the [Unreachable Handling] option. The closeness centrality cannot be obtained from an unconnected network and thus the unreachable node can be ignored in this case. However, depending on the choice of the researcher, the distance of the unreachable node can be given a diameter of 1 within the network and the unreachable node can be reflected into the closeness centrality (Figure 8.4).

4. *Betweenness centrality*: A node that appears more frequently in the two node pairs has a high centrality value. This is termed the betweenness centrality (*Analyze > Centrality > Betweenness (Node or Link*)). Therefore, the betweenness centrality is obtained by the number of times a node appears between the geodesic and shortest path between other nodes. The betweenness centrality can be analyzed based not only on nodes but also on links. The betweenness centrality based on links can be obtained by the number of times a link appears in the shortest path between other node pairs. The betweenness centrality does not consider weights and thus the dichotomize in the preprocess is selected as the default option and by the choice of the researcher the data can be symmetrized according to network without direction. The below example analysis is the result of the symmetrized choice (Figure 8.5).

5. *Prestige centrality*: The prestige centrality analysis proposed by Bonacich is also known as the eigenvector centrality and can be performed by *Analyze > Centrality > Eigenvector.* In the preprocess, the symmetrization of the network is set as the default. The results produce the [R]Main, [T]Eigenvector Centrality Vector, [T]Reflected/Derived/Constant, [M]Spring, [M]Concentric.

   Here, the [T]Reflected/Derived/Constant shows the processing sequence of obtaining the prestige centrality value. The prestige centrality is composed of the centrality that was a reflected part from another node, a derived part from another node, and a constant part (Eigenvector centrality = Constant part + Reflected part + Derived part) (Figure 8.6).

(a)

DISTRIBUTION OF CLOSENESS CENTRALITY SCORES

MEASURES	VALUE	
	In-Closeness	Out-Closeness
MEAN	0.322	0.321
STD.DEV.	0.142	0.055
MIN.	0	0.214
MAX.	0.5	0.468

NETWORK CLOSENESS CENTRALIZATION INDEX
23.504% (IN), 31.424% (OUT)

(b)

	1	2
	In-Closeness	Out-Closeness
John	0.466667	0.376307
Thomas	0.350000	0.280519
Anna	0.287671	0.467532
James	0.000000	0.318342
Peter	0.287671	0.261501
Mary	0.333333	0.266010
Michael	0.333333	0.291105
David	0.456522	0.342857
Anthony	0.446809	0.314869
Bobby	0.287671	0.270677

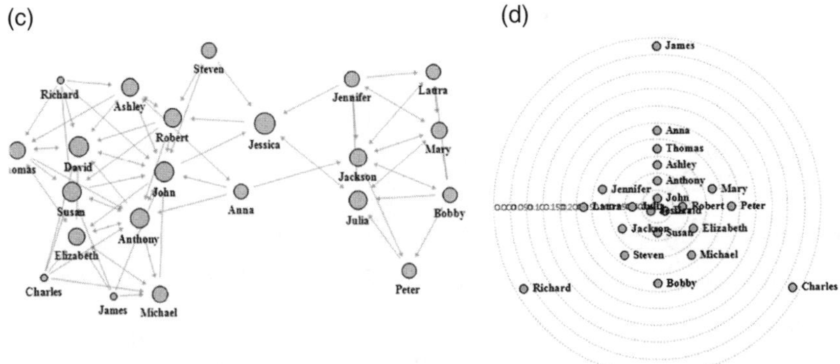

Figure 8.4 Closeness centrality. (a) [R]Main, (b) [T]Closeness centrality vector, (c) [M]Spring (node size: in-closeness centrality), and (d) [M]Concentric.

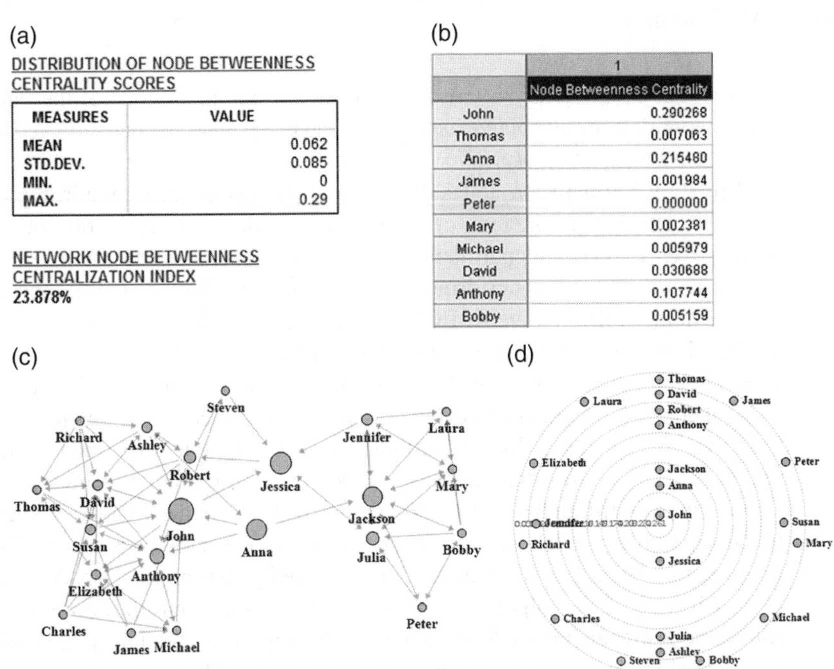

(a)

DISTRIBUTION OF NODE BETWEENNESS CENTRALITY SCORES

MEASURES	VALUE
MEAN	0.062
STD.DEV.	0.085
MIN.	0
MAX.	0.29

NETWORK NODE BETWEENNESS CENTRALIZATION INDEX
23.878%

(b)

	1
	Node Betweenness Centrality
John	0.290268
Thomas	0.007063
Anna	0.215480
James	0.001984
Peter	0.000000
Mary	0.002381
Michael	0.005979
David	0.030688
Anthony	0.107744
Bobby	0.005159

Figure 8.5 Betweenness centrality. (a) [R]Main, (b) [T]Betweenness centrality vector, (c) [M]Spring (node size: betweenness centrality), and (d) [M]Concentric.

(a)

DISTRIBUTION OF EIGENVECTOR CENTRALITY SCORES

MEASURES	VALUE
MEAN	0.167
STD.DEV.	0.132
MIN.	0.009
MAX.	0.466

(b)

	1
	Eigenvector Centrality
John	0.466209
Thomas	0.231480
Anna	0.128138
James	0.132374
Peter	0.009127
Mary	0.015518
Michael	0.187740
David	0.399185
Anthony	0.313707
Bobby	0.010869

(c)

	1	2	3
	Reflected Part	Derived Part	Constant Part
John	0.074459	0.261483	0.131078
Thomas	0.020104	0.080826	0.131078
Anna	0.002335	-0.005182	0.131078
James	0.005232	-0.003653	0.131078
Peter	0.019928	-0.142624	0.131078
Mary	0.026678	-0.143233	0.131078
Michael	0.015772	0.041297	0.131078
David	0.064132	0.204837	0.131078
Anthony	0.033978	0.149278	0.131078
Bobby	0.024285	-0.145394	0.131078

(d) (e)

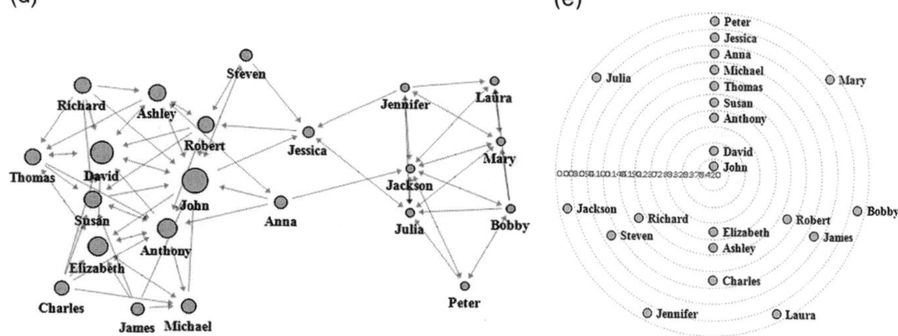

Figure 8.6 Prestige centrality. (a) [R]Main, (b) [T]Eigenvector centrality vector, (c) [T]Reflected/Derived/Constant, (d) [M]Spring (node size: Eigenvector centrality), and (e) [M]Concentric.

6. *Broker*: The broker analysis can be performed in the main node of the one-mode network if the attribute exists, which can be taken as the partition vector (*Analyze > Position > Brokerage*). The role of the individual nodes within the triad relationship between nodes can be divided into the coordinator, representative, gatekeeper, itinerant, or liaison. Here in the work interaction of the *01.Org_Net_Tiny1,* the department attribute was taken as the partition vector and a broker analysis was performed. The product of the broker analysis shows the [R]Main, [T]Brokerage, [M]Clustered, [M]Concentric (Figure 8.7d). In the [R]Main report, the characteristic index (mean, standard deviation, min, max) of each distinct role as the broker of nodes is shown (Figure 8.7a). In the [T]Brokerage, the number of the type of broker role for each individual nodes is shown. For example, John is affiliated to the department of finance and within the triad relationship acts as an itinerant 13 times and as a liaison 21 times (Figure 8.7b). In the [M]Clustered, the clustered map divided according to the department, which was selected as the partition vector, is provided (G1: Finance, G2: Sales, G3: Marketing). The clustered map is produced according to the Clustered-Eades algorithm and the node size is larger as the coordinator role value is higher (Figure 8.7c). If the researcher wishes to change the node size according to the role value, the role can be selected from the [Inspect] tab of the process control panel.

(a)

MEASURES	VALUE					
	COORDINATOR	GATEKEEPER	REPRESEN.	ITINERANT	LIAISON	TOTAL
MEAN	4.045	0.955	0.591	0.591	1.091	7.273
STD.DEV.	4.446	1.988	1.03	2.708	4.358	8.131
MIN.	0	0	0	0	0	0
MAX.	12	8	3	13	21	34

(b)

	1	2	3	4	5	6	7
	Partition Value	Coordinator	Gatekeeper	Representative	Itinerant	Liaison	Total
John	Finance	0	0	0	13	21	34
Thomas	Marketing	8	0	0	0	0	8
Anna	Marketing	1	0	1	0	0	2
James	Marketing	0	0	0	0	0	0
Peter	Sales	0	0	0	0	0	0
Mary	Sales	5	0	0	0	0	5
Michael	Marketing	1	0	2	0	0	3
David	Marketing	11	3	3	0	0	17
Anthony	Marketing	12	2	3	0	0	17
Bobby	Sales	2	0	0	0	0	2

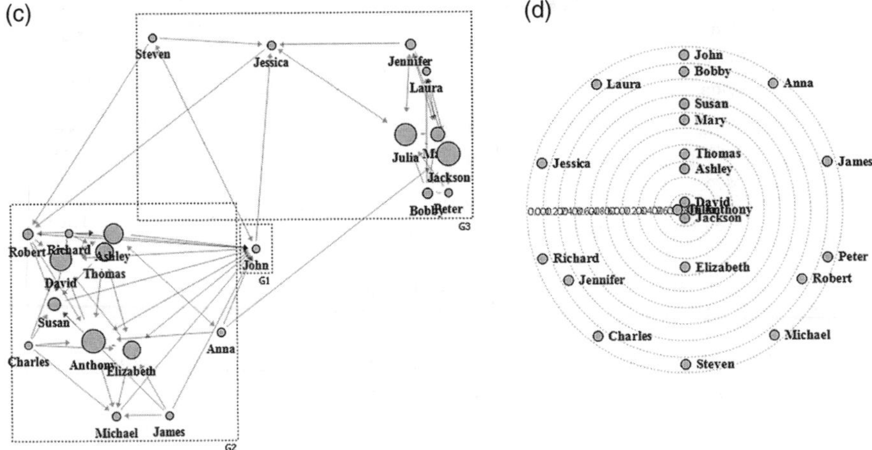

Figure 8.7 Brokerage. (a) [R]Main, (b) [T]Brokerage, (c) [M]Spring (node size: total score of brokerage), and (d) [M]Concentric.

8.1.2 Cohesive Subgroup

1. *Component*: Component is the subgraph of the nodes, which can be connected within the network, and is separated according to a strong component with direction and a weak component without direction. After selecting the *personal knows* of the one-mode network *01.Org_Net_Tiny1* through *Analyze > Cohesion > Component,* the [Minimum size of Component] is 2 and the [Component Type] can be selected as a weak component. The results

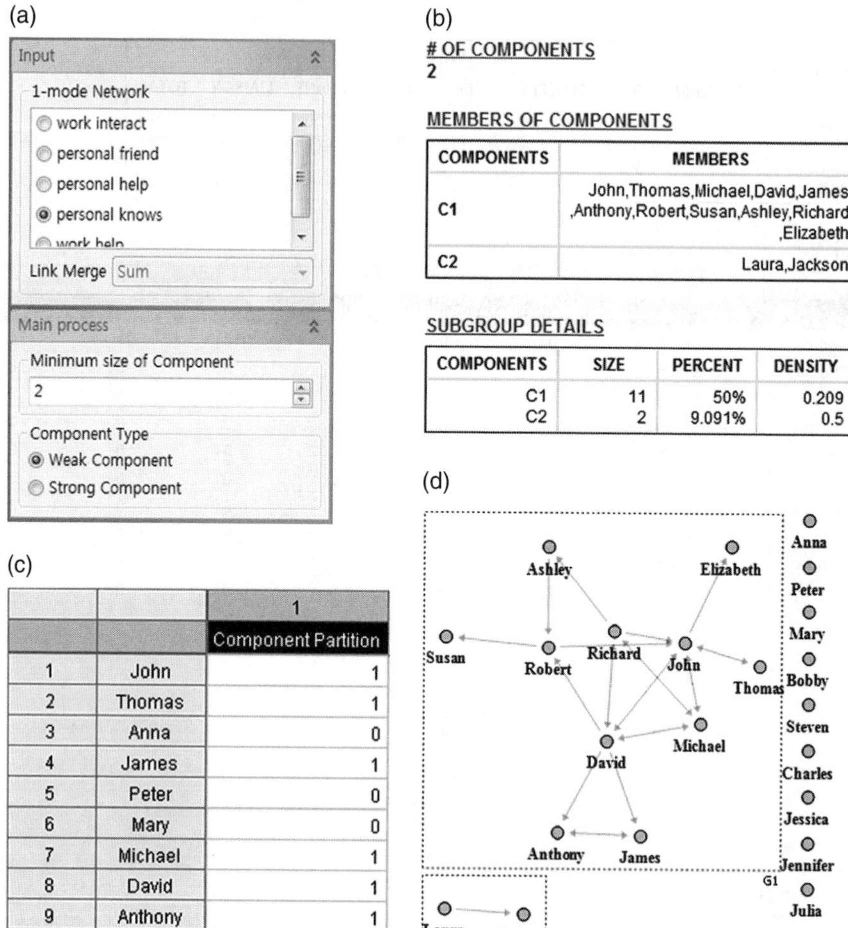

(b)

OF COMPONENTS
2

MEMBERS OF COMPONENTS

COMPONENTS	MEMBERS
C1	John,Thomas,Michael,David,James ,Anthony,Robert,Susan,Ashley,Richard ,Elizabeth
C2	Laura,Jackson

SUBGROUP DETAILS

COMPONENTS	SIZE	PERCENT	DENSITY
C1	11	50%	0.209
C2	2	9.091%	0.5

(c)

		1
		Component Partition
1	John	1
2	Thomas	1
3	Anna	0
4	James	1
5	Peter	0
6	Mary	0
7	Michael	1
8	David	1
9	Anthony	1
10	Bobby	0

Figure 8.8 Component. (a) Input data and main process, (b) [R]Main, (c) [T] Component partition vector, and (d) [M]Clustered.

of the component shows the [R]Main, [T]Component Partition Vector, [M] Clustered. [R]Main contains the number of components, the characteristics of the components, and the node's label belonging to the component. [T] Component From the [T]Component Partition Vector, the researcher can verify which component of the nodes is included (Figure 8.8).

2. *Community*: Community analysis can be performed by either the betweenness or the modularity method (*Analyze > Cohesion > Community > Betweenness(or Modularity)*). If the modularity method is used, the best value of dividing the network into several communities is provided (Figure 8.9a) and the results produces [R]Main, [T]Community Partition, [M]Clustered. In the

(a)

BEST MODULARITY
0.386

(b)

# of Communities	3
Step #	20
Modularity	0.385917
John	3
Thomas	2
Anna	3
James	2
Peter	1
Mary	1
Michael	2

Figure 8.9 Modularity (community). (a) [R]Main and (b) [T]Community Partition.

[T]Community Partition, the number of communities, the modularity, and the community where each node belongs to is presented (Figure 8.9b). Through the modularity method, the work interact one-mode network in the *01.Org_Net_Tiny1* is divided into three communities. The results of the [T]Community Partition can be saved as the attribute in the main node by using the mouse right button(>*Add To Workfile*).

If the betweenness method is applied, the best-cut value is provided in deciding the best number of communities to divide the network. In NetMiner to divide the community according to the best-cut score, four levels is provided (Bad if score < 1.25, normal if 1.25 ≤ score < 2.75, Good if 2.75 ≤ score < 3.5, Excellent if 3.5 ≤ score). According to this standard, the work interact is suggested to be divided into two communities, but the researcher can control the number of communities according to the objective of the research by referring to the community score. The [T]Community Cluster Matrix can also be saved as an attribute of the main node by using the mouse right button (Figure 8.10a). The results of utilizing the betweenness method are comprised of the [R]Main, [T]Community Cluster Matrix, [T]Permutation Vector, [C] Dendrogram, [M]Clustered (Figures 8.10c and 8.10d). The [T]Permutation Vector shows the node sequence within the dendrogram (Figure 8.10b). For example, Anna and James appear in the dendrogram in the first and second corresponding to the permutation vector of 1 and 2.

3. *Clique*: Clique is a sub-group within the network, where three or more nodes are completely connected. The clique within the network can overlap. The analysis can be performed by *Analyze > Cohesion > Clique* and within the [Main process] the [Minimum size of Clique] can be designated. The algorithm that can be applied is the Peamc and Basic, where the analysis subject network is the random network and if the clustering coefficient is low the processing speed is slower than the Basic algorithm. Here, a clique analysis with a minimum size of 5 for the one-mode network *work interact* in the

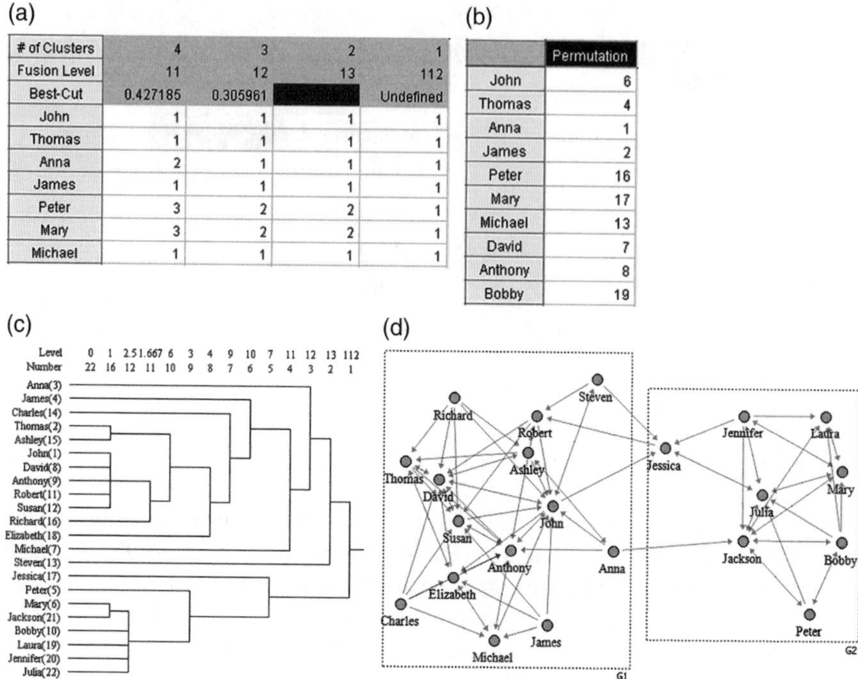

(a)

# of Clusters	4	3	2	1
Fusion Level	11	12	13	112
Best-Cut	0.427185	0.305961		Undefined
John	1	1	1	1
Thomas	1	1	1	1
Anna	2	1	1	1
James	1	1	1	1
Peter	3	2	2	1
Mary	3	2	2	1
Michael	1	1	1	1

(b)

	Permutation
John	6
Thomas	4
Anna	1
James	2
Peter	16
Mary	17
Michael	13
David	7
Anthony	8
Bobby	19

Figure 8.10 Betweenness (community). (a) [T]Community Cluster Matrix, (b) [T] Permutation Vector, (c) [C]Dendrogram, and (d) [M]Clustered.

01.Org_Net_Tiny1 was performed. The analysis results in the [R]Main, [T] Clique Affiliation Matrix, [M]Spring. The cohesion index of the [R]Main is the value obtained from dividing the inner link numbers of the clique with the outer link numbers of the clique. [T]Affiliation Matrix shows, which clique the node is affiliated with. Using the [Inspect] tab in the process control panel within [M]Spring, node affiliations with the clique can be intuitively verified (Figure 8.11).

A less strict standard than the typical clique is the n-clique, where the researcher can designate the maximum distance between nodes. Thus, nodes that are connected less than the distance specified by the researcher can be tied into one clique. By choosing the *work interact* of the *01.Org_Net_Tiny1* and selecting the *Analyze > Cohesion > n-Clique,* the [Maximum Distance (n)] within the [Main process] was taken as 3 and the clique analysis was performed resulting in Figure 8.12. n-clan(*Analyze > Cohesion > n-Clan*) and k-plex(*Analyze > Cohesion > k-plex*) can be performed and results obtained in a similar manner.

4. *k-core*: k-core is an analysis, where each node is connected to at least k number of nodes. In other words, a higher k score in the k-core analysis

(a)

OF CLIQUES
1

MEMBERS OF CLIQUES

CLIQUES	MEMBERS
Clique1	John,David,Anthony,Robert,Susan

SUBGROUP DETAILS

CLIQUES	SIZE	COHESION INDEX
Clique1	5	3.4

(b)

	Clique1
John	1
Thomas	0
Anna	0
James	0
Peter	0
Mary	0
Michael	0
David	1
Anthony	1
Bobby	0

(c)

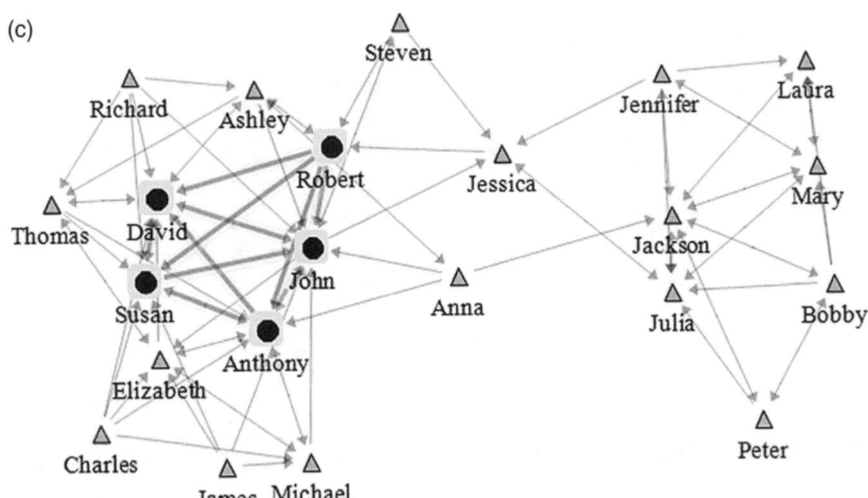

Figure 8.11 Clique. (a) [R]Main, (b) [T]Clique Affiliation Matrix, and (c) [M] Spring.

suggests a stronger relationship between the nodes of the sub-group (*Analyze > Cohesion > k-Core*). The [R]Main provided in the analysis results allow the verification of the number of nodes according to the coreness. Thus, there are 8 nodes that are connected to 5 other nodes and 22 nodes that are connected to 3 other nodes. In the [T]k-Core Affiliation Matrix, a table is provided, where nodes that belong to the k-core is given a 1 and otherwise a 0, and using the mouse right button the attribute of the main node can be added. k-core is typically used, when the peripheral nodes are removed and additional analysis is warranted (Figure 8.13).

(a)

OF N-CLIQUES

3

MEMBERS OF N-CLIQUES

N-CLIQUES	MEMBERS
n-Clique1	John,Anna,Anthony,Robert,Steven ,Ashley,Jessica,Jackson,Jennifer ,Julia,James,Susan,Richard,Michael ,Elizabeth,David
n-Clique2	John,Anna,Anthony,Robert,Steven ,Ashley,Jessica,Jackson,Jennifer ,Julia,Peter,Mary,Laura,Bobby
n-Clique3	John,Anna,Anthony,Robert,Steven ,Ashley,Jessica,Jackson,Charles ,James,Susan,Richard,Michael,Elizabeth ,Thomas,David

SUBGROUP DETAILS

N-CLIQUES	SIZE	DENSITY	COHESION INDEX
n-Clique1	16	0.342	1.64
n-Clique2	14	0.352	2.317
n-Clique3	16	0.392	4.7

(b)

	n-Clique1	n-Clique2	n-Clique3
John	1	1	1
Thomas	0	0	1
Anna	1	1	1
James	1	0	1
Peter	0	1	0
Mary	0	1	0
Michael	1	0	1
David	1	0	1
Anthony	1	1	1
Bobby	0	1	0

(c)

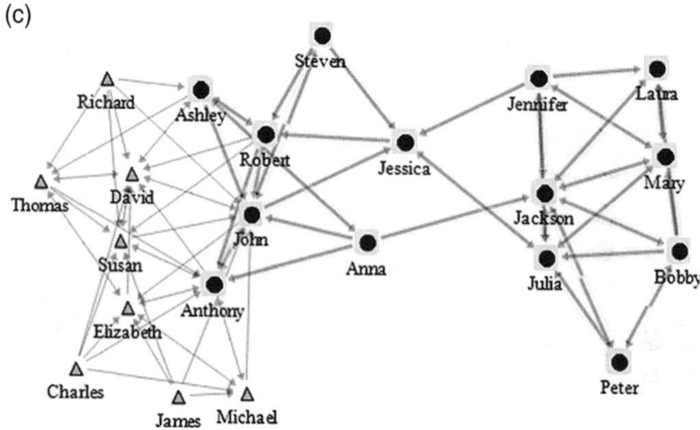

Figure 8.12 *n-Clique. (a) [R]Main, (b) [T]n-Clique Affiliation Matrix, and (c) [M] Spring (n-clique 2).*

(a)

K-CORE

CORENESS	# OF NODES	# OF COMPONENT
5	8	1
4	20	1
3	22	1

(b)

	5-Core	4-Core	3-Core
John	1	1	1
Thomas	1	1	1
Anna	0	1	1
James	0	1	1
Peter	0	0	1
Mary	0	1	1
Michael	0	1	1
David	1	1	1
Anthony	1	1	1
Bobby	0	1	1

Figure 8.13 *k-core. (a) [R]Main and (b) [T]k-Core Affiliation Matrix.*

8.2 Connectivity and Equivalence

8.2.1 Connectivity

1. *Connectivity*: Node (link) connectivity is used to analyze the weakness of the connectivity of the node (link) within the network and is the minimum number of node(link) to remove so that the two nodes are not connected. The analysis can be performed by *Analyze > Connection > Connectivity > N ode (Link)* resulting in the [R]Main, [T]Node(Link) Connectivity Matrix, [M]Spring. Here, the node connectivity analysis was performed on the one-mode network *Trust* of the *02.Org/_Net_Tiny2.* Each cell in the [T] Node(Link) Connectivity Matrix describes the necessary number of nodes(links) so that the connections of the node pairs does not become disconnected. Using the [M]Spring through the [Inspect] tab of the process control panel, the connectivity between the nodes can be intuitively visualized (Figure 8.14).

2. *Reciprocity and Transitivity*: Reciprocity and transitivity can be identified by the dyad census and triad census (*Analyze > Subgraph > Dyad Census (Triad Census)*). Figure 8.15a shows the results of the dyad (triad) census applied on the *Trust* of the *02.Org_Net_Tiny2.* In the Dyad census, # Mutual (node pairs connected in both directions), # Asymmetric (node pairs connected in one direction), # Null (unconnected node pairs) can be verified and the reciprocity score can be calculated by [# Mutual/(# Mutual + # Asymmetric)]. The results of the triad census are shown in Figure 8.15b. The results show the number of networks existing that correspond to the 16 triad isomorphism classes. The transitivity score is calculated from [# Transitive triad/(# Transitive triad + # Intransitive triad)]. The reciprocity and transitivity score can also be verified from the network properties.

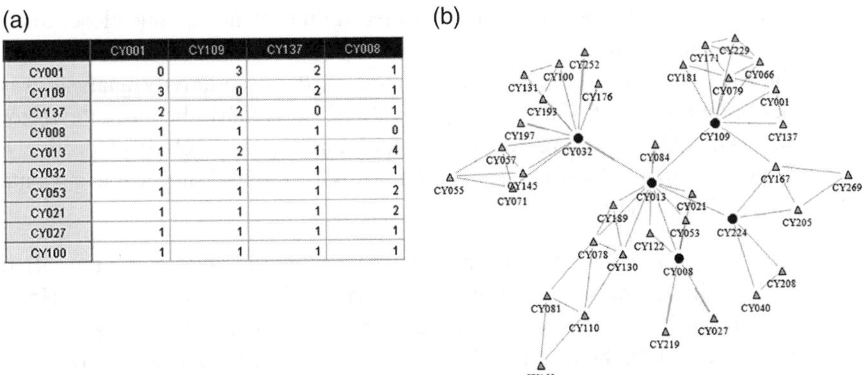

(a)

	CY001	CY109	CY137	CY008
CY001	0	3	2	1
CY109	3	0	2	1
CY137	2	2	0	1
CY008	1	1	1	0
CY013	1	2	1	4
CY032	1	1	1	1
CY053	1	1	1	2
CY021	1	1	1	2
CY027	1	1	1	1
CY100	1	1	1	1

Figure 8.14 Connectivity. (a) [T]Node Connectivity Matrix and (b) [M]Spring.

(a)

DYAD CENSUS

	Observed
# Mutuals	4
# Asymmetrics	61
# Nulls	676

(b)

TRIAD CENSUS

	Observed
003	6,960
012	1,847
102	135
021D	9
021U	123
021C	29
111D	2
111U	5
030T	24
030C	0
201	0
120D	0
120U	4
120C	0
210	1
300	0

Figure 8.15 Reciprocity and transitivity. (a) Dyad census and (b) triad census.

3. *Assortativity*: Assortativity checks for connection between nodes with similar attributes. In other words, a node with a high degree connected with another node with a high degree results in a higher assortativity score. Whereas, if a node with a high degree is connected to a node with a low degree, the assortativity score becomes lower. The assortativity score is between −1 and 1, where a value closer to 1 has a positive similarity and a value closer to −1 has a negative similarity. A value close to 0 suggests a low similarity. Through the *Analyze > Neighbor > Assortativity* menu, the assortativity analysis was performed on *Trust* of the *02.Org_Net_Tiny2*. In [Input], the attribute vector was assigned degree (Figure 8.16a,c) and Team (Figure 8.16b,d), respectively. [R]Main and [T]Assortativity results. [T]Assortativity shows the attribute value of the node pairs.

4. *Network properties*: Various characteristics of the network can be verified with a single analysis (*Analyze > Properties > Network > Multiple*). Here, the properties of the one-mode network *Trust* in the *02.Org_Net_Tiny2* were verified. In the results of Figure 8.17, *Output List > Dimension (Row*Col*Table) > Measure*Significance*Network* was selected from the [Output] option.

(a)

RESULT OF AUTOCORRELATION ASSORTATIVITY

Observed
-0.261

(b)

RESULT OF AUTOCORRELATION ASSORTATIVITY

Observed
0.725

(c)

	Source	Target
CY001,CY109	3	9
CY001,CY137	3	2
CY001,CY079	3	5
CY109,CY001	9	3
CY109,CY137	9	2
CY109,CY013	9	11
CY109,CY066	9	4
CY109,CY079	9	5
CY109,CY181	9	2
CY109,CY167	9	4

(d)

	Source	Target
CY001,CY109	Sales	Sales
CY001,CY137	Sales	Sales
CY001,CY079	Sales	Sales
CY109,CY001	Sales	Sales
CY109,CY137	Sales	Sales
CY109,CY013	Sales	Department Manager
CY109,CY066	Sales	Sales
CY109,CY079	Sales	Sales
CY109,CY181	Sales	Sales
CY109,CY167	Sales	Management

Figure 8.16 Assortativity. (a) [R]Main–Degree, (b) [R]Main–Team, (c) [T]Assortativity–Degree, and (d) [T]Assortativity–Team.

	Observed
# of Links : O(m)	69.000
Density : O(m)	0.047
Average Degree : O(m)	1.769
# of Components(Weak) : O(m)	1.000
# of Components(Strong) : O(m)	35.000
Inclusiveness : O(m)	1.000
Reciprocity(Arc) : O(m)	0.116
Reciprocity(Dyad) : O(m)	0.062
Transitivity : O(nm)	0.486
Clustering Coefficient : O(n^3)	0.707
Mean Distance : O(nm)	1.362
Diameter : O(nm)	3.000
Node Connectivity : O(n^2*m)	0.000
Link Connectivity : O(n^2*m)	0.000
Connectedness : O(m)	0.007
Efficiency : O(m)	0.979
Hierarchy : O(nm)	0.950
LUB O(n^3)	0.101

Figure 8.17 Network properties.

8.2.2 Equivalence

1. *Structural equivalence*: The structural equivalence analysis is possible by the Profile or the CONvergence of iterated CORrelation (CONCOR) method. Profile analysis is possible be executing the *Analyze > Equivalence > Structural > Profile,* where in the [Main process] the measurement indexes of [Direction], [Diagonal Handling Option], [Proximity Measure] are selected. [Clustering Methods] can be selected in the [Post-process]. Possible options to select are the *Single, Complete, Average, Ward* methods. *Single* is a method to calculate the distance between two clusters by the nearest distance between nodes affiliated to separate clusters and *complete* is a method to calculate the distance between two clusters by the furthest distance between nodes affiliated to separate clusters. *Average* is a method to calculate the distance between two clusters and *ward* calculates the homogeneity of the cluster. Here, Trust in the *02.Org_Net_Tinly2* is assigned as a one-mode network, where the [Direction] is in and out, [Diagonal Handling Option] is retain, and [Proximity Measure] is the euclidean distance. The ward method was selected as the [Clustering Methods] in [Post-process]. The results of the profile include [R] Main, [T]Profile Matrix, [T]Profile Cluster Matrix, [T]Permutation Vector, [C]Dendrogram, [M]MDS (multi-dimensional scaling). The structural equivalence score of the nodes is shown in [T]Profile Matrix (Figure 8.18a). [Proximity Measure] was measured with the Euclidean distance and the score in each cell correspond to the euclidean distance between the nodes. Therefore, if each node is equivalent to each other, the score would be close to 0 and if non-equivalent the score would increase. Through the [T]Profile Cluster Matrix, the optimal cluster can be found and two nodes belonging to one cluster suggests node to be structural equivalent.

   The similarity and dissimilarity between each node is reflected in [M] MDS and is arranged to optimally satisfy the relationship between nodes

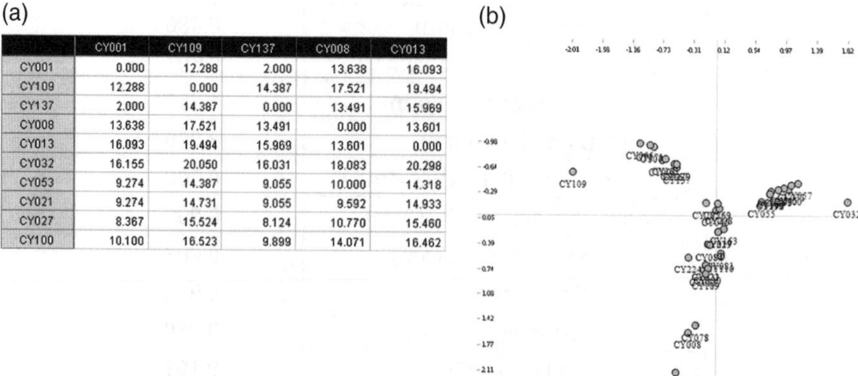

(a)

	CY001	CY109	CY137	CY008	CY013
CY001	0.000	12.288	2.000	13.638	16.093
CY109	12.288	0.000	14.387	17.521	19.494
CY137	2.000	14.387	0.000	13.491	15.969
CY008	13.638	17.521	13.491	0.000	13.601
CY013	16.093	19.494	15.969	13.601	0.000
CY032	16.155	20.050	16.031	18.083	20.298
CY053	9.274	14.387	9.055	10.000	14.318
CY021	9.274	14.731	9.055	9.592	14.933
CY027	8.367	15.524	8.124	10.770	15.460
CY100	10.100	16.523	9.899	14.071	16.462

(b)

Figure 8.18 Structural equivalence (profile). (a) [T]Profile Matrix and (b) [M]MDS.

(Figure 8.18b). Within the [Display] tab of the process control panel, the similarity and dissimilarity related to the options of the [M]MDS can be selected, where shorter euclidean distances between nodes suggest a closer similarity for the selected similarity option. Here, a Euclidean distance close to 0 suggests an equivalence the dissimilarity option is chosen. Therefore, nodes that are close to the [M]MDS are said to be equivalent.

CONCOR is used to identify the structural equivalence through the correlations and can be performed by *Analyze > Equivalence > Structural > CONCOR*. The basic calculation method is to reiterate the calculation until the correlation score of the row and column of the raw matrix is either a +1 or −1 and grouping the nodes with high correlation, where nodes divided into identical groups can be assumed to be structurally equivalent. In the [Main Process], [Direction], [# of Iterations], [Maximum Depth of Split], [Diagonal Handling Option], [Convergence Criteria] option must be chosen. Here, [Maximum Depth of Split] is an option to set the depth of the cluster diagram and dendrogram, the [Convergence criteria] is an option to close the arithmetic operation by setting the criteria value if the correlation variation absolute value becomes smaller than the convergence criteria. A value of 0.1 is set as the default. The results of the CONCOR is similar to the Profile and includes [R]Main, [T]CONCOR Matrix, [T]CONCOR cluster matrix, [T]Permutation Vector, [C]Dendrogram, [M]MDS (Figure 8.19).

2. *Role equivalence*: To check the role equivalence, the Triad and Local method can be used. First, after the network to analyze is dichotomized, the Triad calculates the equivalent by the Euclidean distance of the triad relationship pattern for all nodes and the Local considers the nodes to be equivalent if the connection method of node i with other nodes and node j with other nodes is similar. Role equivalence can be obtained by selecting *Analyze > Equivalence > Role > Triad (or Local)* in the menu. The results include [R]Main, [T]Role

(a)

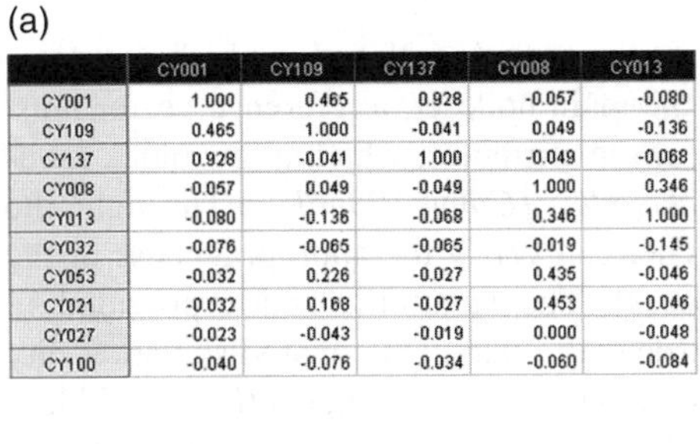

	CY001	CY109	CY137	CY008	CY013
CY001	1.000	0.465	0.928	-0.057	-0.080
CY109	0.465	1.000	-0.041	0.049	-0.136
CY137	0.928	-0.041	1.000	-0.049	-0.068
CY008	-0.057	0.049	-0.049	1.000	0.346
CY013	-0.080	-0.136	-0.068	0.346	1.000
CY032	-0.076	-0.065	-0.065	-0.019	-0.145
CY053	-0.032	0.226	-0.027	0.435	-0.046
CY021	-0.032	0.168	-0.027	0.453	-0.046
CY027	-0.023	-0.043	-0.019	0.000	-0.048
CY100	-0.040	-0.076	-0.034	-0.060	-0.084

(b)

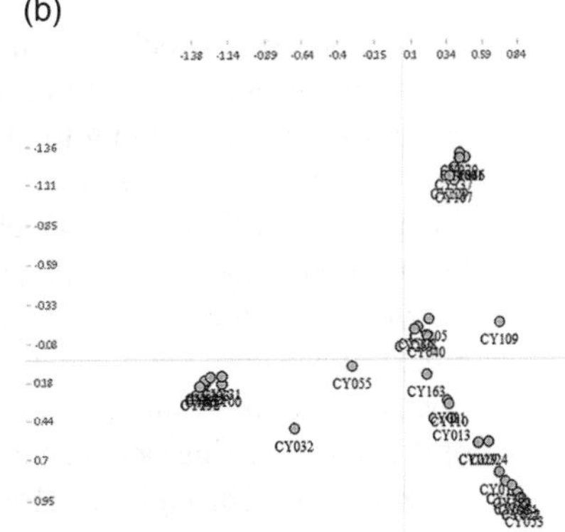

Figure 8.19 Structural equivalence (CONCOR). (a) [T]CONCOR Matrix and (b) [M]MDS.

(a)

	CY001	CY109	CY137	CY008	CY013
CY001	0.000	0.340	0.117	0.192	0.433
CY109	0.340	0.000	0.444	0.149	0.107
CY137	0.117	0.444	0.000	0.298	0.537
CY008	0.192	0.149	0.298	0.000	0.246
CY013	0.433	0.107	0.537	0.246	0.000
CY032	0.392	0.056	0.495	0.202	0.069
CY053	0.118	0.447	0.015	0.301	0.541
CY021	0.118	0.447	0.015	0.301	0.541
CY027	0.131	0.470	0.064	0.323	0.562
CY100	0.007	0.335	0.122	0.187	0.428

(b)

	CY001	CY109	CY137	CY008	CY013
CY001	0.000	1.000	1.000	1.000	2.000
CY109	1.000	0.000	2.000	0.000	1.000
CY137	1.000	2.000	0.000	2.000	4.000
CY008	1.000	0.000	2.000	0.000	1.000
CY013	2.000	1.000	4.000	1.000	0.000
CY032	1.000	0.000	2.000	0.000	1.000
CY053	2.000	1.000	1.000	1.000	3.000
CY021	2.000	1.000	1.000	1.000	3.000
CY027	0.000	1.000	1.000	1.000	2.000
CY100	0.000	1.000	1.000	1.000	2.000

Figure 8.20 Role equivalence. (a) [T]Triad Role Matrix and (b) [T]Local Role Matrix.

Matrix, [T]Role cluster matrix, [T]Permutation Vector, [C]Dendrogram, [M] MDS. Figure 7.38 shows the role equivalence of the Triad analysis result (Figure 8.20a) and the Local analysis result (Figure 8.20b) in the [T]Role Matrix. A value close to 0 in the role matrix suggests an equivalent relationship.

3. *Regular equivalence*: The regular equivalence analysis is carried out by the REGGE (*Analyze > Equivalence > Regular > REGGE*)와 CatRE (*Analyze > Equivalence > Regular > CatRE*). REGGE is a method suitable for data with direction, CatRE is useful for obtaining the equivalent group through the multiplexed matrix. Recommended nodes from similar nodes according to SimRank are at a similar state and can be assumed to be equivalent (*Analyze > Equivalence > Sim Rank*). In the SimRank analysis, [Direction], [# of Iterations], [Dampening Parameter] must be defined within the [Main process]. [Direction] indicates the in or out direction of the network to be analyzed and [Dampening Parameter] is set as the default value of 0.8. In SimRank, the nodes pairs starts at the same value and is continuously calculated resulting in new values at each step. The basic [Dampening Parameter] is the basic value before the calculations begin (Figure 8.21).

4. *Block modeling*: Block modeling is the grouping of nodes which are structurally equivalent. Therefore, in the main nodeset, a reference vector must be set to group according to one of the attributes, which allow block modeling (*Analyze > Position > Blockmodel (Conventional)*). Through the goodness of fit index, the researcher can verify the appropriateness of the block model in the [Main process]. The suitability index provided in NetMiner includes the city block(density), max, chi-squared statistics, city block(adjacency), match coefficient, matrix correlation, coefficient of identity. Next, in the [Main process], the image matrix containing the summary of the links existing between groups can be created by selecting the dichotomize option. Through the [Role Typology Threshold] in the [Post-process], the thresholds for distinguishing the roles of the group can be configured. In NetMiner, the role typology of the group can be classified according to Table 8.1. For example, when some of the out-link in a particular group,

(a)

	CY001	CY109	CY137	CY008	CY013
CY001	1.000	0.742	0.651	0.849	0.595
CY109	0.742	1.000	0.221	0.874	0.863
CY137	0.651	0.221	1.000	0.308	0.000
CY008	0.849	0.874	0.308	1.000	0.709
CY013	0.595	0.863	0.000	0.709	1.000
CY032	0.737	0.892	0.135	0.900	0.870
CY053	0.639	0.244	0.905	0.340	0.000
CY021	0.633	0.220	0.899	0.307	0.000
CY027	0.562	0.149	0.894	0.215	0.000
CY100	0.866	0.817	0.487	0.941	0.647

(b)

	CY001	CY109	CY137	CY008	CY013
CY001	3	1	1	1	1
CY109	1	3	1	2	1
CY137	1	1	3	1	1
CY008	1	2	1	3	1
CY013	1	1	1	1	3
CY032	1	1	1	1	1
CY053	1	1	2	1	1
CY021	1	1	2	1	1
CY027	1	1	1	1	1
CY100	1	1	1	1	1

(c)

	CY001	CY109	CY137	CY008	CY013
CY001	1.000	0.105	0.000	0.000	0.008
CY109	0.105	1.000	0.000	0.000	0.006
CY137	0.000	0.000	1.000	0.000	0.000
CY008	0.000	0.000	0.000	1.000	0.044
CY013	0.008	0.006	0.000	0.044	1.000
CY032	0.000	0.000	0.000	0.000	0.003
CY053	0.000	0.000	0.000	0.000	0.000
CY021	0.000	0.000	0.000	0.000	0.000
CY027	0.000	0.000	0.000	0.000	0.000
CY100	0.000	0.000	0.000	0.000	0.000

Figure 8.21 Regular equivalence. (a) [T]REGGE Matrix, (b) [T]CatRE Matrix, and (c) [T]SimRank Equivalence Matrix (direction: in, dampening parameter: 0.8).

Table 8.1 Role typology of group.

Proportion of Links Sent by Group	Proportion of Links Received by Group	Proportion of Links within Group	
		≥Expected Value	≤Expected Value
>0	>0	Primary position	Broker
	≤0	Low status clique	Sycophant
≤0	>0	High status clique	Snob
	≤0	Isolated clique	Isolate

which has an out-group sending link density, but not an in-group greater than the sending threshold and amongst the in-link of the group, which has an out-group receiving link density, but not an in-group greater than the receiving threshold, the group's role would be a broker if the link density of the in-group within the out-link is equal to or less than the expected value (group's density).

The results of the block modeling includes [R]Main, [T]Block Image Matrix, [T]Block Density Matrix, [T]Block Sum Matrix, [T]Block-Node Affiliation Matrix, [T]# Nodes, [T]Block Role Typology, [M]Clustered. Here, an analysis of the *Trust* network in the *02.Org_Net_Tiny2* was performed, where the node attribute was Team from the [Select Vector] and the City Block (density) was configured within the [Goodness of Fit Index]. The [T] Block Image Matrix of the block modeling results is the matrix after

(a)

	Department Manager	Finance	HR	Management	Marketing	Sales
Department Manager	0	0	0	0	0	0
Finance	1	1	0	0	0	0
HR	1	0	1	0	0	0
Management	1	0	0	1	0	0
Marketing	1	0	0	0	1	0
Sales	1	0	0	0	0	1

(b)

	Department Manager	Finance	HR	Management	Marketing	Sales
Department Manager	0.000	0.000	0.000	0.000	0.000	0.000
Finance	1.000	17.000	0.000	0.000	0.000	0.000
HR	5.000	0.000	5.000	0.000	0.000	0.000
Management	1.000	0.000	0.000	8.000	0.000	1.000
Marketing	3.000	0.000	0.000	0.000	11.000	0.000
Sales	1.000	0.000	0.000	0.000	0.000	16.000

(c)

	Department Manager	Finance	HR	Management	Marketing	Sales
Department Manager	0.000	0.000	0.000	0.000	0.000	0.000
Finance	0.091	0.155	0.000	0.000	0.000	0.000
HR	0.714	0.000	0.119	0.000	0.000	0.000
Management	0.167	0.000	0.000	0.267	0.000	0.021
Marketing	0.500	0.000	0.000	0.000	0.367	0.000
Sales	0.125	0.000	0.000	0.000	0.000	0.286

(d)

	CY001	CY109	CY137	CY008	CY013
Department Manager	0	0	0	0	1
Finance	0	0	0	0	0
HR	0	0	0	1	0
Management	0	0	0	0	0
Marketing	0	0	0	0	0
Sales	1	1	1	0	0

(e)

	# Nodes
Department Manager	1
Finance	11
HR	7
Management	6
Marketing	6
Sales	8

(f)

	Block Role Typology Vector
Department Manager	Snob
Finance	Low Status Clique
HR	Low Status Clique
Management	Low Status Clique
Marketing	Low Status Clique
Sales	Primary Position

(g)

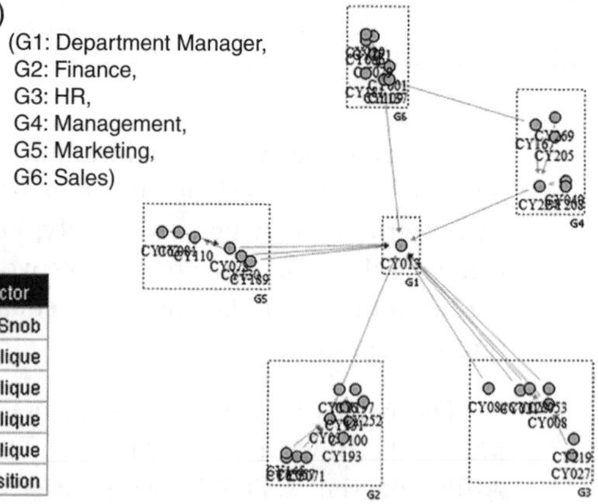

Figure 8.22 Regular equivalence. (a) [T]Block Image Matrix, (b) [T]Block Sum Matrix, (c) [T]Block Density Matrix, (d) [T]Block-Node Affiliation Matrix, (e) [T]# Nodes, (f) [T]Block Role Typology, and (g) [M]Clustered (G1: department manager, G2: finance, G3: HR, G4: management, G5: marketing, G6: sales).

dichotomizing the [T]Block Density Matrix, where the option (default) is set as 1 for density higher than 0 resulting in a value of 1 for density values greater than 0 and 0 for density values less than 0 (Figure 8.22a). [T]Block Sum Matrix is a one-mode network comprised of blocks, where each cell describes the number of links that share two blocks. If the dichotomize option is not selected within the [Preprocess], the number in each cell is the sum of the link weights (Figure 8.22b). The value in the [T]Block Density Matrix is the normalized number of links (Figure 8.22c). In the [T]Block-Node Affiliation Matrix, the researcher can identify which node belongs to which block (Figure 8.22d). [T]#Nodes describes the number of nodes belonging to each block (Figure 8.22e), [T]Block Role Typology shows the role typology of groups (Figure 8.22f) and [M]Clustered expresses the blocks as groups, where the relationship between the blocks and nodes can be visually verified (Figure 8.22g).

8.3 Visualization and Exploratory Analysis

8.3.1 Visualization

1. *Styling of visualized map*: Visualization of the network allows easy perception of the network structure. Therefore, not only is the selection of an optimal visualization algorithm necessary to better express the structure for the visualization of the network, but it is also necessary to effectively use the styling for the node and link. The node and link styling expresses the node or link attribute information within the map. The node and link styling is possible through the [Display] tab within the process control panel by executing the *Node (Link) Style > Node (Link) Attribute Styling,* tool bar (*Node and Link Attribute Styling*), *mouse right button > (multiple) node (link) style.* The color, shape, size can be defined within the node styling and the arrow, direction, weight, color, line style can be defined within the link styling (Figure 8.23).

2. *Detailed setting option of the layout algorithm*: When the data size is large, the coordinates is first set within the Lay 2D (Visualize>Layout) and saved as a node attribute then is visualized through Drawing 2D (Visualize>Drawing). Furthermore, after the visualization is processed, the detailed setting option can be set up using the [Display] tab within the process control panel by (*Display > Node Layout > Node Layout Algorithm > Option*). The instructions of the detailed setting option are provided in Table 8.2.

3. *Chart*: A chart for analysis include the pie chart, matrix diagram, and area bar, box plot, scatter plot, contour plot, surface plot, network contour plot, network surface plot. Here, an analysis on the *01.Org_Net_Tiny1* has been performed. ***Pie chart*** can be expressed with one of the attributes in the main node(*Chart > Pie Chart*). ***Matrix diagram*** expresses the connection relationship of nodes in the form of a matrix, where a colored cell indicates the

(a)

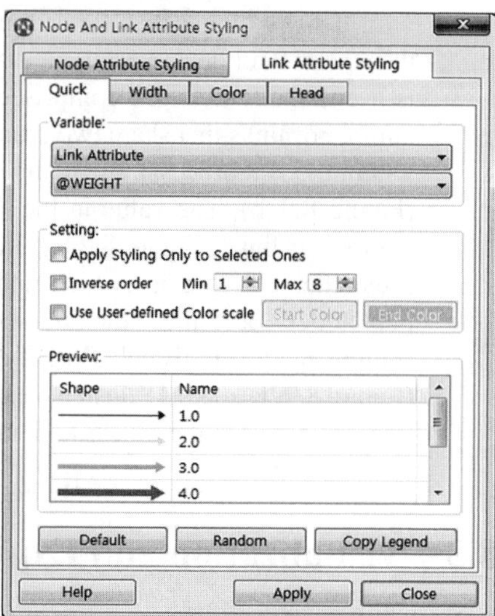

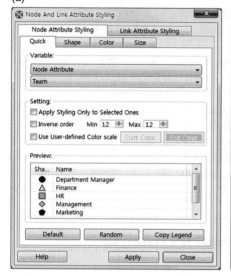

(b)

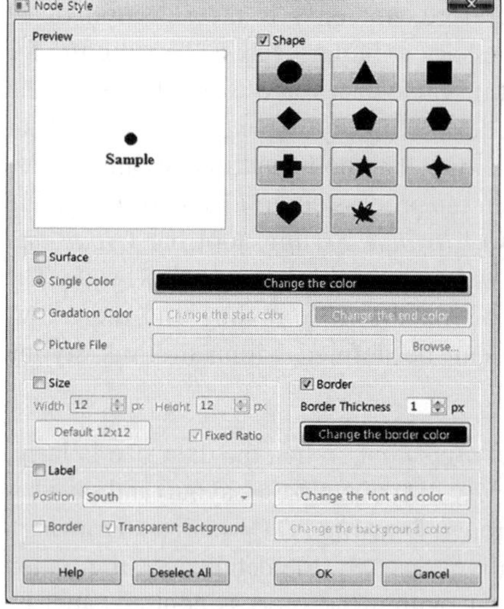

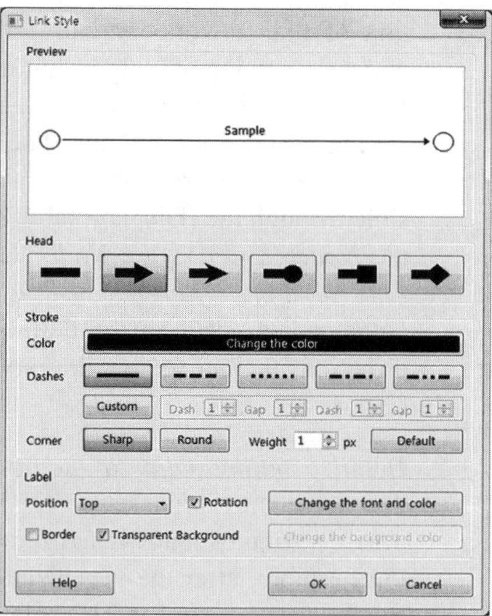

Figure 8.23 Node and link styling. (a) Node and link attribute styling and (b) node and link styling (mouse right button > (Multiple) Node (Link) Style).

existence of a link between nodes and a deeper shade of color indicates a larger link weight (*Chart > Matrix Diagram*). Designation of the [Permutation Vector] within the [Input] allows segmentation of the nodes in the matrix diagram and nodes with the same segment are placed close within the matrix diagram (Figure 8.24).

Table 8.2 Detailed setting option of the layout algorithm.

Setting Option	Description
Alpha oscillation	Oscillation describes the node vibratory. Since the node can continuously oscillate, the node motility (temperature) value[a] should be lowered to reduce the amplitude. Alpha oscillation determines the angle range of node oscillation, where the vibration of the node corresponds to the ratio decrease in the temperature
Alpha rotation	Since the nodes can continuously rotate, the node temperature should be lowered to reduce the rotation range. Alpha rotation determines the range of the rotation angle for the node and the rotation of the node corresponds to a ratio decrease in the temperature
Attenuation factor	When the layout algorithm is performed, the location of the node changes every step and if a large value is used as the attenuation factor the degree of change becomes smaller with time
Between cluster factor	A spring exists between nodes and through this the location of the node is determined. Between cluster factor is the weight multiplied on the force of the spring applied on the clusters, where a smaller value results in the distance between the clusters to become larger
Between component factor	The pulling force on the spring applied between the components is multiplied with the weight, which has a default score set at 2 and a value higher than that would further separate the distance between unconnected components
Cooling coefficient	A large value applied to the cooling coefficient would decrease the degree of movement of the node location with time
Delta oscillation	It is the value of the angle in the oscillation movement of a node with motility
Delta rotation	It is the value of the angle in the rotational movement of a node with motility
Edge length	Between the nodes, there basically exists repulsive forces, but nodes connected with a link will have attractive forces. With a higher edge length value, the repulsive forces between the nodes become comparatively stronger and the attractive forces from the link will become weaker. On the other hand with a lower edge length value, the repulsive forces between the nodes become weaker and the attractive forces from the link will become stronger

(Continued)

Table 8.2 (*Continued*)

Setting Option	Description
Epsilon	In the visualization of the nodes step, if the energy[b] of all nodes becomes smaller than the given value, it is assumed that the node coordinates no longer require optimization and the execution of the algorithm halts. Although a smaller epsilon value results in better visual images, the execution time of the algorithm becomes longer
External cluster factor	The external cluster factor is weighted value multiplied on the attractive forces of the spring applied between nodes affiliated to different clusters, where smaller values correspond to increased distances between connected nodes of different clusters
Final temperature	Describes the target node motility at the end point of the algorithm
Gravitational constant	Value of the force attracted to the center of gravity of each node
Internal cluster factor	Internal cluster factor is a weight multiplied to the attractive forces of the spring applied between nodes of the same cluster, where a higher value used corresponds to nodes within the cluster to come closer
Level closeness (alpha)	A parameter used in the calculation of the hierarchy, where a smaller value corresponds to more hierarchical levels
Level gap (pixels)	Determines the distance between clusters, where the unit is pixel
Maximum iteration	A high value used for the maximum iteration results in greater execution times for the algorithm, but better visual images
Maximum temperature	The maximum motility value of the node
Minimum level depth (beta)	A parameter used when calculating the hierarchy, where a smaller value corresponds to more hierarchical levels
Natural length coefficient	An option to control the basic distance between connected nodes, where the default score is 1. A value less than 1 results in the average distance between connected nodes to be closer than when the default score is used. A value larger than 1 will result in the average distance to be greater than when the default score is used
Random move range	Value of the degree of randomness when the node moves for visualization
Repulsiveness coefficient	An option to control the repulsive forces of the spring applied between unconnected nodes. The default score is configured to be 1 and a value higher than the default will result in the repulsive forces between unconnected nodes to increase and further separate the unconnected nodes

Table 8.2 (*Continued*)

Setting Option	Description
Start temperature	The initial motility of the node
Timeout limit (s)	Time to wait for the algorithm to halt and thus after the set time the algorithm stops

[a] Layout algorithm sums all of the applied force on the nodes and eventually moves the nodes. At this moment, each node retains a motility value and a higher motility value indicates a larger movement of the nodes.

[b] A value proportional to the difference from the ideal distance between nodes.

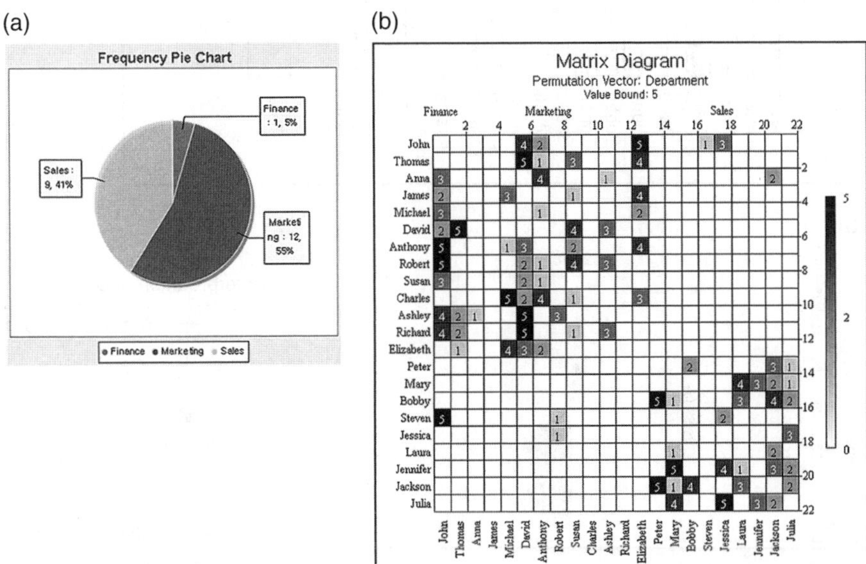

Figure 8.24 Pie chart and matrix diagram. (a) Pie chart (input vector: department) and (b) matrix diagram (input network: work interact, permutation vector: department).

Area bar is chart to express a two-mode network and the main node or sub node can be shown by one vertical bar (*Chart > Area Bar*). ***Box plot*** divides the data into quartiles that depicts the minimum (low limit=$Q1-(Q3-Q1)$), the first quartile (Q1), median, mean, the third quartile (Q3), maximum (upper limit=$Q3+(Q3-1)$) as a picture, where the center position of the distribution, scatter, outlier, and so on, information can be verified (*Chart > Box Plot*). The main node attributer, which is a dependent variable, can be selected to become a main node attribute as an independent variable. For this, the dependent variable must be a variable measured according to the interval and ration scale and the independent variable must be a variable measured in the nominal scale (Figure 8.25).

(a)

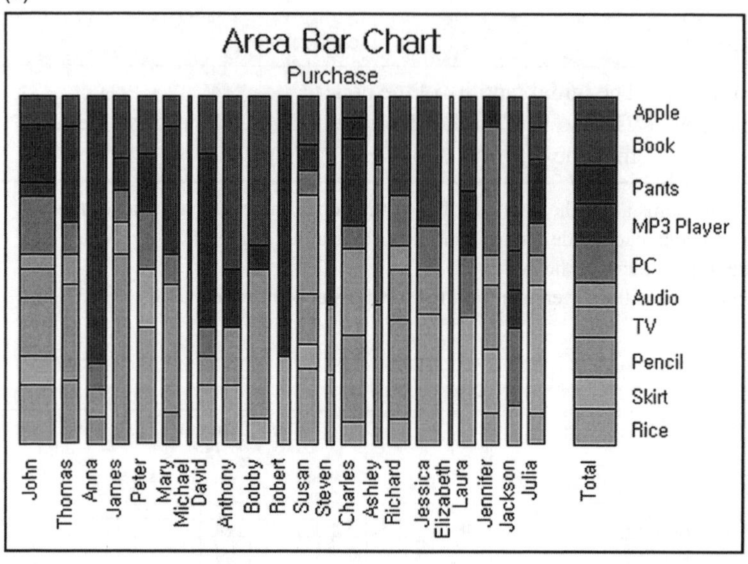

(b)

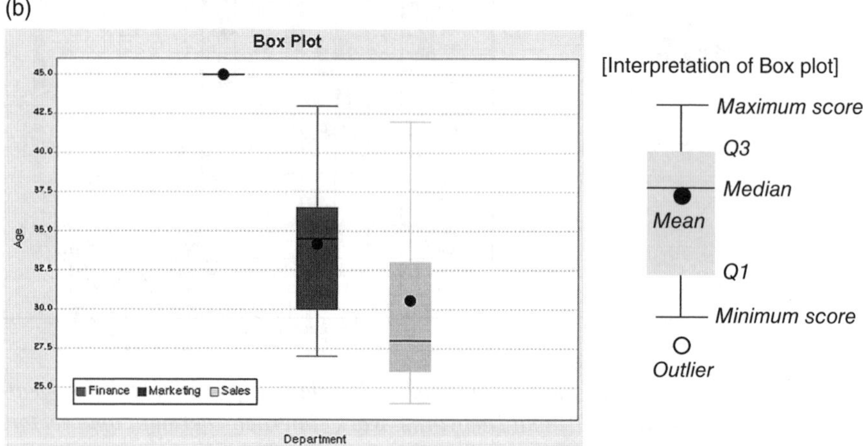

Figure 8.25 Area bar and box plot. (a) Area bar (input two-mode network: purchase) and (b) box plot (dependent variable: age, independent variable: department).

Scatter plot expresses the variable pair by dotting on the X and Y axis (*Chart > Scatter Plot*). The main node attribute for the x axis and the y axis can be selected and expressed. ***Contour plot*** is a three-dimensional plot in the X, Y, Z, where contour shaped plots are cut at a fixed Z axis showing the height using colors (*Chart > Contour Plot*). Regression is used for the contour plot and the position of the dot is determined by regression. Using the [Fitting Method] in the [Main process],

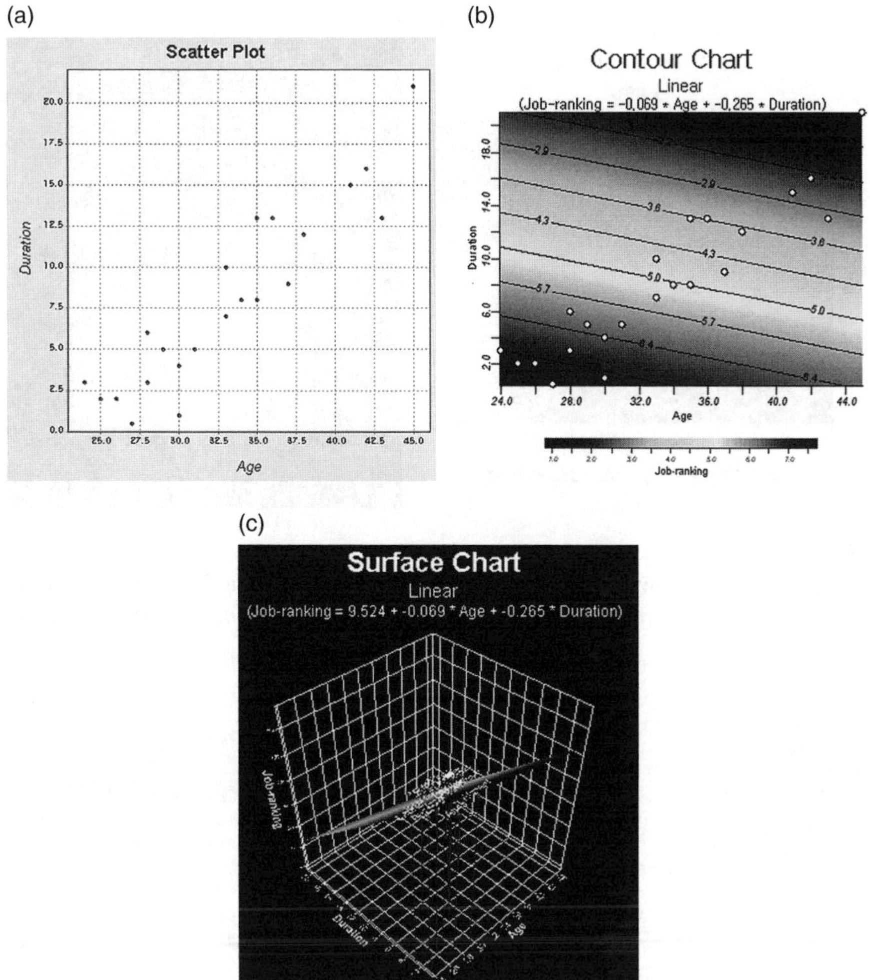

Figure 8.26 Scatter plot, contour plot, and surface chart. (a) Scatter plot (X axis: age, Y axis: duration), (b) contour plot (X axis: Age, Y axis: duration, Z axis: job-ranking, fitting method: linear), and (c) surface chart (X axis: age, Y axis: duration, Z axis: job-ranking, fitting method: linear).

linear regression, quadratic regression, or weighted sum can be selected. ***Surface plot*** is a method to express an X, Y, Z three-dimensional data (*Chart > Surface Plot*). Each surface is determined through regression and the color is determined through the Z score (Figure 8.26).

The ***network contour plot*** and the network surface plot is similar to the contour or surface plot, but in the network contour (surface) plot the X, Y axis is determined the visualized layout algorithm (Kamada and Kawai algorithm) of the one-mode network (*Chart > Network Contour Plot (Network Surface Plot)*) (Figure 8.27).

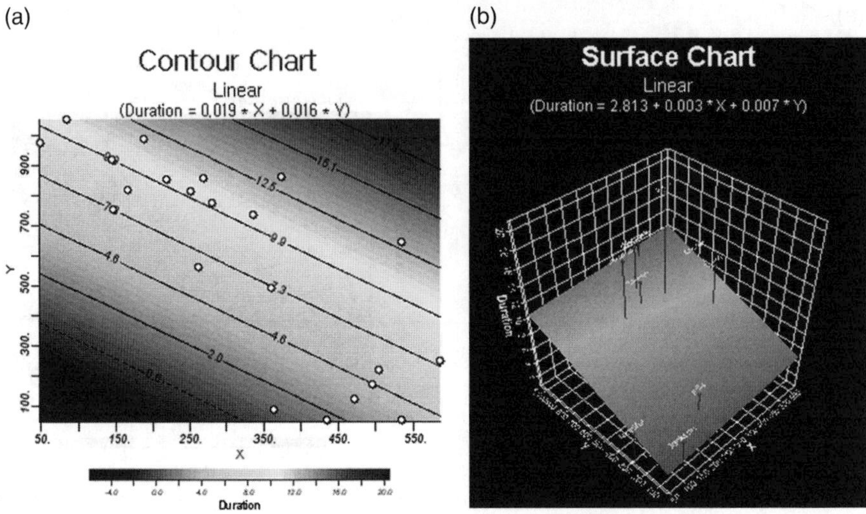

Figure 8.27 Network contour plot and network surface plot. (a) Network contour plot (input network: work interact, vector: duration, fitting method: linear) and (b) network surface plot (input network: work interact, vector: duration, fitting method: linear).

Project
Current Workfile
DataSet ProcessLog
01.Org_Net_Tiny1
Employee [22 * 6]
work interact [89 * 0]
personal friend [63 * 0]
personal help [63 * 0]
personal knows [24 * 0]
work help [66 * 0]
[T] Co-membership(Interested In) [164 * 0]
Clubs [3 * 5]
Club Affiliation [33 * 0]
Interest Items [5 * 1]

[T] Co-membership(Interested In)

		1	2	3
		John	Thomas	Anna
1	John	1.000	0.500	0.000
2	Thomas	0.500	1.000	0.000
3	Anna	0.000	0.000	1.000
4	James	0.333	0.500	0.000
5	Peter	0.000	0.000	1.000
6	Mary	0.000	0.000	0.333
7	Michael	0.000	0.000	0.333
8	David	0.500	1.000	0.000
9	Anthony	0.333	0.000	0.333
10	Bobby	0.333	0.000	0.000

Figure 8.28 Transformation of the two-mode network to a one-mode network.

8.3.2 Transformation of the Two-Mode Network to a One-Mode Network

A two-mode network with disparate characteristics can be transformed into a one-mode network with identical characteristics. The formed matrix is the co-membership matrix of the main node, overlap matrix of the sub node and the bipartite matrix of the main and sub node. Transformation of the two-mode network is initiated by selecting *Transform > Mode > two-mode Network* and choosing the two-mode network to transform and then configuring the [Output Network] and [Proximity

Measures] in the [Main process]. Here, the transformation of the two-mode network *Interested In* to a one-mode network of the *01.Org_Net_Tiny1* was performed, where Co-membership(Main*Main) was designated as the [Output Network] and the *Match > Jaccard Coefficient* was designated for the [Proximity Measures]. If the analysis is performed, the transformed one-mode network in the current workfile can be added through the dialog box. The results of the transformation of the two-mode network to a one-mode network includes [R]Main, [T]Co-membership(Interested In) (Figure 8.28).

Appendix A

Visualization

One of the advantages of social network analysis is the intuitive visualization of the network. The hidden structural relationship can be verified through visualization and can provide insight into the direction of analysis. Furthermore, the numerical analysis can provide a more persuasive reporting. That is why visualization is often a simple representation of the social network analysis data through diagrams. There are various algorithms for the visualization of network. Generally, if the attribute data analysis results are visualized in the form of a chart or a plot, the network is visualized using a graph drawing algorithm. Visualization of the network considers the relationship between nodes and after calculating the coordinates, a particular algorithm is selected depending on how we want to place the nodes on a network map.

In the steel product analysis here, a trade relationship network with more than 10 000 tons such as S. Korea, China, Japan, and USA is visualized depending on each algorithm, where the results are visualized according to the different algorithms.

A.1 Spring Algorithm

The spring layout algorithm assumes a virtual spring between nodes, where the nodes are placed according to the pushing and pulling forces between the nodes. As the nodes are distributed within the map, adjacent nodes are closely

Fundamentals of Big Data Network Analysis for Research and Industry, First Edition. Hyunjoung Lee and Il Sohn.

placed within a defined interval and are visualized so that there are fewer repetition or intersections in the links.

1. *Kamada and Kawai* [1]: Each node pair has identical distance and the distance between nodes is determined according to the path, where the pair of nodes is positioned proportional to the shortest path.
2. *Stress majorization* [2]: Similar results are obtained compared to the Kamada and Kawai, but is obtained more quickly.
3. *Eades* [3]: The initial indicator value for each node is randomly given, where neighboring node pairs are pulled within a defined interval distance and nonneighboring nodes are placed further away.
4. *Fruchterman and Reingold* [4]: Similar results are obtained to the Eades and results are obtained more quickly but are different in expressing the pulling and pushing forces between nodes. Neighboring nodes are pulled together closely but are not placed too close to each other.
5. *GEM (Graph EMbedder)* [5]: Similar results to the Fruchterman and Reingold are obtained but are more effective in visualization of complex large data. Neighboring nodes are pulled closer together but refrain from overlapping nodes or minimizing leaning toward a unidirection.
6. *HDE (high dimensional embedding)* [6]: The maps are not quite detailed and precise but allow rapid visualization of large quantities of network data (Figure A.1).

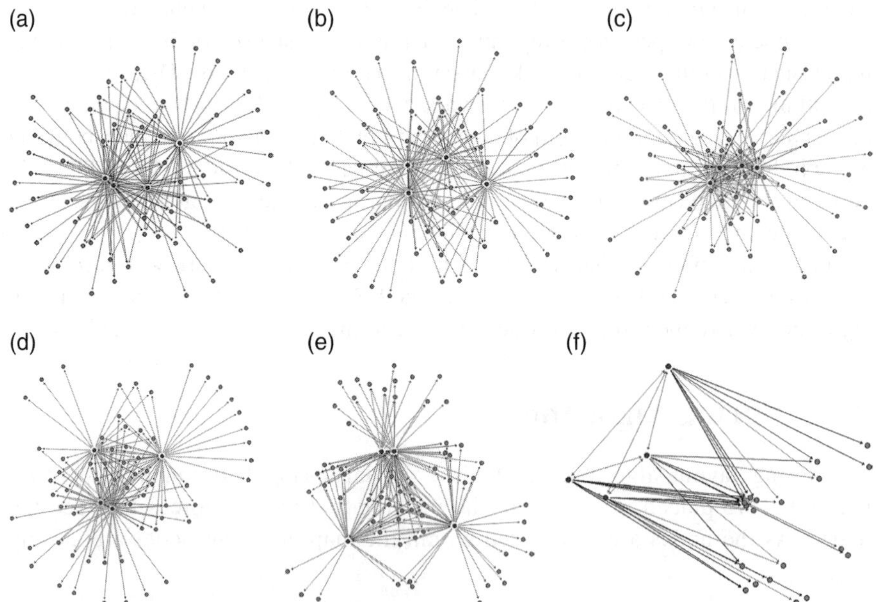

Figure A.1 Spring algorithm. (a) Kamada and Kawai, (b) stress majorization, (c) Eades, (d) Fruchterman and Reingold, (e) GEM, and (f) HDE.

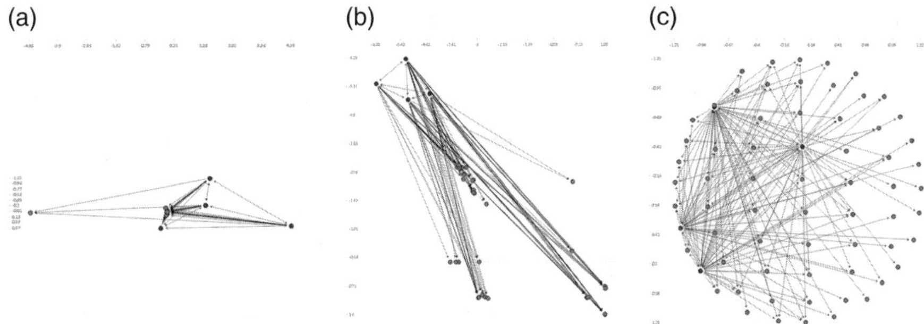

Figure A.2 Multidimensional scaling algorithm. (a) Classical MDS, (b) nonmetric MDS, and (c) Kn-MDS.

A.2 Multidimensional Scaling Algorithm

The multidimensional scaling (MDS) algorithm applies the dissimilarity or similarity data of all node pairs and is an algorithm that allows placement of all nodes with maximum satisfaction of the relationship between nodes.

1. *Classical MDS* [7]: Data with an interval scale or ratio scale can be applied, where the matrix is normalized and the eigenvector calculated resulting in the coordinate value of each node.
2. *Nonmetric MDS* [8]: Data with an ordinary scale can be applied, where the coordinate value of the classical MDS is used. The distance sequence of the matrix corresponds to the distance of nodes within the map and uses a coordinate value for each node that minimizes the stress by estimation of the best fit coordinate value through repetition.
3. *Kn-MDS* [9]: One method of a nonmetric MDS, where the conditions of minimum stress are applied by various methods (Figure A.2).

A.3 Cluster Algorithm

To express the cluster structure using the cluster algorithm, a spring algorithm is used, nodes affiliated with identical clusters are gathered, and nodes of a different cluster are pushed away from the map.

1. *Clustered Eades* [10]: A modified Eades algorithm, where nodes of the same cluster are pulled together and nodes of different clusters are pushed away.
2. *Clustered Cola* [3]: A modified Eades algorithm, where nodes of the same cluster are pulled together and nodes of different clusters are pushed away (Figure A.3).

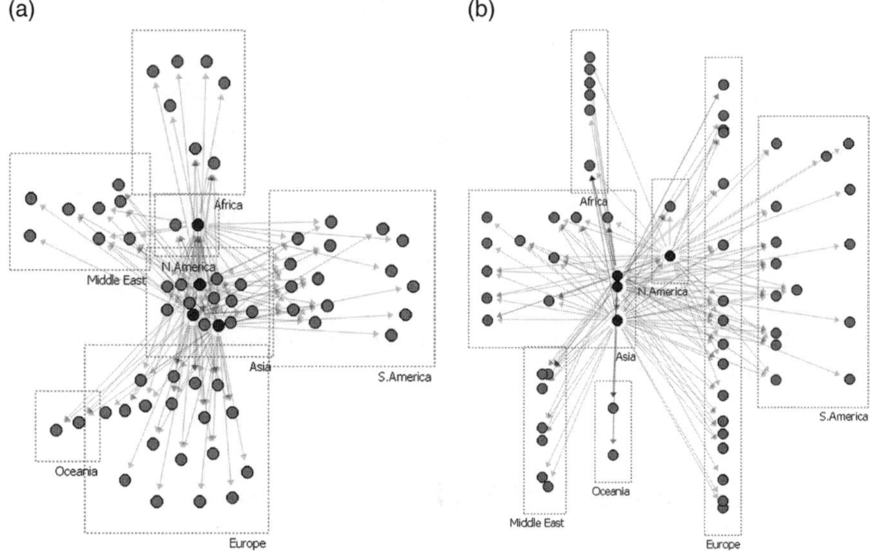

Figure A.3 Cluster algorithm. (a) Clustered Eades and (b) clustered Cola.

A.4 Layered Algorithm

Similar layouts are obtained to the Kamada and Kawai, but the layered algorithm is an algorithm that allows identification of the flow in the graph by placing the nodes above one another [11]. The algorithm in the layered is the Dig-CoLa algorithm. The Dig-CoLa algorithm is the clustering of the hierarchical position between nodes and forms the hierarchical cluster of nodes (Figure A.4).

A.5 Circular Algorithm

The layout algorithm is useful, where nodes are placed at defined intervals within a circumference and allow the identification of concentrated nodes within the network and the relative separation of nodes from one another, allowing a rough outline.

1. *Circumference* [12]: Each node is placed within a defined circular distance and a split vector value is inserted that allows the sequential placement of the node, and nodes that are defined to be within the same category are placed within the similar regions.

2. *Concentric* [13]: Higher centrality will place the node within the center of the map and a lower centrality will place the node farther from the center.

3. *Radical* [1]: Similar to the concentric, nodes with high centrality will place it near the center of the map with a lower centrality at the periphery. However,

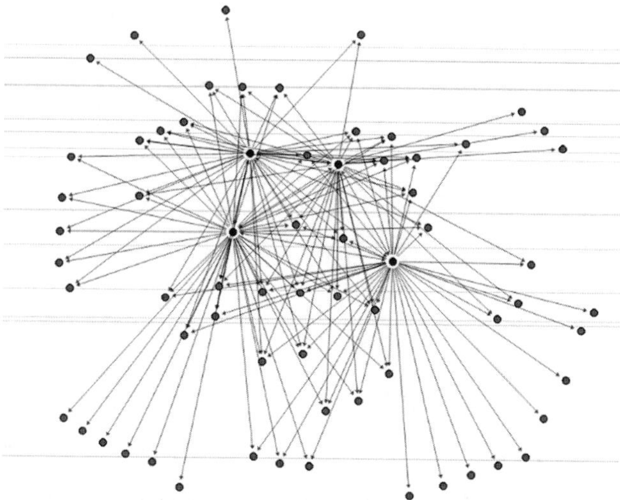

Figure A.4 Layered algorithm.

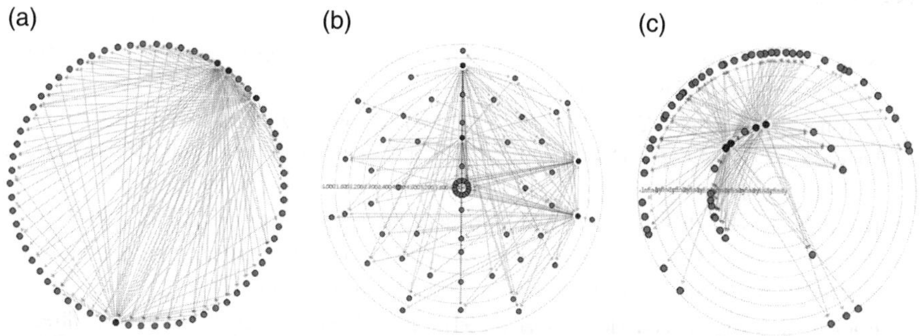

Figure A.5 Circular algorithm. (a) Circumference, (b) concentric, and (c) radical.

the node pairs are placed proportional to the shortest path according to the Kamada and Kawai algorithm, making the radical different from the concentric (Figure A.5).

A.6 Simple Algorithm

The simple algorithm places the nodes randomly according to the coordinate value.

1. *Fixed* [14]: The researcher places the nodes according to a predefined coordinate value.

2. *Random* [15]: Nodes are placed randomly (Figure A.6).

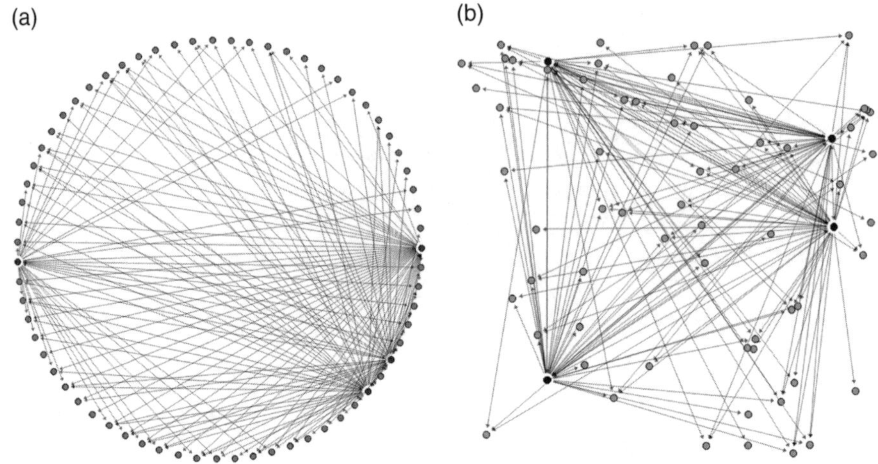

Figure A.6 Simple algorithm. (a) Fixed and (b) random.

References

1 Kamada, T., Kawai, S. (1989) An algorithm for drawing general undirected graphs. *Information Processing Letters*, **31**(1), 7–15.

2 Gansner, E.R., Koren, Y., and North, S. (2004) Graph drawing: stress majorization, In Pach, J. (Ed.), *Graph Drawing*, Lecture Notes in Computer Science, Vol. **3383**, 239–250, Heidelberg: Springer.

3 Eades, P. (1984) A heuristic for graph drawing *Congressus Numerantium* **42**, 149–160.

4 Fruchterman, T.M.J. and Reingold, E.M. (1991), Graph drawing by force-directed placement, *Software-Practice and Experience*, **21**(11), 1129–1164.

5 Frick, A., Ludwig, A., and Mehldau, H. (1994) A fast adaptive layout algorithm for undirected graphs, In R. Tamassia and I.G. Tollis (Eds.), *Proceedings of the DIMACS International Workshop on Graph Drawing (GD)*, Vol. **894**, pp. 388–403, Springer-Verlag: Berlin.

6 Harel, D. and Koren, Y. (2004) Graph drawing by high-dimensional embedding, *Journal of Graph Algorithms and Applications*, **8**(2), 195–214.

7 (a) Borg, I. and Groenen, P. (1997) *Modern Multi-Dimensional Scaling: Theory and Applications*, New York: Springer; (b) Gower, J.C. (1966) Some distance properties of latent root and vector methods used in multivariate analysis, *Biometrika*, **53**, 325–328.

8 (a) Kruskal, J.B. (1964) Nonmetric multidimensional scaling: a numerical method *Psychometrika*, **29**, 115–129; (b) Shepard, R.N. (1962) The analysis of proximities: multi-dimensional scaling with an unknown distance function, *Psychometrika*, **27**, 125–139.

9 Torgerson, W.S. (1952) Multi-dimensional scaling: I. Theory and method, *Psychometrika*, **17**, 401–419.

10 Dwyer, T., Koren, Y., and Marriott, K. (2006) IPSEP-COLA; an incremental procedure for separation constraint layout of graphs, *IEEE Transactions on Visualization and Computer Graphics*, **12**(5), 821–828.

11 Dwyer, T., Koren, Y., and Marriott, K. (2007) Constrained graph layout by stress majorization and gradient projection, *Discrete Mathematics*, **309**(7), 1895–1908.

12 Becker, M.Y. and Rojas, I. (2001) A graph layout algorithm for drawing metabolic pathways, *Bioinformatics*, **17** (5): 461–467.

13 Silverira, M. (2005) An Algorithm for the detection of multiple concentric circles, *Pattern Recognition and Image Analysis*, **3523**, 271–278.

14 Kowalski, K. and Lev, B. (2014) A fast and simple branching algorithm for solving small scale fixed charge transportation problem, *Operations Research Perspectives*, **1**(1), 1–5.

15 McGuffin, M.J. (2012) Simple algorithms for network visualization: a tutorial, *Tsinghua Science and Technology*, **17**(4), 1–16.

Appendix B

Case Study: Knowledge Structure of Steel Research

We deal with the data in our daily life as many or as few. Nations consider national income or economic growth rate to be important, while enterprises are concerned with sales. Researchers deal with data and figures from research, and students use their grades as useful data to be accepted into a university. In this sense, there is nobody who lives without being related to any kind of data.

However, we cannot easily find out any information just by fixing our eyes on the data. It really does in this era of Big Data, in which various kinds of data are accumulated rapidly and largely. Data in a way indicate reality itself, but still we can understand nothing just by looking at it. In this sense, data are just like a reality. Therefore, we need to analyze the data to obtain available information.

We intended to offer the useful information to the researchers by analyzing the data existing in reality. Then we attempted "knowledge structure" analysis on the field of steel research with the theses published in "Steel Research International". By this, we tried to systematize the steel research so far and to provide the useful guide for academic development in the steel industry. The research in the steel industry has been developed rapidly in both academic and practical aspects. Then, which unique characteristics can be found in this process of the development? For those who are used to interpreting data or those who have researched in the relevant field, it is not so difficult to find out some features just by looking over some research papers or figures. However, to ordinary people, this may just seem to be

Fundamentals of Big Data Network Analysis for Research and Industry, First Edition. Hyunjoung Lee and Il Sohn.

the list of figures and similar items. For this reason, we needed a method to find out some features or structures from the data itself, that is, reality itself. This is what we call "Big Data network analysis." Here, are the details of how we collect and analyze the data, and they are published in the January 2015 issue of *Steel Research International* [1]. The way to understand the knowledge structure of steel industry is as follows.

Step 1: *Collecting the data*: Collect bibliographic information of articles published in *Steel Research International.* These articles include academic articles, reviews, case studies, corrections, book reviews, editing guidelines, and so on. Among these types, we excluded other types except academic articles, reviews, and case studies because they do not have a direct influence on the knowledge structure of steel research.

Step 2: *Extracting the data*: Extract keywords from the collected articles. Those keywords represent the research topic of the articles so they can be extracted from keyword list, abstract, and title of articles.

Step 3: *Cleansing the data*: Mostly, keywords of articles can be written differently depending on authors so it is necessary to standardize them. Then, we cleansed the keywords through experts in the steel industry.

Step 4: *Organizing the data*: To conduct the network analysis for the knowledge structure, the data should be organized in an analyzable format. About these data, construct a two-mode network for articles and keywords and apply published years later when making annual analysis (Figure B.1).

Step 5: *Transforming the data as a one-mode network*: It is difficult to detect the structure of keywords through a directed relationship of two-mode network that is the relationship between articles and keywords (Figure B.2).

Step 6: *Perform the network analysis of the data*: Network analysis performs centrality and cohesive subgroup analysis.

Step 6.1: In centrality analysis, high degree centrality score of certain keywords indicates that there are many keywords that are co-occurring in one article. High closeness centrality score shows the short geodesic distance from other keywords in a network so it reveals a position that can affect the entire steel research most rapidly. A keyword showing high betweenness centrality score connects sub research areas in steel industry. These keywords lead to convergence of the research.

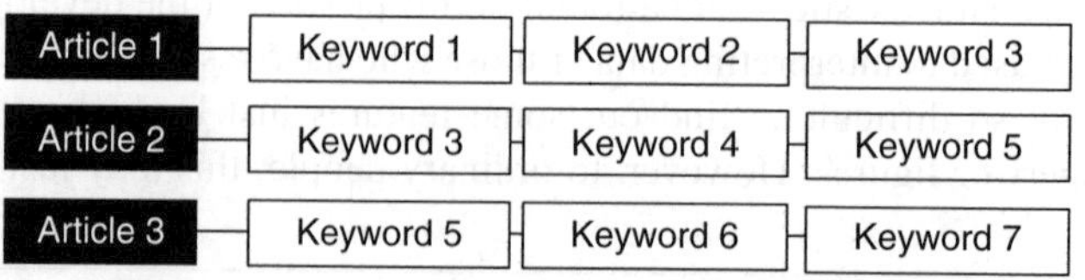

Figure B.1 two-mode network (article–keyword).

Step 6.2: Conduct cohesive subgroup analysis to understand a sub research area in the steel research. A set of keywords shown in many articles concurrently can be recognized as segment research areas.

Step 7: *Conduct additional analyses of the data*: Conduct additional exploratory analyses according to the purpose of the research. Here, we made research mapping to apprehend the development direction of the steel research based on cohesive subgroups.

Then, conduct a task of the analysis to apprehend the knowledge structure of the steel research. Here, we deal with the fourth step of organizing the data. We used NetMiner for network analysis.

Step 4: The organization of collected data starts from constructing two-mode network like Figure B.3a. Import collected data into NetMiner (*File > Import > Text Files or Excel Files*).

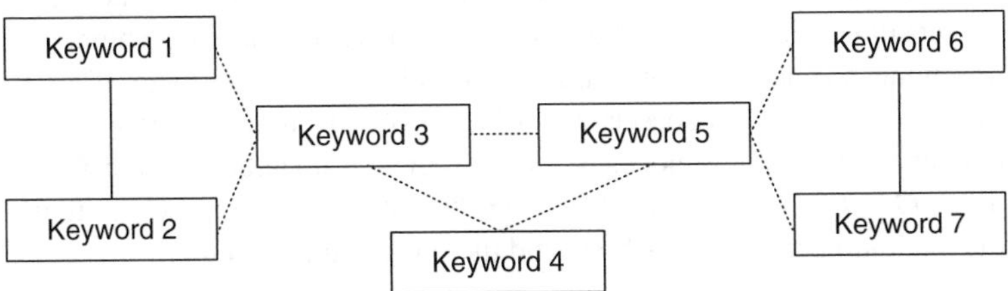

Figure B.2 one-mode network (keyword–keyword).

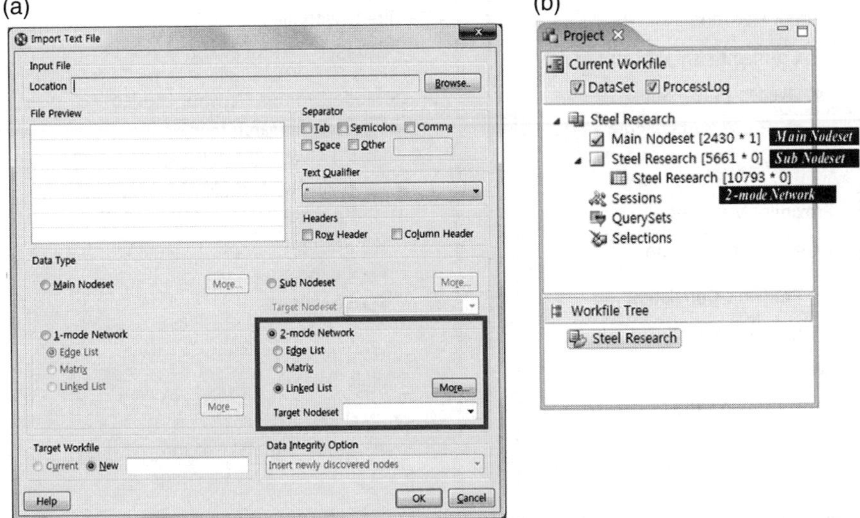

Figure B.3 The screen for importing. (a) Importing on network data and (b) workfile after data importing of NetMiner.

If the EXCEL data are imported, it is not necessary to set up an extra separator, but in the case of text file data, divide data column by using *Separator*. Also, choose *two-mode Network > Linked List* in import option because collected data are constructed in the form of linked list in two-mode network. After importing data, Main Nodeset, Sub Nodeset, two-mode networks are generated in *Current Workfile* of NetMiner. In *Workfile Tree,* we can see that workfile is generated with an imported file's name (Figure B.3b).

Step 5: Data imported in NetMiner are two-mode network composed by article–keyword. To understand the knowledge structure of research area, it is necessary to transform it into the one-mode network with the form of keyword-keyword. We can transform two-mode network into one-mode network through *Transform > Mode > two-mode Network.* At this point, select *Output Network > Overlab(Sub*Sub), Proximity Measures > Type > Correlation > Inner Product* in the main process like Figure B.4a. Finally, click Run Process and pop-up menu to ask whether make workfile appears. If we click yes, then existing data are preserved and transformed child workfile is generated like Figure B.4b. In NetMiner, each number after nodeset and network means the number of node and node attribute and the number of link and link attribute. That is, *Steel Research [5661*0],* nodeset of newly generated one-mode network, signifies that the total number of nodes is 5661 and there is no node attribute. On the other hand, *Overlap(Steel Research) [26385*0]* of one-mode network signifies that the total number of links is 5661 and there is no link attribute.

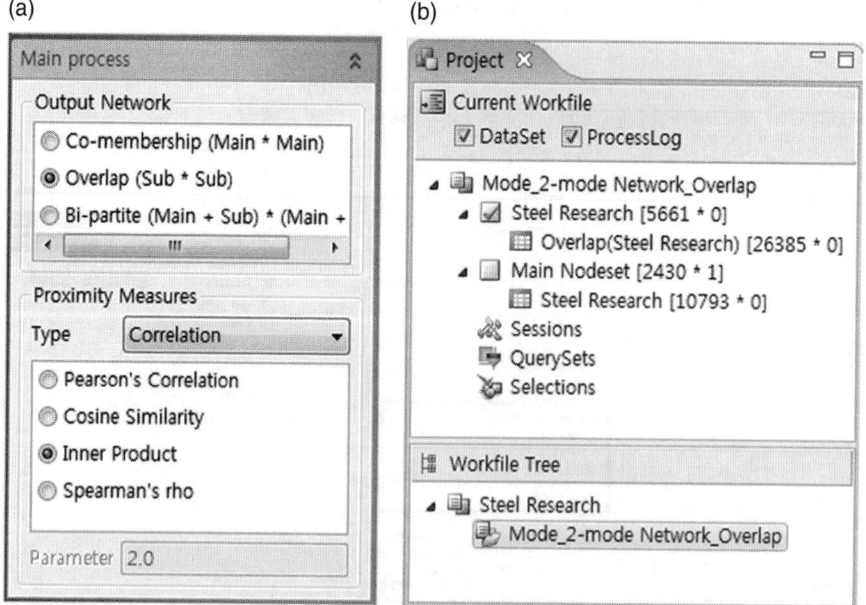

Figure B.4 Transforming a two-mode network into a one-mode network. (a) Network transform and (b) child workfile.

Co-occurrence matrix of keywords is generated like Table B.1. The generated matrix can be confirmed through the *Overlap (Steel Research)* of one-mode network. Each cell from co-occurrence matrix indicates co-occurrence frequency of *keyword i* and *keyword j* within the research period, from 1990 to 2013 while diagonal shows occurrence frequency of *keyword i* in the same period. Specifically, through co-occurrence matrix, we can see that microstructure appears as a keyword in 95 theses during 24 years and it appears with duplex stainless steel in 4 theses.

Through co-occurrence matrix, we can find out frequency of occurrence of keywords during the research period. Moreover, we can figure out which research was mainly going on each year by separating it annually Table B.2.

In addition, we can check out keywords along with research through keyword pairs like Table B.3. With this, we can have the merit of finding out keywords, which are necessary for a research conducted with an arbitrary keyword. Therefore if we visualize it, we can navigate keywords as well as we explore other keywords in a research.

Step 6: Through the data transformed into one-mode network, it is possible to apprehend keywords and sub research areas which are considered important in the steel research. For this, we perform centrality and cohesive subgroup analysis.

Step 6.1: To conduct a centrality analysis, select a method of analysis that researchers need from *Analyze > Centrality.* Here, we conducted *Degree, Betweenness > Node, and Closeness* Analyses. First, when we select degree centrality, we can choose a method to obtain a degree centrality score in the *Main Process.* At this point, we can choose whether nodes would be the number of another node and connected link or they would be the sum of link weight. Generally, we assume that the existence of link is more important than link weight so we measure degree centrality with this assumption but in some cases we measure degree centrality score according to link weight value. Closeness centrality considers reachability of whole network as important so *Dichotomize* option must be set as default in the *Preprocess.* However, for closeness centrality, we must set up *Unreachable Handling* option in the Main Process. Basically, unreachable nodes are set to be

Table B.1 Keyword–keyword paired co-occurrence matrix.

	Nitrogen	Annealing	Duplex Stainless Steel	Microstructure	Direct Reduction
Nitrogen	28	1	1	1	
Annealing	1	10	1		
Duplex stainless steel	1	1	11	4	
Microstructure	1		4	95	
Direct reduction					5

Table B.2 Frequency of keywords from 1990 to 2013.

Keywords	Overall Period #	Keywords	1990–1994	Keywords	1995–1999	Keywords	2000–2004	Keywords	2005–2009	Keywords	2010–2013
Microstructure	95	Microstructure	14	Kinetics	15	Transformation induced plasticity	17	Finite element method	37	Microstructure	34
Finite element method	79	Heat transfer	10	Liquid iron	11	Continuous casting	14	Microstructure	29	Transformation induced plasticity	33
Transformation induced plasticity	72	Kinetics	10	Heat transfer	8	Mechanical properties	14	Continuous casting	22	Twinning induced plasticity	24
Mechanical properties	64	Mass transfer	9	Mechanical properties	8	Microstructure	12	Inclusion	20	Finite element method	21
Continuous casting	62	Nitrogen	9	Nitrogen	8	Finite element method	10	Slag	19	Blast furnace	20
Slag	54	Hot rolling	8	Finite element method	7	Slag	10	Transformation induced plasticity	19	Continuous casting	19
Blast furnace	50	Liquid iron	8	High temperature	6	Aluminum	7	Blast furnace	18	Mechanical properties	19
Kinetics	42	Thermodynamic	8	Iron	6	Blast furnace	7	Mechanical properties	16	Precipitation	19
Stainless steel	41	Mechanical properties	7	Liquid steel	6	Low carbon steel	7	Stainless steel	14	Slag	15
Heat transfer	39	Niobium	7	Low carbon steel	6	Solidification	7	High strength steel	11	Phase transformation	14

Table B.3 Keyword–keyword pair co-occurrence frequency.

Keyword Pairs	Frequency	Keyword Pairs	Frequency
Mechanical properties – microstructure	21	Kinetic – reduction	7
Transformation induced plasticity – twinning induced plasticity	12	Viscosity – slag	7
Nitrogen – carbon	10	Al_2O_3 – MgO	6
Transformation induced plasticity – retained austenite	9	Blast furnace – ironmaking	6
Microstructure – heat treatment	8	Desulfurization – hot metal	6

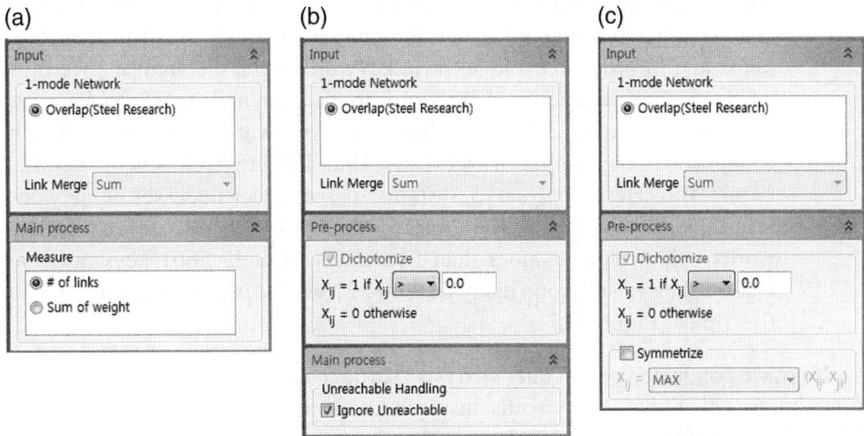

Figure B.5 Process control area of centrality. (a) Degree centrality, (b) closeness centrality, and (c) betweenness centrality.

ignored. Betweenness centrality also deals with nodes and position so there is no need to consider the weight. Therefore in NetMiner, *Dichotomize* option, not considering link and weight in the *Pre-Process,* is set as default (Figure B.5).

The result of centrality analysis is presented as *[R]Main Report, [T]Centrality Vector, [M]Spring, [M]Concentric.* In NetMiner, [R] stands for Report, [T] stands for Table, [M] stands for Map. Therefore, one report, one table, and two maps are calculated by the centrality analysis. In *[R]Main Report,* process information and output summary are presented. Distribution of centrality score and network centralization index are presented as output memory. Centrality scores of each nod are presented in *[T] Centrality Vector.* A visualized map from Spring algorithm is presented in *[M]*

Spring. In display tab at the bottom, styling of the visualized map can be done. *[M] Concentric* is a map to make a node with a higher centrality score located closer to the center so we can easily find out which node has the highest score on the map. Here, the result of degree centrality analysis is presented. Co-occurrence matrix does not consider direction so in-degree centrality score and out-degree centrality score are identical.

The result of centrality analysis for steel research is arranged and presented like Table B.4. The result of centrality analysis and "microstructure, finite element method" show both high degree and betweenness centrality score so these two keywords are always considered in steel research as well as they connect sub research areas of steel research so they promote converged study keywords. In addition, microstructure, mechanical properties, and continuous casting are in the positions, which can be diffused most successfully in steel research. Therefore, researchers who first study steel research must concern these keywords.

Step 6.2: Prior to cohesive subgroup analysis, from 1993 to 2013, 94.2% of entire keywords appear under five times so we excluded them from the analysis after we concluded that they had a relatively small influence on the study. In order to exclude those keywords from the analysis, we must add frequency occurrence of keywords to the main node set *(Steel Research [5661*0])* as node attribute in advance. Afterward, if we select *Query Composer* in the toolbar of NetMiner, Data Editing Area is generated like Figure B.6. Here, in *QuerySet Status,* if we select node set or network, insert *Query,* and select *Try > Apply > Run* in order, we can extract keywords, which appear more than five times. Among 5661 keywords, we made cohesive subgroup analysis with 321 words, which appear more than five times (Figure B.7).

Next, we conducted community analysis. Through community analysis, we made more intraconnections of keywords inside a group than interconnections among groupssoastoapprehendsubresearchareas.Weselect*Analyze > Cohesion > Community* for an analysis. Here, we must select *Algorithms* for community analysis in the *Main Process* of Process Control Area. In this case, CNM is the most famous algorithm, and it guarantees a fine result but it has the slowest speed of analysis among listed algorithms. *Include Nonoptional Output* is used when a researcher wants to divide a network into a certain number of communities regardless of modularity score. As a result of community analysis, *[R]Main, [T]Community Partition, [M]Clustered* are generated. *[R]Main* presents best modularity score whereas *[T]Community Partition* presents that certain nodes belong to which subgroup as a form of table. In *[M] Clustered,* a clustered map of a cohesive subgroup is divided with the best modularity. Here, clustered maps of each cohesive subgroup are shown with different shapes and colors at the bottom tab, *Display > Node Style > Node Attribute Styling* (Figure B.8).

As a result of cohesive subgroup analysis for steel research, total eight subgroups were found shown in Table B.5. Here, *Keywords #, Link #, Intraconnection (Density)*

Table B.4 Keyword centrality analysis.

Keyword	Degree Centrality	Keyword	Closeness Centrality	Keyword	Betweenness Centrality
Microstructure	5.05	Microstructure	34.40	Microstructure	9.53
Finite element method	4.72	Mechanical properties	32.57	Finite element method	7.71
Continuous casting	3.87	Continuous casting	32.41	Continuous casting	6.43
Transformation-induced plasticity	3.50	Slag	31.87	Slag	5.35
Mechanical properties	3.30	Kinetics	31.74	Mechanical properties	5.05
Slag	3.29	Solidification	31.55	Transformation-induced plasticity	4.67
Blast furnace	2.90	Stainless steel	31.52	Kinetics	4.66
Kinetics	2.44	Transformation-induced plasticity	31.38	Blast furnace	4.03
Stainless steel	2.33	Phase transformation	31.35	Stainless steel	3.61
Precipitation	2.07	Precipitation	31.33	Solidification	2.85

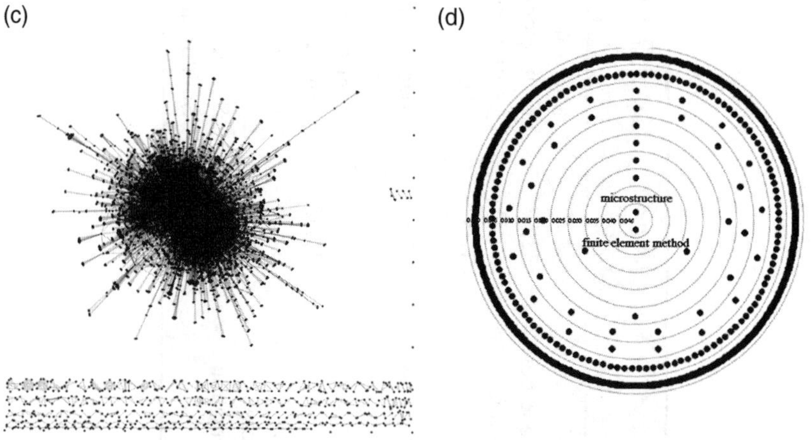

Figure B.6 The results of degree centrality. (a) [R]Main Report, (b) [T]Degree Centrality Vector, (c) [M]Spring, and (d) [M]Concentric.

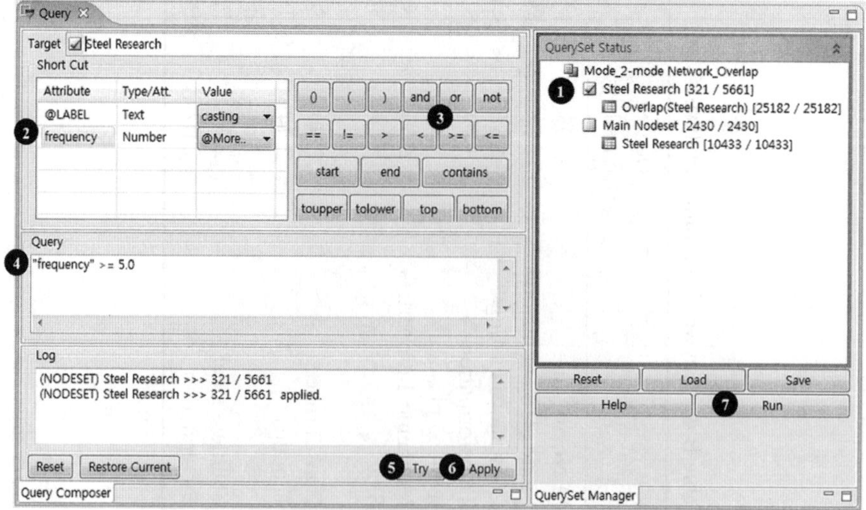

Figure B.7 Query composer.

(a)

# of Communities	8
Step #	63
Modularity	0.652088
twinning induced plasticity	1.0
mechanical propertie	2.0
flow stress	1.0
tensile test	1.0
ironmaking	5.0
blast furnace	5.0
solidification	7.0
stainless steel	6.0
hot metal	5.0
vanadium	4.0
high strength steel	2.0
hydroforming	2.0
martensite	3.0
kinetics	5.0
microstructure	3.0
niobium	8.0
retained austenite	3.0
nitrogen	4.0
thermodynamic	5.0
titanium	8.0

(b)

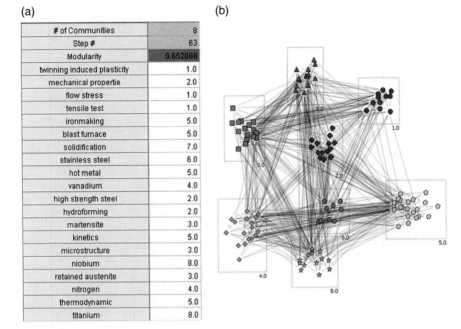

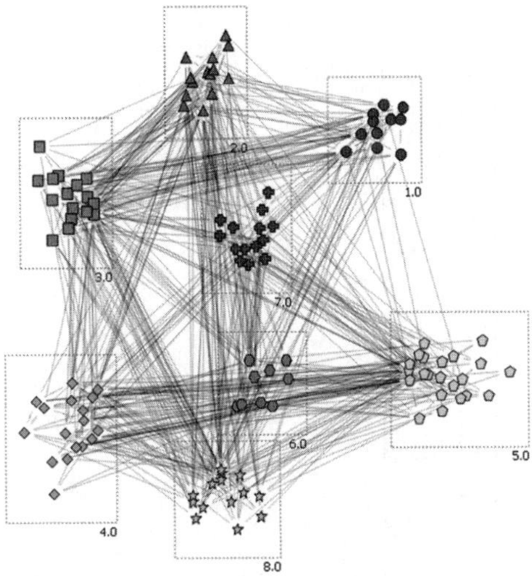

Figure B.8 The results of cohesive subgroup. (a) [T]Community Partition and (b) [M]Clustered.

can be found from *Analyze > Properties > Group. Interconnection* is a result of additional exploratory analysis.

Step 7: Research Category is divided considering intraconnection and interconnection like Figure B.9 to understand sub research areas of steel research. Subgroups in a sub research area that have both high interconnection and intraconnection score are a *main stream research area (I)* receiving attention as a developed field of study. Subgroups, which have high intraconnection score but have low interconnection score, are independent *growth research area (II)*, and subgroups, which have both low intraconnection and interconnection score, are *next generation research area (III)* that is not yet structuralized and still studied separately. Last, subgroups, which have low intraconnection score but have high interconnection score, are a *trend research area (IV)* that has high scalability in study.

This case is conducted to understand the knowledge structure of steel research published in "Steel Research International" based on big data network analysis. The result of analysis has a significance that it makes us effectively understand accumulated steel research so far. Furthermore, through the mapping of subgroup areas, it provides an important guide to establish direction of next study. However, still it is necessary to examine the steel research more comprehensively including dealing with various steel research journals that we could not deal with here.

Table B.5 Subgroup research area of steel research.

Cohesive subgroups		Keywords #	Link #	Intra connection (%)	Inter connection (%)	Research category
No.	Keywords within the subgroup					
G1	Austenitic steel, ferritic stainless steel, flow stress, grain size, hot deformation, martensitic transformation, and so on	11	56	50.90	8.15	I
G2	Austenite, austenitic stainless steel, ductility, fatigue, finite element method, high strength steel, hot stamping, and so on	14	82	45.10	9.36	I
G3	Annealing, cold rolling, deformation, dual phase steel, duplex stainless steel, electron backscattered diffraction, formability, and so on	16	108	45.00	9.90	I
G4	Activity, alloy, aluminum, copper, high speed steel, iron, liquid iron, and so on	17	80	29.40	7.76	IV
G5	Basic oxygen furnaces, basic oxygen furnaces slag, blast furnace, carburization, computational fluid dynamic, decarburization, dephosphorization, and so on	22	138	29.90	6.32	IV
G6	Continuous casting, high temperature, molten steel, mold, optimization, physical modeling, surface tension, and so on	9	28	38.90	7.20	I
G7	Casting, characterization, composition, fluid flow, heat transfer, inclusion, ladle, and so on	14	62	34.10	0.06	III
G8	Carbide, carbon, corrosion, creep, hardness, microalloy, microalloyed steel, and so on	14	72	39.60	0.08	II

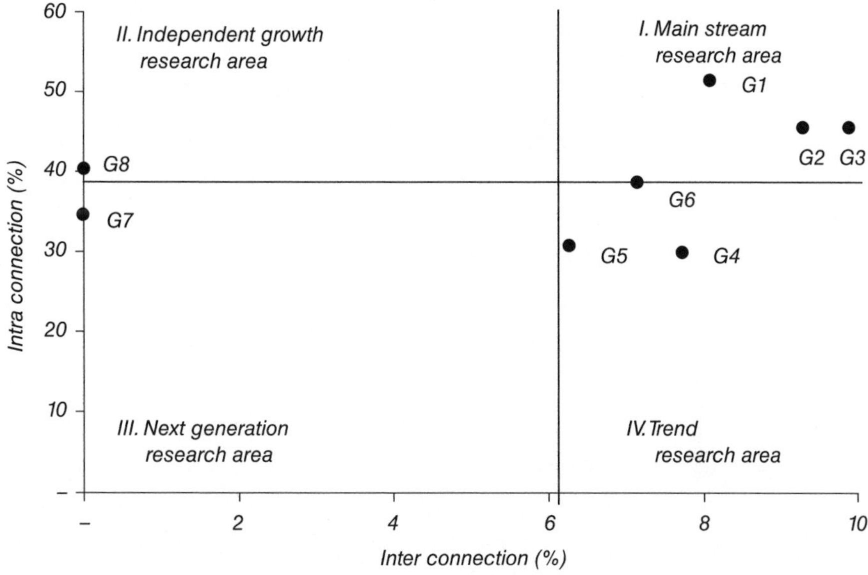

Figure B.9 Subgroup area mapping in steel research.

Reference

1 Lee, H. and Sohn, I. (2015) Looking back at Steel Research International and its future, *Steel Research International*, **86** (1), 10–24.

Index

Fundamentals of Big Data Network Analysis for Research and Industry, First Edition. Hyunjoung Lee and Il Sohn.